HOW TO PLAY THE
OPENING IN CHESS

HOW TO PLAY THE
OPENING
IN CHESS

RAYMOND D. KEENE and
DAVID N. L. LEVY

RHM PRESS
a division of RHM Associates of Delaware, Inc.
Albertson, Long Island, New York 11507

Published in the United States by R.H.M. Press
New York, New York

Published by arrangement with the Bobbs-Merrill Company Inc.

Published in Great Britain by William Collins Sons & Co. Ltd.

ISBN 0-89058-021-9
Library of Congress Catalog Card No.: 75-9232

Printed in the United States of America

PREFACE

Many more books have been written about the openings in chess than about the middle game and endgame together. This is quite natural when one considers that the memorization of a sufficient number of opening variations can guarantee even the inexperienced player a satisfactory position against any opponent. But memorization is useless without understanding. First, if one occasionally forgets a long variation, or if one's opponent varies it, an understanding of the underlying principles is essential to finding the correct moves. Secondly, if one understands why a particular move is correct, one is far more likely to be able to manage the transition from opening to middle game. The correct middle game ideas will suggest themselves as an extension of the opening strategy.

The book is in three sections. The first describes in some detail those principles that underlie all sound chess openings. Readers who conscientiously master these principles will find themselves able to understand the many advanced books that have been written on the subject, and the comments made by annotators in books and chess columns.

In particular, they will be able to follow the second and third sections of this book – studies of twelve varied chess openings, which have been carefully chosen to present a cross-section of styles and ideas.

Each opening is studied in four contrasting main lines, giving forty-eight main lines in all. Each main line is followed by briefer studies of the principal variations on it, usually four or five to each main line. These are all annotated at a level calculated to widen the keen student's horizons and lead him to further explorations.

As well as giving good coverage to these twelve, we offer the reader brief notes on most other openings, so that he will not feel baffled when he encounters a name, such as Alekhine's Defence, in a chess magazine or newspaper column.

To get the best out of the book the reader is strongly recommended to read through the first chapter twice, before going any further. The third chapter, too, should be read a second time, after the reader has familiarized himself with the individual openings and can therefore appreciate better, remarks made on the characteristics of different openings.

After that we suggest a quick reading of the rest of the book before settling down to a lengthy and careful study of all that it contains. This will familiarize the reader with the terms used and he will be all the more able to go from the generalization to the particular instance.

Pawn positions play a vital role not only in the opening, but throughout the game, and the reader is urged to keep returning to the chapter on The Importance of Pawns until he has a thorough grasp of its contents.

One further point: when exploring the variations from the main lines, do not think it a waste of time to start from the beginning each time and play quickly through the moves all over again. True, for every variant, a small diagram gives the position at the point of departure from the main line, but to play the moves over from the beginning is the best way there is to impress upon the mind the different patterns of opening play, and to register the points at which playable alternatives occur.

We would like to thank W. G. Raines and Jacqueline Keene for helping to prepare our original typescript, also W. T. McLeod and R. Mongredien for their constant encouragement and many helpful suggestions.

RDK DNLL

NOTE ON DIAGRAMS

Each main line is illustrated by two large diagrams. The first shows the position after the moves which define the opening have been made. (These are shown in bold type in the summary of moves that come before this diagram.) The second shows the position at the conclusion of the analysis.

Each alternative move is illustrated by a smaller diagram. This, placed at or near the beginning of the analysis of the variation, shows the position at the point at which the player has to decide whether to play this variation or continue with the main line.

CONTENTS

1

DEVELOPMENT AND TACTICS

The opening in chess is the phase of the game in which each side tries to place his army as advantageously as possible for the struggle that comes in the middle game.

Development
This process of moving the pieces forward from their original squares is called development.

When deciding on which square a piece will be best situated (or developed) various factors must be borne in mind. It is not usually a good idea to develop a piece to a particular square if the only reason for doing so is to exercise some tactical threat. This is because when the threat has been nullified by our opponent's reply, the developed piece is misplaced – it is not serving any useful purpose. One simple example is a move often played by rank beginners: after 1 P—K4, P—K4, the move 2 Q—R5 carries the crude threat of 3 Q×KP ch, and the slightly deeper idea of 3 B—B4, followed by 4 Q×BP mate (Scholar's Mate). Black replies to 2 Q—R5 with 2...N—QB3. His KP is then protected and he can help speed up his development by attacking White's queen, either by 3...N—KB3, or 3...P—KN3, followed by...B—N2.

In contrast, *it is normally a good tactic to make a move that both develops a piece to a useful square, and, carries with it some threat.* In this way we may save a "tempo" (another word for a move) because our opponent must use his reply move to react to the threat. If his reply does not contribute to his own development, then our last move has been made free of charge – we have "gained a tempo". If our opponent's reply is also a developing move however, we have not actually gained anything, because *each* side has made one more developing move. But neither have we lost anything in the transaction.

Consider, for example, the following sequence of moves: 1 P—K4, N—KB3 (Alekhine's Defence); 2 P—K5, N—Q4. White seems to be able to get a free developing move by playing 3 B—B4, because that move attacks the black knight; but if Black retreats the knight by 3...N—N3, White's bishop is now under fire, and the tempo that was "gained" on move three must be given back on move four when the bishop retreats (4 B—N3 or 4 B—K2).

The Initiative
The word "initiative" occurs time and again in chess books. Let us consider exactly what is meant by initiative and why it is so important.

At the start of the game White has the advantage, because it is his turn to move. This advantage of the move has often been compared to the advantage of the serve in tennis, but whereas the serve brings victory in almost 90 per cent of the games in top class tennis, the advantage of the white pieces corresponds to a win in only about 32 per cent of master games (roughly, 22 per cent are won by Black and 46 per cent drawn). These figures indicate an average overall advantage for White of approximately 57 to 43.

One obvious characteristic of the initiative is that if Black makes the same moves as White for as long as is legal, White will sooner or later have an overwhelming advantage. Arguing on a less artificial level, it is nearly always the case that symmetrical positions are favourable to the player who is to move. The only exceptions to this rule occur in the endgame, and do not concern us here.

Because of the undesirability of maintaining a symmetrical position, Black normally breaks the symmetry within the first two moves. Every move by Black should play some part in countering White's plan of development. If Black's opening strategy is successful he either neutralizes White's initiative or, even better, snatches the initiative for himself. If Black fails in this respect, White can use his initiative to mount an attack, win material, or gain some significant positional advantage.

How is it possible to tell who has the initiative? This question is not so naïve as it might appear, because many players often confuse the initiative with a short series of easily countered threats. In fact, only experienced players can judge whether an initiative is imaginary (temporary) or real. An example of a real (useful) initiative is seen in the variation of the Caro-Kann Defence, which we examine on page 128. An imaginary (temporary) initiative is seen in the main line of the Giuoco Piano (page 62).

The initiative itself does not constitute a tangible advantage. Its worth lies in its ability to be exchanged for an advantage of a different sort: for material, for an attack, or for an advantageous ending. It probably seems paradoxical to the reader that we so glibly discuss reaching an advantageous ending when we are engaged on explaining the principles of openings. It is quite common however, to find in a book on chess openings, a statement such as ". . . and Black has the better of the ending." In the Exchange Variation of the Ruy Lopez (page 84) we have an excellent example of White actually utilizing his initiative by playing for the better ending from as early as move four.

The fight for the initiative is one of the underlying motifs in opening play. White starts with the advantage of one move (or tempo), and while he is developing his forces he tries to maintain, or even increase, this advantage. It is therefore most important not only to develop pieces on good squares but to develop them as quickly as possible. During the nineteenth century, when the scientific study of chess openings had not yet begun, speed of development was generally regarded as so important that players would gladly sacrifice material, in the interests of obtaining a big initiative. The Muzio Gambit (page 49) is an example of this theme. White sacrifices first a pawn and then a knight in order to build up a substantial lead in development.

There is only one general principle that can be given as a guideline for those who wish to use their tempi correctly, to develop their pieces quickly, and to avoid handing an important initiative to their opponents. *Do not move the same piece twice in the opening.* This is a principle rather than a hard and fast rule. The reasoning behind it is easy to see – if we move a piece that has already been moved we have wasted a tempo that could have been used to develop another unit. Naturally such a principle has many exceptions. If a piece is attacked it may be forced to move. If the attacker is a piece which our opponent is moving for the first time, then we may have lost a tempo because his development has been augmented by his last move, whereas ours has not been helped by the moving of an attacked piece. If, on the other hand, the attacker is a piece which has itself already moved, then we have not lost a tempo.

The Pawn Centre

While control of the centre is primarily the task of the pieces during the early stages of the game, the actual occupation of the centre is normally left to the pawns. There are two contrasting views on the subject of the pawn centre. The classical approach favours the idea of installing as many pawns as possible in the vicinity of the centre, and supporting these pawns by whatever means is necessary. Thus, the classicists would relish having White's pawn centre in many variations of the King's Indian Defence: **1 P—Q4, N—KB3; 2 P—QB4, P—KN3; 3 N—QB3, B—N2; 4 P—K4.**

White's pawns control the squares QB5, Q5, K5 and KB5. But are they really as imposing as they look?

There are many pawn formations which, being typical of some particular opening or variation, have appeared thousands of times in master chess. Another such impressive looking pawn centre is the one arising from the Exchange Variation of the Grünfeld Defence: **1 P—Q4,**

N—KB3; 2 P—QB4, P—KN3; 3 N—QB3, P—Q4; 4 P×P, N×P; 5 P—K4, N×N; 6 P×N. These two positions have in common the fact

that White's pawns appear to exert so much influence in the centre, that it would seem to be extremely difficult for Black to contest White's centre control. Yet, it is the very act of undermining White's pawn centre that reflects the second approach to the whole problem, which is the hypermodern approach.

The hypermodern school, which was founded by Breyer, Réti, and Nimzowitch, subscribed to the view that the opponent could be permitted to build a strong-looking pawn wall provided that measures could later be taken to undermine and (hopefully) demolish it. Thus, in the Grünfeld Defence position shown in the above diagram, Black hits out at the white centre with an early ...P—QB4, so that tension is introduced on White's Q4 square. Eventually there may be an exchange of pawns on this square, in which case White's QP would suddenly be vulnerable and exposed to the full wrath of Black's fianchettoed KB. The methods used by Black to counter White's pawn centre in the King's Indian Defence will be discussed in the relevant chapter (pages 165–178).

It is not difficult to appreciate that the strongest central pawn structures are those in which the QP and KP are both on the fourth rank. In this way they control between them four central squares in the opponent's half of the board. But it is not often possible to maintain pawns at Q4 and K4. In the French Defence for example, after the moves 1 P—K4, P—K3; 2 P—Q4, P—Q4, White's KP is attacked and in most variations eventually advances to K5. Black then has two ways in which he can set about undermining White's central pawn structure. He can attack it from the front by ...P—KB3 or from behind by ...P—QB4. Both methods will be illustrated in the chapter on the French Defence (pages 106–122), but let us take a quick look at one particular variation: 1 P—K4, P—K3; 2 P—Q4, P—Q4; 3 N—QB3, N—KB3; 4 P—K5, KN—Q2; 5 QN—K2, P—QB4. White's pawn base is attacked, so: 6 P—QB3, N—QB3; 7 P—KB4, P—QN4; 8 N—B3, P—N5. White's pawn chain is again attacked from near its base.

Black's idea is to exchange pawns twice, by ...NP×P, followed by ...BP×P. In this way, the base of White's pawn chain is moved up the board to where it is more vulnerable to attack from Black's pieces. This strategy for undermining a pawn chain is useful in a variety of positions. The principle is *when the base of a pawn chain moves up the board it becomes more vulnerable.*

Centre Control

The most important concept connected with development is control of the centre of the board. By counting the moves that can be made by a knight or bishop which is placed, first, on one of the four central squares of an empty board, then on one of the squares on (say) the second rank, and finally on one of the squares at an edge or corner of the board, it is easy to see that a piece situated in the centre usually attacks more squares than one which is not. From this simple experiment we can draw the logical conclusion that our pieces should, if possible, be placed on squares from which they help to control the centre. In this way it will hopefully be possible to occupy the centre later in the game and thereby control a greater part of the board.

The reader might now be tempted to ask the question "On which squares should I develop my pieces?" If it were possible to give a simple answer, then many of the more advanced books on chess openings would become obsolete! There are many different plans of development that can be adopted by White. In reply to each of these plans Black also has a wide choice of systems of development. It is the combination of both plans that gives rise to a particular opening, or variation within that opening.

Rather than try to give general rules for the development of pieces it will be of more value to the reader to list the advantages and disadvantages of developing the knights and bishops on particular squares. Normally, the development of the queen and rooks depends more on the middle game strategy. Only one general rule can be given: *Do not develop the queen early in the game.* In the main body of this book the reader will come across various positions that help to illustrate this principle. There will also be, as with all generalizations, a few counter examples.

Development of the Knights

The traditional squares for the knights are KB3 and QB3. From KB3 for example, a knight attacks the two central squares, Q4 and K5, and it may eventually move to KN5 in order to join in an attack against the opponent's KB2 or KR2. When developing a knight at KB3 there is one important counterstroke that must be remembered and safeguarded against where necessary: if the KP has been moved, then the pin B—KN5 can be a strong blow by the opponent. Consider the following variation of the Giuoco Piano: **1 P—K4, P—K4; 2 N—KB3, N—QB3; 3 B—B4, B—B4; 4 N—B3, N—B3; 5 P—Q3, P—Q3.** We have already

mentioned that symmetrical positions favour the side whose turn it is to move, and this one is no exception. After **6 B—KN5,** White's initiative virtually guarantees him some advantage (see page 63 for a fuller discussion of this variation). If, however, White plays **6 O—O** instead, it is now Black who takes the initiative with **6...B—KN5!**, and it is White's knight which is pinned against its queen. Trying to relieve the pin by **7 P—KR3** turns out to be an error, because rather than move his bishop away (or exchange it for White's knight) Black can play **7...P—KR4!**.

This kind of position is well known in symmetrical king's pawn openings (those openings which start 1 P—K4, P—K4). Black's last move does not really sacrifice a piece because, after **8 P×B, P×P**, White's KN is attacked and to move it would allow a mating attack along the KR-file; e.g., **9 N—Q2, N×P!; 10 P—KN3,** (if White captures the knight, then 10. . .Q—R5 is killing); **10. . .N×NP!,** and now White cannot prevent Black's . . .Q—R5, etc.

So White's 7 P—KR3 has served no useful purpose. Instead it has reacted to White's disadvantage, because it has weakened the area around his king (cf. the section on king safety, pages 23–24). For White to move his queen out of the line of fire of the bishop (i.e. off the Q1—KR5 diagonal) would be to permit Black to rupture White's king position by . . .B×N. Such a weakening should normally be avoided if at all possible.

There are two common methods of dealing with the pin B—KN5:

(1) Prevent it by playing P—KR3. (See, for example, White's 9th move, page 78.)

(2) The effect of the pin can be substantially reduced by the move B—K2. (See, for example, Black's 4th move, page 107.)

The pin B—QN5 is usually less dangerous than the corresponding move on the king's side. This is because king's-side castling is much more common than queen's-side castling, and the exchange B×N, doubling the QBP, is therefore not usually a threat. The reader will find a thorough discussion of the pin, B—QN5, in the chapter on the Nimzo-Indian Defence.

The alternative squares for the knights are K2 and Q2. The KN is usually developed at KB3, partly because as well as exerting its influence on the centre and carrying the possibility of N—KN5, it provides protection for the KR2 square, a square which often becomes vulnerable after king's-side castling. The move QN—Q2 is therefore played more often than KN—K2. From these squares on the second rank the knights control only one of the four central squares (K4 or Q4), but this does not necessarily mean that the moves are inferior from the point of view of centre control. The move QN—Q2 for example, leaves the QBP free to advance. After P—QB3 the square Q4 receives additional support, while P—QB4 adds pressure on the Q5 square. An example of QN—Q2 being played in conjunction with P—QB3, is found in the Closed Defence of the Ruy Lopez (page 77).

A more aggressive purpose of developing a knight on the second rank is that it may later be redeployed to KB4 or QB4, from where its influence is felt as far as the sixth rank. During the opening (or early middle game) the move N—KB4 (or N—QB4) is normally played only after the opponent's KP (or QP) has either advanced to the fifth rank, or been removed from the board altogether. Clearly, if our opponent still has a pawn at Q2 or Q3 when we play N—QB4, he can drive the knight away at will by playing P—Q4, unless of course his QP is immobile (blockaded by our own QP). It is not only from the central pawns, however, that knights on KB4 and QB4 must fear an attack. It is quite normal for the move P—QN4 to be played, so as to drive away an enemy knight at the same time as staking a claim to more space on the queen's side. Consider, for example, the following variation of the King's Indian Defence:

> 1 P—Q4, N—KB3; 2 P—QB4, P—KN3; 3 N—QB3, B—N2; 4 P—K4, P—Q3; 5 N—B3, O—O; 6 B—K2, P—K4; 7 O—O, QN—Q2; 8 P—Q5, N—B4.

Black's QN cannot be driven away at once by 9 P—QN4, because White's KP is *en prise*. So White continues with **9 Q—B2,** defending the KP, and now Black must take immediate action to prevent 10 P—QN4!. The thematic move for Black is **9...P—QR4.** This prevents an immediate 10 P—QN4. If White tries to prepare the advance by P—QR3 and R—QN1, Black can reply to P—QR3 with ...P—R5, so that an eventual P—QN4 can be met by P × P e.p.

In this example, Black was able to play ...N—QB4 before ...P—QR4, because White had to take time off in order to come to the defence of his KP. In many positions of this type, however, Black's ...N—B4 does not carry any immediate threat, and Black must therefore play ...P—QR4 before ...N—B4. This motif is seen frequently in the King's Indian Defence.

One final comment on the development of knights. *It is rarely a good idea to place a knight at the edge of the board.* Developing a knight to KR3 or QR3 is usually a poor long-term investment because it exerts no influence on the centre. Occasionally the move N—R3 is played as part of a manoeuvre to take the knight to B4. One such example is the Réti Gambit: 1 N—KB3, P—Q4; 2 P—B4, P×P. Now White frequently plays 3 N—R3, followed by 4 N×P. This is one of relatively few exceptions to the above "rule".

Development of the Bishops

Bishops, by virtue of their greater freedom of movement, have a wider range of development possibilities. On KN5 or QN5 a bishop frequently pins a knight against the enemy king or queen. The value of such a pin is a rather variable quantity. Sometimes it may help restrict the opponent to a defensive set-up (the classic example is White's 3 B—N5 in the Ruy Lopez). In other positions it may help the opponent gain momentum for a flank attack as in the following example.

White's last move was **7 B—KN5**, pinning the black knight against the queen. Play continues: **7. . . P—KR3; 8 B—R4.**

If White retreats the bishop to KB4, then 8. . .P—KN4 also gains momentum for Black's assault on White's king's side. 8 B ×N, concedes Black the advantage of the two bishops without extracting any compensation.

8. . .B—N2; 9 P—K4, P—KN4; 10 B—N3, N—R4.

Black's 7th and 9th moves have been the preliminaries to a king's side attack. White's QB, having been driven around the king's side by Black's advancing pawns, is about to be exchanged off (see Black's last move). White has thus conceded the advantage of the two bishops, but he hopes that by doing so he will be able to take advantage of Black's weakened king's side. As we shall see, Black's demonstration on the king's side works out in his favour, because of the possibility of a further advance of the KNP and KRP. This position has been reached a few times in master play. Experience suggests that Black's coming attack is so strong that he already has a big advantage.

We shall now follow one master game that reached this position. The reader is not expected to understand the point behind most of the moves – the purpose of this example is to illustrate how easily Black's attack is built up after White has castled, and to show the part played in the attack by the pawns that have advanced with gain of tempo. Play continued:

11 B—N5 ch, K—B1.

Black does not mind losing his right to castle, because his KR is needed on the R file to help in the attack.

12 B—K2, N×B; 13 RP×N, N—Q2; 14 N—Q2, Q—K2; 15 P—KN4 (hoping to hold up the advance of Black's pawns); **15...P—R3; 16 P—R4, B—Q5!.**

Adding pressure to the area around White's king and preparing for the possibility of 17...Q—B3, which would threaten both mate at KB7 and the win of a pawn by 18...B×N; 19 P×B, Q×QBP.

17 O—O, N—B3; 18 N—B4, P—KR4!.

Now the attack starts in earnest and in a few moves the game is over.

19 P×P.

If White tries to win material by 19 N—N6, P×P; 20 N×R, he finds himself being mated after 20...Q—K4.

19...P—N5; 20 N—K3, N×RP.

White is helpless. Black threatens both 21...Q—R5 and 21...N—N6.

21 B×NP, Q—R5; 22 P—KN3, N×P; 23 K—N2, N×R; 24 K×N, B×N(K6), and White resigns.

This attack was possible because Black's king was safely situated on KB1. If a player has already castled king's side he is much less likely to be able to afford the luxury of playing P—KR3 followed by P—KN4, because it leaves his king dangerously exposed. As a rough guide we can state that *the pin, B—KN5, is more likely to be advantageous if the enemy king is already committed to the king's side.* The same can be said of the corresponding situation on the queen's side.

Other aspects of the pinning move B—KN5 have been discussed or referred to in the section on the development of knights (page 14).

On the squares QB4 or KB4, a bishop exerts pressure along the diagonal from R2 to N8. This pressure is often very useful in the case of the bishop developed at QB4 in a king's pawn opening. The reason for this will become clear in the section on the weakness of the KB2 square (page 22). It is rather less common to see the QB developed at KB4 in a queen's pawn opening, because the diagonal from KR2 to QN8 is of relatively minor importance unless the opponent has castled queen's side.

When developing the KB at QB4 it is necessary to consider whether or not it is (or will be) to the opponent's advantage to attack this bishop with the move N—QR4. As with most fundamental questions in chess, the answer depends on the exact nature of the position, and it is not possible to give a satisfactory generalization. We can, however, give the reader two questions that he should ask himself when trying to decide on the merit of the opposing move N—QR4 in such positions:

(1) If the bishop retreats to Q3 or K2, is the enemy knight at QR4 well placed or not? Unless the knight can later occupy the square QB5 the answer is nearly always "No," because there is little else for the knight to do other than return to QB3 from whence it came. In many

positions arising from the Sicilian Defence, it *will* be possible to establish the knight at QB5 by first supporting that square with any or all of the moves ...P—QN4, ...R—QB1, or ...Q—B2. Even then, it is sometimes the case that the knight at QB5 accomplishes very little.

(2) If the bishop retreats to QN3, does the exchange N×B give the advantage to one side or the other? Usually this exchange leaves one player with the advantage of the two bishops. In contrast, by recapturing the knight with the QRP, the QR-file will have been half opened, thereby putting pressure on the opponent's QRP, and introducing the possibility of bringing the QR quickly to the centre, or the king's side, after R—R4 or R—R5. Both of these factors must be considered, together with the short term effects of the exchange. Only then can an accurate assessment be made.

A more important counterstroke, which is nearly always strong, is a tactical resource known as the "fork trick", which is usually employed by Black. The fork trick requires for its basis the arrangement shown in

the above diagram, although it is unimportant whether the black QP is on Q2 or Q3 and whether White's QP is on Q2 or Q4. Black plays... N×KP!. If White replies N×N, Black regains the "sacrificed" piece by...P—Q4, forking the bishop and knight. The idea of the fork trick is that it results in the liquidation of the enemy centre. In the above position White has two pawns in the four central squares, and two pieces supporting the centre. After the forking manoeuvre has been completed, White has had one of the pawns and one of the pieces exchanged; his control of the centre has been substantially reduced. The following example of the fork trick working out well in practice, is taken from a recent game played between Grandmasters LJUBOJEVIC and DONNER. The game opened thus:

1 P—K4, P—Q3; 2 P—Q4, N—KB3; 3 N—QB3, P—KN3; 4 P—B4, B—N2; 5 B—B4, N×P!.

When Black is allowed to use the fork trick, White must adopt one of two courses of action. He may either capture the knight as described in the skeleton example above or he may first try to weaken Black's king position. It is this second course that Ljubojevic adopted in the game in question:

6 B×P ch, K×B; 7 N×N.

Now the material balance has been restored, but Black has the advantage of the two bishops and White's centre is not so strong as it was two moves ago. The only disadvantage of the transaction from Black's point of view is the fact that his king is apparently insecure, but this problem can be solved without much difficulty. The game continued:

> **7. . .R—K1; 8 N—KB3, K—N1; 9 0—0, N—Q2; 10 P—B3, P—N3; 11 Q—N3 ch, P—K3; 12 N(B3)—N5, N—B1,** and White had no advantage.

On K3 or Q3, a bishop supports the centre usually without fear of attack. The commonest way for a bishop on the third rank to be attacked, is by an enemy knight appearing at its N5. Usually the sequence N—N5 and N×B is prevented by either P—B3 or P—R3. In some situations however, this manoeuvre can be permitted because, after N×B, the recapture BP×N, produces a strong pawn centre which provides at least adequate compensation for the "loss" of bishop for knight. Examples of this will be seen in the Taimanov Variation of the Sicilian Defence (page 105) and in the Pirc Defence (page 223).

One guideline, in fact virtually a golden rule, concerning the development of bishops on the third rank is: *Do not develop a bishop on the third rank in front of an unmoved KP or QP.* The central pawns should be free to move, to occupy or add support to the centre, and to make way for the development of the pieces.

K2 and Q2 are squares that are normally only occupied by bishops being employed for defence. This is partly because the scope of such a bishop will be limited by a knight at B3. The most notable exception to this "rule" is seen in many variations of the Sicilian Defence, in which White's bishop at K2 is often used in the middle game both in attack and defence. In the Dragon Variation, for example (page 99), White's 7 B—K2, prevents Black from playing . . .N—N5, which would attack the bishop at K3, and later this bishop supports the advance, P—KN4.

The Fianchetto

The fianchetto is the name of the sequence P—N3, followed by B—N2, in which a bishop is developed on one of the "long" diagonals (KR1—QR8 or QR1—KR8). A bishop developed in this way is called a fianchettoed bishop. In some modern defence systems (see e.g. page 193), Black's very first operation is to fianchetto his KB: **1 P—K4, P—KN3; 2 P—Q4, B—N2.** From KN2 or QN2, a bishop adds support to the

centre, as well as applying latent pressure to the more distant squares on the diagonal (N7 and R8). In the early days of chess theory, bishops were seldom developed on the long diagonals. During the past half-century however, the fianchetto has become a well understood motif and is now seen frequently in games played at all levels. Not only can a fianchettoed bishop be used as an offensive weapon, it can also provide a defence for a castled king which sits behind it on N1 (cf. the section on king safety, page 23).

It is sometimes desirable to exchange off an opposing fianchettoed bishop. The usual means of accomplishing this is shown in the following diagram. White has developed his QB at K3, making sure (by playing

P—KB3), that Black cannot attack this bishop by . . . N—N5. Then White places his queen behind the bishop so that now, after the move B—KR6, the bishop will be defended. On KR6 White threatens to exchange bishops on KN7. Black cannot retreat his bishop to KR1, because that would expose his rook to attack and capture. He must therefore either exchange bishops himself by . . . B × B, or allow White to exchange bishops at will.

Of course Black can recognize the sequence P—B3, B—K3, Q—Q2, B—KR6 while it is in the making, and he can take measures to prevent the exchange of his fianchettoed bishop. He might, for example, move his KR from KB1 so that when White plays B—KR6 the fianchettoed bishop can retreat to KR1, from where its influence will still be felt through the long diagonal. A different method consists of replying to B—K3 with . . .P—KR3, and to Q—Q2 with . . .K—R2. In this way White has been denied the possibility of playing his bishop to KR6 because that square is now guarded by both Black's king and his bishop.

The Vulnerability of KB2

For both players the square KB2 is the most vulnerable to an early attack. Much of the former theory of king's pawn openings was built around this vulnerability; hence the King's Gambit (pages 46–60) and Giuoco Piano (pages 61–69) were extremely popular during the last century and the early part of this.

The KB2 square owes its importance and its vulnerability to the fact that at the beginning of the game it is defended by the king and no other piece. This gives rise to various mate possibilities which can sometimes be employed against helpful opponents. The reader will almost certainly have fallen into scholar's mate at some time shortly after learning the game. Such an early disaster can only come as a result of gross neglect, yet even experienced players sometimes lose quickly because of a tactical trick based on the attack on KB2. Here are some examples:

(1) 1 P—K4, P—K4; 2 N—KB3, P—Q3; 3 B—B4, B—N5; 4 N—B3, P—KR3?; 5 N×P!, B×Q? (if 5. . .P×N, 6 Q×B, and White is a pawn ahead with much the better game); 6 B×P ch, K—K2; 7 N—Q5 mate.

(2) 1 P—K4, P—K4; 2 N—KB3, P—Q3; 3 B—B4, B—K2; 4 P—Q4, P×P; 5 N×P, N—KB3; 6 N—QB3, N—B3; 7 O—O, O—O; 8 P—KR3, R—K1; 9 R—K1, N—Q2?; 10 B×P ch!, K×B (if the king moves to B1 or R1, then 11 N—K6 wins the queen); 11 N—K6!!, K×N; 12 Q—Q5 ch, K—B3; 13 Q—KB5 mate.

(3) 1 P—K4, P—K4; 2 N—KB3, N—QB3; 3 B—N5, P—QR3; 4 B—R4, P—QN4; 5 B—N3, N—B3; 6 P—Q4, N×QP?; 7 B×P ch!, K×B; 8 N×P ch, K—K1; 9 Q×N. White has regained the piece with a pawn as interest.

(4) 1 P—Q4, P—KN3; 2 P—K4, B—N2; 3 N—KB3, P—Q3; 4 N—B3, N—Q2; 5 B—QB4, KN—B3; 6 P—K5!, P×P; 7 P×P, N—R4; 8 B×P ch!, K×B (8. . .K—B1 loses a piece to 9 P—K6); 9 N—N5 ch, K—N1 (the other king moves result in the loss of the queen after 10 N—K6); 10 Q—Q5 ch, Resigns (mate at KB2 cannot be prevented).

(5) 1 P—K4, P—K3; 2 P—Q4, P—Q4; 3 N—Q2, P—QB4; 4 KP×P, KP×P; 5 P×P, B×P; 6 N—K2??, Q—N3, and White is lost – he must give up a knight to prevent being mated. If, for example, 7 N—KB3, Black wins by 7. . .B×P ch; 8 K—Q2, Q—K6 mate.

(6) 1 P—K4, P—QB4; 2 N—KB3, N—QB3; 3 P—Q4, P×P; 4 N×P, N—B3; 5 N—QB3, P—Q3; 6 B—QB4, P—KN3?; 7 N×N,

P×N; 8 P—K5, P×P??; 9 B×P ch!, K×B; 10 Q×Q, and wins.

In each of the above examples one side has quickly reached a lost position, because he failed to keep a proper watch over his KB2 square. These are not isolated examples – there are literally thousands hidden away in chess literature. The reader will come across further examples during his study of the second part of this volume. We cannot emphasize too strongly the importance of the KB2 squares in the opening. *Always be on the lookout for attacks and sacrifices on the KB2 squares.*

King Safety

The king is the most important piece on the board. It should always be looked after with the greatest care. At the beginning of the game the kings are rather vulnerably situated in the centre of the board. If the play becomes sharp and tactical in nature it is a great disadvantage to have one's king in the centre, because it is likely to be brought into the skirmish, possibly with disastrous results.

Fortunately the rules of chess provide us with a means of extricating the king from the centre – castling. *It is usually advisable to castle rather early in the game.* Castling normally takes place as part of the opening strategy. It is rare for castling to be left until the middle game, but under some circumstances, particularly if queens have been exchanged, it may be possible to omit castling altogether. After all, the idea of castling is principally to put the king in a safe place. Once queens have been exchanged the danger of an attack on the king is very much reduced, so much so that Black, satisfied to equalize in the opening, sometimes gives up the right to castle in order to exchange queens. The following variation is an example: **1 P—Q4, N—KB3; 2 P—QB4, P—Q3** (the Old Indian Defence); **3 N—QB3, P—K4.** White now has the option of depriving Black of his right to castle: **4 P×P, P×P; 5 Q×Q ch, K×Q.**

Black will soon make a haven for his king by . . .P—QB3, so that it can sit safely on QB2 in readiness for the endgame. With the exchange of queens, White's opening advantage has been minimized, and careful play should secure Black the draw.

In most openings both players usually castle. The reader would therefore do well to study carefully the various kinds of weakness that exist in castled king positions, to learn how to avoid creating such weaknesses in his own king position and to examine the various attacking plans of development that take advantage of such a weakness in the opponent's position.

The key factor in the safety of a castled king is the formation of pawns that protect the king. A pawn structure which is both safe and flexible is the basic arrangement of pawns at KR2, KN2, and KB2 (assuming that king's-side castling has taken place). The pawn at KR2 is usually supported by a knight at KB3 as well as the king at KN1. Should there be a strong attack on the KR2 square along the KR2—QN8 diagonal, it is possible to blunt this attack by playing P—KN3. If the KRP is at KR3 instead of KR2 the opponent has a target which can be used to speed up a king-side attack, either through the advance P—KN4—N5, or by threatening to sacrifice a bishop or knight on the KR6 square.

Because of the inherent weakness of the pawn structure KR3, KN2, KB2, the move P—KR3 must not be played casually. Another disadvantageous aspect of the move P—KR3 is seen in the section on the development of knights (page 14). The move does create a certain weakness but frequently it is necessary and beneficial. Being able to judge when the move P—KR3 should or should not be played, like all other aspects of judgment in chess, comes only with experience.

We have already come across the fianchetto in the section on the development of bishops (page 16). A castled king is usually well hidden behind a fianchettoed bishop. In order to penetrate the king's domain the enemy must find some point of entry. The usual method of attacking such positions is to open up the KR file by advancing P—KR4—R5 and RP×P. In this way, once the fianchettoed bishop has been exchanged by the manoeuvre described earlier (page 21), the way may be open for a mating attack along the KR file. An example of this strategy is to be found in the chapter on the Sicilian Defence (page 100).

Castling behind a far advanced KNP (or rushing up the board with the KNP in front of a castled king) is a very aggressive tactic which frequently rebounds. If the attack does not work, the attacker's king is left exposed to the wrath of his opponent's counter-attack.

While the advance of the KRP and KNP often weaken a castled king, the advance of the KBP does not usually carry such a dangerous hazard. The advance is often a useful part of king-side attack or it may help to support a central breakthrough by P—K5. The one weakness which is incurred when the KBP moves is along the KN1—QR7 diagonal. Sooner or later an enemy bishop or queen might appear on that diagonal, and the results could be unpleasant. Remember the old motto "Never miss a check!"

To summarize: *Avoid creating unnecessary weaknesses in the structure of pawns that guard your castled king – sooner or later these weaknesses may cause your downfall. This holds for queen's-side castling also.*

2

THE IMPORTANCE OF PAWNS

Pawns are the soul of chess – PHILIDOR

Nobody can hope to master the intricacies of chess unless he has some grasp of the proper way to handle his own pawns, and some inkling of the correct attitude to adopt towards his opponent's foot soldiery. Pawns are the bone-structure, the skeleton of the chess board, and if your pawns are weak your whole position may be diseased. On the other hand, if your pawns are strong your whole position is probably healthy and flourishing.

The pawn structure may well determine the activity of your pieces. You can be tied down to the defence of a weak pawn or your pieces can be shut out of play by pawns unfortunately placed. Further, it is on the pawn configuration that such factors as weak squares depend.

Let us now enter into a systematic examination of this most important realm.

Pawn Weaknesses
Pawns can become weak in two rather different ways – they can be weak in defence, and weak in attack ("static" and "dynamic" weaknesses are the usual terms). First, let us consider pawns which are weak in defence. Pawns are the least mobile of chessmen, so when a pawn is threatened with capture it is sometimes quite difficult to move it out of range of the attacking forces. The most economical way to defend an endangered pawn is with another pawn; guarding such a pawn with a piece can result in a loss of activity for the piece which has thus been relegated to a defensive role.

Any pawn which cannot be protected by another pawn should be regarded with suspicion – it may be a latent weakness. The prototypes for this sort of weakness are the isolated pawn and the backward pawn. A pawn is "isolated" if the friendly pawns on adjacent files have disappeared, and "backward" if the friendly pawns on adjacent files are too advanced to defend it.

Of course, the remarks of the preceding paragraph are, at most, useful generalizations. Whether isolated or backward pawns really are weak depends on the configuration on the board as a whole. As you read and play through the openings in this book, you will find examples (notably in the Queen's Gambit Accepted) of positions in which an isolated QP turns out to be a powerful instrument of attack. In the Sicilian Defence, also, there are several lines where Black plays an early

...P—K4, leaving himself with a backward QP, and yet still gets a good game, because White's army is not well-placed to exploit this defect. However, these are the exceptions rather than the rule. The following striking example should convince the reader just how serious pawn weaknesses can be:

14 *Black to move*

This position arose in the game SIR GEORGE THOMAS–ALEKHINE, Baden-Baden 1925. Its notable features are White's two pawn weaknesses – the isolated QRP and the backward QBP. These in turn have led to general demoralization in the White camp. White's pieces are forced to occupy defensive posts – in particular, White's bishop is more like a glorified pawn than a pillar of the Church. Although the winning process is lengthy, there is never any real doubt about the final outcome, for White is never allowed a shred of active play. From the diagram the game concluded:

    1...Q—Q4; 2 Q—K3, Q—QN4; 3 Q—Q2, R—Q4; 4 P—KR3, P—K3; 5 R—K1, Q—R5; 6 R—R1, P—QN4; 7 Q—Q1, R—B5; 8 Q—N3, R—Q3; 9 K—R2, R—R3; 10 R(B3)—B1, B—K2; 11 K—R1, R(B5)—B3.

This plans the regrouping ...Q—B5, ...R—R5, and ...R(3)—R3, after which the QRP cannot be defended. Because of this threat White will soon be forced to exchange queens.

    12 R(B1)—QN1, B—R5; 13 R—KB1, Q—B5; 14 Q×Q, R×Q; 15 P—R3, B—K2; 16 R(B1)—QN1, B—Q3; 17 P—N3, K—B1; 18 K—N2, K—K2; 19 K—B2, K—Q2; 20 K—K2, K—B3; 21 R—R2, R(B5)—QR5; 22 R(N1)—QR1, K—Q4; 23 K—Q3, R(R3)—R4; 24 B—B1, P—QR3: 25 R—N2, P—R4.

With all White's pieces tied down it is easy to force new weaknesses on the K side. The threat is ...P—R5.

    26 P—R4, P—B3; 27 B—B1, P—K4.

Forcing the final collapse.

    28 BP×P, P×P; 29 B—N2, P×P; 30 P×P, P—N5; 31 P×P, R×R; 32 P×R, R×B; 33 Resigns.

This example illustrates the relative permanence of pawn weaknesses – once they appear they are difficult to eradicate. In the position shown in Diagram 14, although there is no immediate way for Black to win material, Black has a decisive advantage. White's game is reduced to complete passivity due to the constant need to defend his weak pawns and Black can build up his position at leisure.

Before continuing, let us mention two obvious, but important, general points. First, a backward or isolated pawn situated on an open file is usually much weaker than one which is not in an open file. This is because a pawn on an open file can be attacked frontally by the opponent's major pieces. Second, it is not only the pawn itself, but also the square in front of the pawn, which may become weak. For instance, in the Thomas–Alekhine game above, White's QB4 square was firmly in Black's control, and served as an excellent outpost for the black pieces.

As the material on the board is reduced by exchanges, the disadvantages of weak pawns tend to grow rather than diminish, for it becomes increasingly hard to combine the defence of the weaklings with active play elsewhere. An illustration of this is seen in Diagram 15, which occurred in the game RUBINSTEIN–MARSHALL, Breslau 1912.

15. *White to play*

In the previous course of play Rubinstein had spurned a promising middle game, in which he had two bishops against Marshall's two knights, in order to reach this major piece ending. His decision was undoubtedly correct – both subjectively (Marshall was better at attacking than at playing endgames) and objectively. In a middle game the KB file could be used by Black as a staging point for an assault on White's king, whereas in the ending actually reached, the control of this file is not of great importance and Black has no compensation for his isolated QB and K pawns. The weakness of these pawns was sufficient to decide the outcome of the game. Play went:

1 P—K4!, Q—KR4; 2 P—B4!.

2 Q×BP?, R—R3; 3 P—KR4, Q—N5 leaves Black with play on the K side and good drawing chances – he can usually sacrifice a rook to give perpetual check. White need not be in a hurry to win the weak pawns – they will not run away – and he should first ensure the safety of his king.

2...Q—R4; 3 P—K5, R—R3; 4 R—QB2, Q—N3 ch; 5 K—N2, R—Q1; 6 R(B1)—B2.

Now Black has run out of tactical threats and his position collapses.

6...R—QB1; 7 R(KB2)—Q2, K—R1; 8 R—Q6, Q—N8; 9 R × BP, R—KN1; 10 R—B8.

White wins.

The isolated QP is a law unto itself. Tarrasch once said "He who fears the isolated queen's pawn should give up chess." The static weakness of this pawn is often counter-balanced by great dynamic strength. Two examples may help to make this more clear:

16. *White to play*

17. *White to play*

In Diagram 16 White has been successful in his fight against the isolated QP. White's rooks are actively placed on the open file and his beautifully posted knights dominate the position. The weakest piece on the board is clearly Black's bishop which is hemmed in by the QP. It is hardly surprising, in view of White's great positional superiority, that there is available a combination which will translate this superiority into material terms. From the diagram play continued: **1 Q × R!, Q × Q; 2 N(B5) × B, Q × R** (if the queen moves away White simply wins two rooks and a bishop for the sacrificed queen); **3 R × Q, P × N; 4 N × P,** and White emerges with an extra pawn into an easily won ending.

Now consider Diagram 17. Again, White has a great advantage, but this time we see the isolated QP in attack. Because of the pawn on Q4 White has been able to post a knight on the aggressive square K5. The other White pieces are also actively posted. In contrast, Black's forces are very passive and Black has not been able to blockade the White QP by establishing a piece on his own Q4 square. In such a position White should be looking out for combinations based upon the disruptive advance, P—Q5. White won now with:

1 N × P!, K × N; 2 P—Q5, N × P; 3 N × N, Q—N1.

3...P × N would be met by 4 B × P ch, K—N3; 5 B × B, R × B; 6 Q × R, N × Q; 7 R × Q, winning.

4 N × B, R × N.

Or 4...N × N; 5 R × B, R × R; 6 Q × P ch.

5 B × R, etc.

In general, we can say that the dynamic strength of the isolated QP arises from the control of the useful outpost squares K5 and QB5, and also from the possibilities of opening up the game at an advantageous moment with P—Q5. In the normal positions where the pawn on Q4 is opposed by an enemy pawn on K3, the owner of the isolated QP will also have some spatial advantage in the centre. When playing against it, care must be taken to neutralize these benefits by blockading the pawn and guarding against direct attacks against the castled king or along the open QB file. If an ending is reached, the isolated QP will usually be a distinct (possibly fatal) weakness.

Another frequently-seen pawn configuration which can either be weak or strong is shown in the two Diagrams which follow.

18. *White to move*   19. *Black to move*

Black's pawns on Q4 and QB4 are called "hanging pawns." The strength or weakness of hanging pawns depends on which side has the initiative, and whether the pawns themselves are tied down or free to advance. Diagram 18 is a position from the 6th game of the Spassky-Fischer 1972 World Championship Match. Here the pawns are somewhat suspect, for they are under attack and Black is unable to advance them. Black has defended the pawns with pieces, but as a result of the defensive measures taken to protect the pawns Black's forces have become somewhat disorganized. Note, in particular, that the QBP is pinned, which fact White (Fischer) exploited with his next move **1 N— Q4.** Play then continued:

    1...Q—B1; 2 N×B, P×N; 3 P—K4!, P—Q5.

After 3...P×P, Black's pawn structure is hopelessly shattered, and Fischer would easily have regained the pawn with interest.

    4 P—B4, Q—K2; 5 P—K5, R—N1; 6 B—B4, K—R1; 7 Q—KR3, N—B1; 8 P—QN3.

We can see how easily Spassky's game has slipped downhill – Fischer has gained the advantage of bishop *v* knight and is about to start a decisive K-side attack with P—B5. The exchange of Spassky's QB has left the light squares around his king very weak. Black's formation is lifeless and holds out little hope of counter-attack. The Black king and QB pawns are exposed to severe pressure, and Black's passed QP does not help since it is heavily blockaded by White's bishop and queen.

Turning now to Diagram 19 we find a different situation. Here Black's hanging pawns are well-supported by active pieces, and by advancing them immediately Black can create a very strong passed pawn. The finish was:

1...P—Q5!; 2 Q—K2, N—K4; 3 P×P, P×P.

3...B×R?; 4 P×N.

4 R×R, B×R; 5 R—K1, P—Q6!; 6 Q—Q1.

6 Q×N, Q×Q; 7 R×Q, P—Q7 is even worse.

6...B—N5; 7 Q—R1, P—Q7; 8 R×N, P—Q8=Q; 9 R—K8 ch, R×R; 10 Q×Q(B6), B—K7; 11 N—N3, B—N2; 12 Q—B6, B—N4; 13 Q—B1, Q×Q; 14 B×Q, R—K8; 15 B—K3, R—R8; 16 P—QR4, B—Q6; 17 P—B4, R—N8; 18 K—B2, B×B; 19 N×B, R×P; 20 Resigns.

The ending is an easy win for Black.

The general conclusion to be drawn is that hanging pawns are weak in defence (they are, in effect, two backward pawns on adjacent files) but can be an attacking force if they are free to advance.

As we said in our opening remarks, weakness in defence is not the only sort of pawn weakness that can manifest itself. Consider the somewhat artificial position shown in Diagram 20:

20. *Either side to move*

This is a simple king and pawn ending. Material is equal but the pawn position is not balanced – Black has a majority of three to two on the K side, while White has a similar majority on the Q side. The only difference between the two positions lies in White's doubled QN pawns – little enough you might think. However, if this position arose in a master game, few players of the White pieces would hesitate before resigning, for White's situation is hopeless. To what should we attribute White's loss? None of White's pawns is weak in defence – they can all be defended as easily as their Black counterparts. However, owing to the doubled QN pawns, White's Q-side pawns are very weak in attack. Black can advance his K-side pawn majority and quickly produce a passed pawn but, against correct play, there is no way for White to create a passed pawn from his Q-side majority.

21. *White to move*

A different form of weakness in attack is shown in Diagram 21. White has an imposing pawn centre as well as a bishop against knight, and at first sight it looks as though he is doing well. Closer examination reveals, however, that all the winning chances lie with Black. White's proud centre is fine so long as it remains stationary, but if it attempts to advance it will fall apart and crumble into dust. The reader should remember that a pawn centre is never sought as an end in itself, but rather as the means to an attacking break-through.

In this position the normal advance P—K5 is positional suicide, for it will leave White with two sets of doubled and isolated pawns. The attempt to attack on the Q side by pushing a pawn to QB5 is also doomed to failure, since there is no pawn on the QN file to support such an advance. All White can do is sit behind his massive but immobile centre hoping for something to turn up, while Black starts to organize an attack on the K side. The continuation was:

    1 R—QN5, Q—R3; 2 R(N5)—N5, P—KB3; 3 R(N5)—N4, P—N3; 4 B—Q3, R—K2; 5 P—B4, N—N2; 6 P—B3.
6 Q×P, Q×Q; 7 R×Q, N—K3, followed by 8. . .N×QP, is also good for Black.

    6. . .N—K3; 7 B—B1, P—KB4; 8 R(N4)—N2, R—B3; 9 B—Q3, P—KN4.
Threatening. . .Q×RP ch.

    10 R—KR1, P—N5; 11 B—K2, N—N4; 12 BP×P, P—B6; 13 R—N3, P×B; 14 Resigns (JANOWSKI-LASKER, World Championship Match, 1909).

As we see from these examples, groups of pawns containing doubled pawns are often weak in attack. However, it would be unfair to say that every doubled pawn complex is a weakness. For instance, when you come to read the section on the Nimzo-Indian Defence you will find examples of positions in which the impaired mobility of the doubled pawn complex is compensated for by the strength which the doubled pawns impart to the centre. Another illustration of doubled pawns strengthening the centre is provided by the game Gelfer-Keene later in this chapter.

The reader should already be convinced that *isolated* doubled pawns are a serious weakness in almost all positions, for the usual difficulties associated with isolated pawns are added to by the fact that the foremost pawn cannot be defended by major pieces from behind.

22. *White to move*

In Diagram 22 we have another example which shows that the real weakness can often be the square in front of the pawns. White's blockading knight dominates Black's position and prevents Black's pieces from getting to the defence of the king. There was a pretty mating finish: **1 R—K3, K—R1; 2 P—KN4, R—KN1; 3 Q×P ch!!, K×Q; 4 R—R3 ch, N—R5; 5 R×N ch, K—N3; 6 R—R6 ch, K—N4; 7 P—B4 ch, K×P; 8 N—K3 mate.**

A common tactical theme is the sacrifice of the exchange to produce isolated doubled pawns. This is usually most effective when the defences are shattered in the process. The best-known examples of this motif are found in the Dragon Variation of the Sicilian Defence, but here are two instances to give you the idea.

23. *Black to move*

The continuation in Diagram 23 was **1...R×B!?; 2 P×R, Q×P.** Black's sacrifice does not lead to a forced win, but gives excellent practical chances against White's exposed king and weak pawns. The game ended:

3 N—K5?, N×N; 4 P×N, R—B1; 5 Q—N3, Q—B5; 6 QR—R1, R—B5; 7 P—B3, N—B4; 8 Q—N6, N×P; 9 Q×KP ch, K—R2; 10 Q—R3, Q×BP; 11 P—K6, N×P ch; 12 K—N2, Q×P ch; 13

K—N3, R—R5; 14 R×N, Q—N3 ch; 15 K—R2, R×Q ch; 16 R×R, Q×P; 17 R—KN3, Q—K5; 18 Resigns.

24. *Black to move*

From Diagram 24 play went;

1...R×N; 2 P×R, Q—K1; 3 Q—B2.

After 3 K—B2 Black simply plays 3...Q—K3 and 4...R—K1.

3...Q×P ch; 4 K—R1, N—K4; 5 R—KB1, R—K1; 6 R—B4, P—B3; 7 Q—K4, N—N3.

7...Q×BP; 8 R×QP is unclear.

8 Q×Q, R×Q; 9 R×QP.

Black also wins after 9 R—B2, N—K4, for both QB pawns will soon fall.

9...N×R; 10 P×N, R×KP; 11 R×RP, R—KB7; 12 R—N7, R×BP; 13 R×QNP, R×P; 14 R—N3, K—B2.

It was not difficult for Black to win the ending.

Since any connected group of pawns must contain at least one which is not defended by its fellows, it follows that a position with many pawn islands will usually contain more weak pawns than one with few. To end this section, here is a cautionary tale to illustrate this principle.

25. *Black to move*

The position in Diagram 25 arose in the game PETROSIAN–BARCZA, Budapest 1955. In his book of Petrosian's best games P. H. Clarke had this to say: "White's formation is in perfect order, Black's is in shreds. As a general rule, the fewer one's pawn groups (sometimes they are called 'islands') the better. Here we have 1 v 4, and a finer demonstration could not be wished for. Throughout the remainder of the game the black pawns fall like over-ripe plums." The game ended:

1...B—K2; 2 R×NP, R—B3; 3 R×R, R×R; 4 R—R8 ch, K—Q2; 5 R—R7 ch, R—B2; 6 R×R ch, K×R; 7 Q×P, Q—R7 ch; 8 K—B3, Q—Q7; 9 Q—N1, P—B4; 10 N—N3, B—R5; 11 N—K2, B—K2; 12 P—R3, B—N5; 13 N—N3, K—B3; 14 N×P, K—N4; 15 N—Q6 ch, K—R5; 16 N×P, B—R6; 17 N—K5, Resigns.

Pawn Structures

Apart from the weakness of individual pawns, several other types of positional defects can arise which are directly attributable to an inferior pawn structure. Usually these occur when too many pawns have become fixed on squares of the same colour. The commonest manifestations are the "bad" bishop (a bishop whose mobility is impeded by its own pawns), and the appearance of weak squares ("holes"). Here is a striking example:

26. *White to move*

In Diagram 26 White has an enormous advantage because of the holes on Black's KB4 and KR4, which he can use as outposts for his pieces, and because of Black's hopeless KB, which in this position is hardly more valuable than a pawn. Black's difficulties are multiplied by a severe case of cramp – the White pawns have gained so much space that Black is choking. The winning plan is not hard to spot – White merely has to regroup his pieces to support an eventual sacrifice N×QP. Against this Black is helpless, for he has no active play and can only shuffle his pieces around. The game continued:

1 Q—B1, R—Q1; 2 Q—R3, B—B1; 3 B—K3, R—Q2; 4 QR—B1, R—Q1; 5 KR—Q1, B—Q2; 6 N×QP!, N×N; 7 B×BP, B—B1; 8 B—KN4!, B×B; 9 P×B, R—Q2; 10 N—B5, Q—Q1; 11 B×N, N—B1; 12 P—B5, N—N3; 13 P—B6, P×P; 14 P×P, R×B; 15 Q×R, Q×Q; 16 R×Q, Resigns.

The bad bishop is an occupational hazard of certain openings, notably the French Defence. If the pawn structure is blocked, the weakness of this piece can persist throughout the game.

27. *White to move*

In Diagram 27 we see the triumph of a good knight over a bad bishop in an ending. The general rule in all bishop *v* knight positions is, that the player with the bishop should try not to put his pawns on the same colour squares as his bishop. In the diagram position Black's bishop is so reduced in scope that even the protected passed QBP is not enough to save the game. The game concluded:

    1 P—B5.

A pseudo-sacrifice to free the outpost KB4 for the knight.

    1...P—N4; 2 P—KR4, P—B3; 3 RP×P, P×NP; 4 N—N1, B—Q2; 5 P—B6 ch, K—K1; 6 N—B3, P—N5; 7 N—R4, B—K3; 8 N—N6, B—B2; 9 N—B4, K—Q2; 10 K—K2, P—R4; 11 K—K3.

Black is now virtually in "zugzwang". Any move he makes must lose material, for his king must stay on Q2 to stop P—K6, and his bishop must remain on B2 to guard the Q and KR pawns.

    11...B—N1; 12 N×RP, B—B2; 13 N—B4, B—N1; 14 N—K2, B—K3; 15 K—B4, K—K1; 16 K—N5, K—B2; 17 N—B3, K—B1; 18 K—N6, K—N1; 19 P—B7 ch, K—B1.

19...B×P ch; 20 K—B6, K—B1 transposes.

    20 K—B6, B×P; 21 P—K6, B—R4; 22 N×P, B—K1; 23 N—B3, Resigns.

The advance of the QP is immediately decisive.

28. *Black to move*

Turning to Diagram 28, we see another type of disadvantage arising from placing too many pawns on squares of the same colour. Here

Black's pawns on KR2, KN3, and KB4 are all on light squares, and as a result the dark-squares on the K side have been seriously weakened. The weakness of these squares is enhanced because Black's KB, which would normally cover them, has been exchanged. The holes on Black's KB3 and KR3 are especially prominent. White won quickly after **1...Q—KB2; 2 P×P, P×P; 3 P—N6!, Q×P** (3...P×P; 4 N—N5 leads to mate); **4 B×N, Q×Q ch** (4...Q×B; 5 KR—N1); **5 B×Q**, etc.

It is well-known that balanced or symmetrical pawns structures tend to lead to drawish positions. The most aggressive chess openings strive to produce unbalanced pawn positions and thus create greater winning chances. In unbalanced positions we should distinguish between two kinds of pawn majority: the pawn majority in the centre and the pawn majority on a wing.

29. *Black to move*

In Diagram 29 White has a beautiful mobile central pawn majority ably supported by two bishops. Bishops do not like blocked positions, but in open positions like that in the diagram, possession of the two bishops constitutes an important advantage. The rapid advance of White's pawns will make it difficult for Black to co-ordinate his forces. Play continued:

1...K—Q2; 2 KR—K1, P—K3; 3 QR—Q1, N—Q1; 4 B—B4, R—QB1; 5 P—B4, R—K1; 6 P—B5, K—K2; 7 B—Q6 ch, K—Q2; 8 P—QN4, P—QR3; 9 B—N3, R—K2; 10 B—R4, P—B3; 11 P—Q5, P×P; 12 B—N4 ch, N—K3; 13 R×P ch, K—B3; 14 R—Q6 ch, K—N4; 15 R—N6 ch, Resigns.

Here is an illustrative game which shows the devastating effect which a mobile central pawn army can exert. GELFER–KEENE, Student Olympiad, Dresden 1969:

1 P—QB4, P—QB4; 2 N—QB3, P—KN3; 3 P—KN3, B—N2; 4 B—N2, N—QB3; 5 N—B3, P—K3; 6 P—Q3, KN—K2; 7 B—B4, P—K4; 8 B—N5, P—KR3; 9 B—K3, P—Q3; 10 Q—B1, P—R3; 11 R—QN1, R—QN1; 12 P—QR3, P—QN4; 13 P×P, P×P; 14 P—QN4, P—B5; 15 P×P, P×P; 16 O—O, N—Q5; 17 Q—Q1, KN—B4; 18 N—Q2, B—K3; 19 B—Q5, R—QB1; 20 R—B1, O—O; 21 B×B, P×B.

The doubled pawn here is no weakness – it only helps to strengthen Black's centre.

22 B×N, P×B.

The strength of Black's pawns – especially the passed QBP – is overwhelming. White's two passed Q-side pawns are relatively valueless, since he cannot position his pieces effectively to support their advance.

23 N(B3)—K4, P—B6; 24 N—N3, Q—N3; 25 Q—Q3, P—K4; 26 KR—Q1, R—KB2; 27 R—R1, R(B1)—B1; 28 R—KB1, P—Q4; 29 N(K4)—B5, P—K5; 30 Q—Q1, N—K6!; 31 N—Q7, Q—Q3; **32 Resigns.**

The final position deserves a diagram:

30. *Final position Gelfer-Keene*

A very common type of unbalanced position is the kind where the two contestants have pawn majorities on opposite wings. If both sides have castled short, the player with the Q-side pawn majority often has an advantage. This happens for two reasons. In the middle game, the Q-side pawns are normally free to advance, while K-side pawns can only be advanced with great caution, because of the possibility that their forward march will create weaknesses in front of the castled king. Also, in the ending, when both players are trying to create passed pawns, it can be an asset to have a passed pawn on the Q side which cannot be blockaded by the opposing monarch.

An important strategical plan designed to counteract the latent superiority of the Q-side pawn majority is the "minority attack." A minority attack consists of the advance of a pawn minority against an opposing pawn majority on the same wing. The minority attacker hopes that, after the smoke of battle has cleared, the "extra" pawn in his opponent's majority will become weak and exposed. As an example of the strategy involved we give the game KEENE–PATTERSON, Match 1963, which was an extreme case of a successful minority attack:

1 P—Q4, N—KB3; 2 P—QB4, P—KN3; 3 N—QB3, P—Q4; 4 N—B3, B—N2; 5 B—N5!, N—K5; 6 P×P, N×B; 7 N×N, P—K3; 8 Q—Q2, P—KR3; 9 N—R3, P×P; 10 N—B4, P—QB3; 11 P—K3, B—B4; 12 B—Q3, Q—B3; 13 O—O, O—O.

The stage is now set for a minority attack: White will advance his QN and QR pawns. After these have been exchanged, Black's remaining Q-side pawns will become weak.

    14 P—QN4, N—Q2; 15 P—N5, B×B; 16 Q×B, N—N3; 17 P—QR4, QR—B1; 18 P—R5, N—B5; 19 P—R6, Q—K2; 20 P×NP, Q×NP; 21 P×P, R×P.

White's strategy has triumphed and the QP cannot be defended.

    22 KR—N1, Q—Q2; 23 KN×QP, KR—B1; 24 N—N4, N—K4; 25 Q—K4, P—KB4?.

An error – but Black was losing anyway.

    26 Q—Q5 ch, Q×Q; 27 N(B3)×Q, Resigns.

Pawns and Control of Space

As a general rule, it is a good idea to gain space whenever possible, provided that in so doing you do not expose weaknesses in your own camp. The most important way of securing territory is through pawn advances. We have already seen a striking example (Diagram 13) of the difficulties which can accompany a cramped position. The reader will find no shortage of other examples in the rest of this book.

A word of warning, however – beware of flanking blows! Consider Diagram 31:

31. *Black to move*

In this position White has attempted to gain extra space in the centre by advancing his QP to Q5. Because of this the central position has become blocked. Traditionally, the correct way to meet a flank attack is by counter-attack in the centre. White will find this impossible here because he has no play in the centre, and so Black can commence a K-side pawn avalanche against which White is powerless. The continuation was:

    1...P—KB4; 2 B—R6, P—B5; 3 B×B, K×B; 4 Q—Q3, P—KN4.

The win is almost automatic.

    5 N—R2, N—B3; 6 P—B3, P—KR4; 7 K—B2, P—N5; 8 RP×P, RP×P; 9 K—K2.

Trying to evacuate the disaster area – but this loses immediately.

    9...P—N6; 10 N—N4, N×N; 11 P×N, B×P ch.

Black wins.

A Note on Passed Pawns

The study of passed pawns really belongs to a manual of endings rather than a book on opening theory, for it is usually in the ending that the passed pawn comes into its own. But the standard division of chess into opening, middle game, and ending is somewhat arbitrary, and passed pawns can arise very early in the game. Creating a passed pawn is normally a good idea. The Gelfer-Keene game quoted above is a fine illustration of how strong a protected passed pawn can be. Another instructive example is the passed KP from the 6th game of the Spassky-Fischer 1972 World Championship Match see page 29.

Of course, passed pawns can also be weak – especially if isolated – so make sure you can support your passed pawn once it is born. It is often a good idea not to advance a passed pawn too rapidly in the middle game, but rather to nurse it along until an ending can be reached. If the pawn strays too far from home, the enemy forces may gobble it up.

32. *White to move*

In Diagram 32 Black's QRP may look terrifying, but in fact it will soon be lost, for Black has no defence to the threatened KR—QB1, R—B2, and R ×P. Deserting your offspring is a crime!

3

PSYCHOLOGY IN OPENING PLAY

Lasker points out that "in many positions it is impossible to speak of the best move; there are, rather, several possibilities, and from these one move may be the best against a particular opponent and under particular conditions." With these words Lasker acknowledges that play in chess is affected by factors extraneous to the position on the board. In this section before going on to study specific openings we attempt to analyse some of those factors.

We wish to show the reader that the correct handling of an opening is not totally dependent on the objective factor of knowing the opening thoroughly, and sticking to the relevant strategies and tactics to produce an advantage. It is also dependent on subjective factors; the mood of the player, whether he is at home with the chosen opening, whether he is stronger than his opponent, whether he wants to win or draw; and all this will be reflected in his play. Thus, when a player is faced by the choice between several equally good moves, he will apply these psychological criteria to help make his decision.

One of the most important of these psychological factors is that of the player's own style. It is therefore necessary for you to scrutinize your own play, and to recognize the set-ups with which you feel most comfortable. You will soon discover the basic outlines of your style. Are you a cautious player? Does losing upset you? Do you want the excitement of a quick win, or do you prefer to win by refusing to be diverted from a planned, slow and careful build-up? Or do you want the game to be an interesting one in which you consider a well-fought loss to be as exciting as a win? The openings in this book won't all suit you: the ideal player is an all-rounder who can switch to play any opening; but, assuming that as a student you are not an ideal player, you must decide what kind of games you want.

If, as White, you want a quiet game, you will find that the Flank openings, the Queen's Gambit, the Réti, and the English, suit strategical players who do not want to learn set theoretical lines. If you open with 1 P—K4 as White, you may get involved in a heavily-analyzed theoretical fight such as the Dragon. Similarly, as Black you should play the Caro-Kann for a quiet game, and the Sicilian for the fireworks.

In this book one aim is to help the reader to choose openings appropriate to his own style, and we have tried to avoid the mistake, made by many openings books, of being mere encyclopaedic compilations. Such books give endless, indigestible variations with little commentary, and the amateur is often completely lost as to what is happening. There are so many cross-references, games, variations, and deviations catalogued before him that he loses sight of the basic aims behind an opening, and in trying to master all the variations becomes bogged down in pure memory work.

In contrast, we have described the basic features of each opening, and the aims behind the play, and have given sufficient variations for the reader to see how these aims can be realized on the board in a number of situations. This approach enables the reader to select an opening that suits his style of play, or his opponent, or his particular needs at the time.

For example, in the section concerning the Nimzo-Indian, we categorically state that it would suit someone who wants to win as Black. It does not create tactical complications but positional ones; it is a quiet opening with the accent on strategy rather than tactics. Again, when dealing with the King's Indian, we have stated that it, too, is a sharp defence, but in the tactical sense; to be at home with this opening you must be able to calculate variations rather than depend on a feel for strategy. Sharp lines, sacrifices, and concrete variations make up this opening, and the accent is on accurate calculation.

These examples raise the question of what type of defence appeals to you as Black? When you play with the Black pieces do you feel it is very important to counter-attack and seize the initiative at all costs? Remember that White moves first – the initiative is his birth-right! Or do you feel automatically that Black should try to defend against White's first move, neutralize his initiative, equalize the position, and only then play for a win? These are two equally valid viewpoints.

There are defences that are stonewalling or "copy-cat" defences, where Black copies White's moves, trying to neutralize White's advantage. In most lines of the Ruy Lopez, White occupies the centre, Black occupies the centre, White attacks Black's KP, Black defends it – he parries all White's threats and retains a solid position, without trying anything special. Eventually, if White does not play very well, his advantage will just peter out, and Black will try to take the initiative himself. The same can be said of the Queen's Gambit Declined – the counter-part of the Lopez on the Q side. This classical approach to the problem of defending with Black is very popular at all levels. It suits many players.

But there is another method. There are defences which seek to exploit the defects created by White's very first move. After 1 P—Q4, White has surrendered some of his control of the K4 square. If Black then plays the Nimzo-Indian, starting with 1...N—KB3, or the Queen's Indian, he is instantly going out to exploit this fact and the fact that White cannot now push 2 P—K4. In the Nimzo-Indian, Black is prepared to let White form a big pawn-centre, but only at the cost of doubled pawns. Similarly, with the King's Indian, White is allowed to build his pawn-centre, for Black regards the pawn-centre itself as a weakness – he does not defend against its erection, but waits to strike it down after it has arisen.

This is a rather more modern concept of the way to play as Black, for Black does not just defend against White's initiative, he exploits the weaknesses created by the fact that White does possess the initiative. This requires a certain attitude to defensive problems on the part of the player himself: if he firmly believes that Black has to equalize before he can start playing for a win, then, of course, playing the Alekhine, the Nimzo-Indian, or the King's Indian Defence will not suit him. The player of these defences must believe in the counter-attack, in the idea that the initiative can create weaknesses.

This contrast between these different approaches to playing as Black can be clearly seen in the games of the 1972 World Championship Match between Spassky and Fischer. In general, Spassky defended classically as Black – he defended the Ruy Lopez twice, and when Fischer opened 1 P—QB4 he tried to transpose into a Queen's Gambit. Once he even replied 1. . .P—QB4, stonewalling. Spassky was not trying to be dynamic as Black and he was content to try to hold down White's initiative. It was as White that he tried to win.

But Fischer as Black tried all sorts of aggressive openings – the Alekhine, the Modern, the Poison Pawn variation of the Sicilian. None of these was in the least defensive. Each tries to weaken White's KP or tries to seize squares weakened by White's first move, for after 1 P—K4, White has neglected his Q4 square. This clash of styles was very interesting; it had been a long time since we had seen such a contrast, as the attitudes of previous contestants were often similar – as Black they defended, and as White they tried to score their wins. Yet in Reykjavik, Fischer went all out for wins, with Black, as well as White, and was ready to play unbalancing defences in order to score points.

One of Fischer's motives for his very lively style of play in this match was his desire to play variations that would not suit Spassky, for just as it is important to know your own style, it is also very useful to study the style of your opponent. If you are playing in a tournament, do not hesitate to look at the previous games of your opponent beforehand – it will help you to understand what might throw him off balance. At the highest level Grandmasters make quite a science of knowing the psychological make-up of their opponents. The Russian players compile comprehensive files on their leading Western rivals, noting the small weaknesses in the way they handle certain positions, whether they succumb to time-trouble frequently, and how they deal with surprising innovations.

So, if you know that you are playing someone cautious, who declines sacrifices on principle, then you will be able to exploit his frame of mind. Play something that may not be sound, but that is sharp, and you will be secure in the knowledge that he will not even attempt to find the sharp refutation. You can gain a good position, which the opening would not obtain against objective play. For instance the Morra Gambit, the King's Gambit, and the Hennig-Schara in the Tarrasch Defence to the Queen's Gambit (1 P—Q4, P—Q4; 2 P—QB4, P—K3; 3 N—QB3, P—QB4; 4 BP×P, BP×P) are not objectively sound, and against a Grandmaster you would lose a pawn for no compensation, for part of the Master's equipment is his courage, and he will not balk at complications but will analyse them. In a club match, however, you may get away with such risky play, and your opponent may decline the pawn and get a poor position from the opening.

By playing something like the English or Caro-Kann against a quiet player you will be entering his kind of game. You should therefore try to win by playing lines he will be afraid of, as well as playing good moves on the board.

Conversely, against a more explosive player you should try to keep the game simple. If he opens 1 P—K4, play the Caro-Kann or the French. As White, avoid gambit lines and open 1 N—KB3 or 1 P—QB4, and then channel the opening into something that will frustrate your opponent's desire for a lively game.

Your choice of opening will also be affected by your attitude to your opponent. For instance, if you are playing in a tournament or club match and find yourself facing opposition much stronger than yourself, you may well be content with a draw, and you will want to keep the position balanced by playing for symmetrical pawn structures, and other features, which increase the likelihood of a draw. Conversely, you may be winning a tournament and come up against your nearest rival, and in this case, in order to score over him, you will have to play more aggressively for the win.

Having got to this point, the question "Why do we play regular set openings at all?" may well have crossed the reader's mind. What is the point of all this theory? Well, opening theory is the distilled essence of what is best – a catalogued reflection of the experience of leading players. For example, at master level one never sees the sequence 1 P—K4, P—KR3 or 1 P—K4, P—KB4 (after 2 P×P White has won a pawn and Black's K side is weakened). Any games played with these irregular moves would quickly show that Black has a poor position, so there are no examples of these in theory. They are never played. The good lines, which recur, are the ones that are accepted as theory. Once they recur, they can be set down and variations can be noted.

More plausible is the line 1 P—Q4, N—KB3; 2 N—QB3 (trying to play P—K4), 2...P—Q4 (preventing P—K4); 3 P—KB3 (trying to play P—K4 again). All this looks reasonable – but we do not deal with it because in fact it is hopeless. It looks as if White will play P—K4 with a big centre, but P—KB3 weakens the K side and robs the KN of the square KB3. If White ever plays P—K4, Black will exchange pawns and pressurize White's QP, which now has the Black queen on it; e.g., 3...N—QB3 (threatening...P—K4), with a tremendous position – free development, the knights on good squares and stopping White from playing P—K4. If he does attempt 4 P—K4, the following could happen 4...P×P; 5 P—Q5, N—K4; 6 P×P, P—K3 – at best White ends up with an isolated KP with a Black knight blocking its passage.

We stick to theory because it does reflect play at the highest level, but there is always room for useful innovation, and the psychological impact of good innovation can be seen in the third game of the Spassky-Fischer 1972 World Championship Match, when Spassky, as White, spent 25 minutes considering his reply to Fischer's innovation on move eleven in a Modern Benoni.

In fact, that 1972 World Championship Match is a good, practical demonstration of the psychological tactics we have discussed. We have already stated that Fischer's attitude was to go all out for the win in every game, and not only did he produce innovations in play to that end, he also innovated in his choice of opening. Fischer was known to play certain openings as White and as Black, and he started by playing these. He then switched and started to play 1 P—QB4 – the English Opening – instead of his usual 1 P—K4. As Black he normally played the Najdorf Sicilian, but in the match he played the Alekhine, and the Pirc. This constant switching to openings that he had never usually played, combined with his playing them well, put great pressure on Spassky, who frequently came out of the openings with a bad position, sometimes as early as move eight or nine. Even as White he often got a dismal position from the opening.

Fischer's success showed that he had analysed how Spassky handled the openings, found certain weak spots, and then exploited them. The fact that he changed to fresh openings for himself indicated that he wished to prevent Spassky doing the same for him.

KING'S PAWN OPENINGS

INTRODUCTION

The move 1 P—K4 is one of White's most natural choices for the opening move of the game, for it stakes a claim in the centre and opens lines for White's KB and queen. Replies to 1 P—K4 can be grouped into two general categories: those in which Black prevents White from forming a full pawn centre with 2 P—Q4, and those in which Black permits such a centre in the hope of using it as a target for his counter-attack later in the game. Into the first class fall all the symmetrical defences starting with 1. . .P—K4 and also the Sicilian Defence (1. . .P—QB4). The second class is represented here by the French Defence (1. . .P—K3), the Caro-Kann (1. . .P—QB3), and the Modern Defence (1. . .P—KN3).

The most obvious reply to consider first is 1. . .P—K4, for it would at least seem that Black cannot have reduced his prospects by playing this move. All the reasons for White's 1 P—K4 apply with equal validity to Black's 1. . .P—K4. Of course, since the position is symmetrical, White still has the advantage of the move – but White started with that advantage anyway. How should White now continue? In accordance with the general principle that one should develop where possible with a threat, the logical course for White is to look for moves which contribute to his development and at the same time attack the unprotected Black KP.

The way in which White sets about these tasks depends largely on the style of game which he prefers. The attacking player often decides on an opening in which the complications begin at an early stage, as for example in the King's Gambit. The positional player will usually choose to maintain the tension for somewhat longer and he is more likely to prefer one of the openings stemming from 2 N—KB3.

This has the merits of bringing a knight into play and paving the way for the eventual thematic advance P—Q4. Black, in turn, should now be looking for developing moves which protect the KP – he usually chooses 2. . .N—QB3. The symmetrical KP openings which we consider start from this position. The next decision White must make is where to put his KB. We shall examine the two most important alternatives, the Ruy Lopez (3 B—N5) and the Giuoco Piano (3 B—B4).

4

KING'S GAMBIT

1 P—K4, P—K4; 2 P—KB4

During the last century the King's Gambit was by far the most popular opening, at all levels of play. White offers the sacrifice of a pawn at move two, with the idea of obtaining speedy development and opening up lines for an early attack against Black's king. In its heyday, the King's Gambit often brought White brilliant victories after he had built up a dangerous attack in the opening; but as the theory of openings evolved it was discovered that Black, by developing his own forces in a sensible manner, could obtain a perfectly satisfactory position.

In offering his KBP on his second move, White plans to utilize the KB-file to attack Black's weak spot at KB2. We have seen in the introduction how this square often comes under pressure from a bishop at White's QB4 and a knight at White's K5 or KN5. Here, White hopes to open up a third line of attack by castling K side. This brings his KR to KB1, from where it can make its influence felt along the KB file.

Another aspect of the gambit is that if Black accepts the pawn (2...P×P) his only central unit is deflected thereby making it easier for White to increase his centre control with a later P—Q4. Nevertheless, Black's best system of defense involves accepting the gambit and returning the pawn in a way which eases the development of his pieces.

By the very nature of the dynamic positions that arise from the King's Gambit, the opening is most popular with beginners and club players who enjoy the cut and thrust tactics that usually develop. In contrast, there is the consideration that the gambit was played so often over such a long period that analysis has shorn it of much of its terror at master level.

KING'S GAMBIT ACCEPTED

1 P—K4	P—K4
2 P—KB4	P×P
3 N—KB3	P—KN4
4 B—B4	P—Q3
5 O—O	P—KR3
6 P—Q4	B—N2
7 P—B3	N—QB3
8 P—KN3	P—N5
9 N—R4	P—B6
10 N—Q2	B—B3
11 N(Q2)×P!	P×N
12 Q×P	R—R2
13 N—N6!	

In this section we shall examine one of the older variations, in which Black captures the gambit pawn and holds on to it.

1 P—K4	P—K4
2 P—KB4	P×P

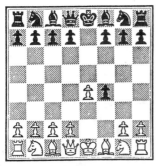

3 N—KB3

This is the most natural move. It prevents the check 3...Q—R5 and conforms to White's general strategy of quick K-side development.

3 . . .   P—KN4

Black is anticipating White to play P—Q4 in the not too distant future, threatening to win back the sacrificed pawn by B×P.

4 B—B4

Once again White pursues his policy of K-side development, at the same time keeping in mind Black's KB2 square.
(For 4 P—KR4 see p. 48)

4 . . .   P—Q3

A solid move, depriving White's knight of the use of his K5 square and opening the way for Black's QB.
(For 4...P—N5 see p. 49)

5 O—O

In return for the gambit pawn White now has a three tempi lead in development. His latest move intensifies the pressure against Black's KB2 square by bringing the rook to the KB file.

5 . . .   P—KR3

Supporting the KNP is essential either now or after 5...B—N2; 6 P—Q4, because White would then be threatening 7 N×P!, Q×N; 8 QB×P, opening the KB file and thereby initiating a very dangerous attack.

6 P—Q4

White cashes in on another aspect of his compensation. When Black made the capture 2...P×P, he removed a pawn from the centre thereby relinquishing his control of that area. White now sets up a formidable pawn centre and only then does he proceed with his K-side attack.
(For 6 P—KN3 see p. 49)

6 . . .   B—N2

This is a better square for the bishop than K2, because White may eventually try to open up the position with P—K5, and it would be useful to have as much control as possible over that square. If the bishop is required on the Q1—KR5 diagonal at some later stage, Black will be free to play B—B3, as in fact he does in the main line. Another reason for leaving the K2 square vacant at this stage is that it might be a good square for Black to develop his KN.

7 P—B3

A dual purpose move, supporting the QP and creating the possibility of Q—N3, which would add support to the attack against Black's KB2.

7 ...   N—QB3

(For 7...B—K3 see p. 50)

8 P—KN3!

Now White is ready to attack. The text soon leads to the opening up of the KB file.

8 ...   P—N5

(For 8...B—R6 see p. 50)

9 N—R4   P—B6

Black has succeeded in keeping the KB file closed. Or has he?

10 N—Q2   B—B3

It seems as though Black is getting the upper hand. He still has his extra pawn and he has now instituted an attack on White's KN, which appears to be stuck out on a limb. The knight cannot retreat and it cannot advance to KB5, because after (11 N—B5), B×N; 12 P×B, Q—Q2, White's KBP is extremely weak, and there is no longer any hope of an attack along the KB file. There is however, one other possibility.

11 N(Q2)×P!   P×N
12 Q×P

White has cleared away the obstructive pawn at KB3, and his pressure on Black's KB2 square is now at its peak.

12 ...   R—R2

Defending his Achilles' Heel.

(For 12...B—R6 see p. 50)

13 N—N6!

A move which is surprising, because on N6 the white knight does not actually attack anything. The point of the move is to bring the knight nearer to the centre by N—B4. This aim cannot be achieved by 13 N—N2 because Black could then play 13...B—R6, pinning the knight against White's rook, and then exchange off the knight for his somewhat useless bishop.

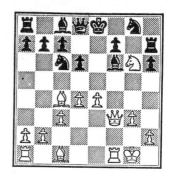

The game SPIELMANN–GRUNFELD, Teplitz Schonau 1922 continued:
13...R—N2.
Not 13...P×N, which loses quickly to 14 B×N, R—N2; 15 B—N3, B—K2 (forced); 16 B×P, R—R2; 17 B—B7 ch, K—Q2; 18 Q—N4 mate.
14 N—B4, B—N5.
White was threatening 15 N—R5.
15 Q—N2, B—N4; 16 P—KR3, B—Q2; 17 N—R5, R—R2; 18 P—K5!.
Opening up another line of attack – the K file, and simultaneously vacating the square K4 for the queen.
18...P×P; 19 Q—K4, P—B4.
Forced, since 19...R—R1 allows 20 N—N7 ch, followed by mate.
20 R×P!, B×R; 21 Q×B.
White had a tremendous position.

---

4 P—KR4

4 P—KR4. White abandons, temporarily, his developing move B—QB4 and pays heed to Black's challenging move 3... P—KN4. Since White's KN cannot use the square KN5 at the moment (the black pawn on that square is guarded by the queen), many games of yesteryear saw the move 4 P—KR4, the idea of which is to precipitate the reply 4...P—N5, and then to follow up with 5 N—N5 or 5 N—K5. White's queen is then attacking Black's KNP and his knight is aimed at the key square, Black's KB2. White's attack will soon be augmented by B—QB4 (and possibly O—O). One example of this strategy working out well is a variation analysed by the nineteenth-century master Jaenisch: From the diagram play continues:

4 . .P—N5; 5 N—K5, P—KR4.
Many other moves are possible here. The text has the advantage of defending Black's KNP while making way for ...R—R2 which protects the KBP.
6 B—QB4, R—R2; 7 P—Q4.
Even though Black's king would be exposed after 7 N×P, R×N; 8 B×R ch, K×B; 9 P—Q4, White does better to keep his active pieces rather than exchange them for a passive rook.
7...P—Q3; 8 N—Q3, P—B6; 9 P×P, B—K2; 10 B—K3, B×P ch; 11 K—Q2, P×P; 12 Q×P.
With White's position so active, Black's extra pawn is of little consequence.
12...B—N5; 13 Q—B4,N—Q2.
After 13...Q—B3, White's lead in development is so significant that he can afford to allow the exchange of queens; e.g., 14 N—B3, P—B3; 15 P—K5!, Q×Q; 16 N×Q, P×P; 17 P×P, B—N4; 18 QR—KN1, and White's pressure along the KN file gives him an enormous advantage.
14 N—B3, N—N3; 15 B—N3, R—N2; 16 QR—KB1, B—N4; 17 Q—B2.
17 B×P ch loses the bishop after 17...K—B1; 18 Q moves, B×B ch; and 19...R×B.
17...B×B ch; 18 Q×B, Q—K2; 19 P—K5.
White is still a pawn down but his pieces are by far the more active. According to Jaenisch, White has the advantage.

4...P—N5

4...P—N5. A more forceful move than

4...P—Q3. By pushing on his NP, Black compels White to declare his intentions at once. The most interesting possibility now at White's disposal is the **Muzio Gambit, 5 O—O.** White sacrifices a knight and in return he gets the compensation that is traditional in the King's Gambit Accepted – strong pressure along the KB file and a huge lead in development.
5...P×N; 6 Q×P, Q—B3.
There are other ways to defend the KBP, but this is the most usual.
7 P—K5.
This pawn sacrifice opens up a new line of attack.
7...Q×P; 8 P—Q3.
It is necessary to defend the bishop against the threat of 8...Q—QB4 ch.
8...B—R3; 9 N—B3, N—K2; 10 B—Q2, QN—B3; 11 QR—K1, Q—B4; 12 N—Q5, K—Q1.
In return for the sacrificed material White has achieved a harmonious development of his forces. In addition, Black's king is none too well placed, and his rooks and QB are completely out of play. All in all the chances are about even, though a proof of this assessment is well beyond the scope of this book.

---

6 P—KN3

---

6 P—KN3. This is an attempt to open up the KB file even earlier than in the main line. If Black captures the pawn he loses by force: (6...P×P); 7 B×P ch!, K×B; 8 N—K5 dbl ch, K—K2; 9 R—B7 ch, K—K1; 10 Q—R5, etc. Black's best line is probably **6...P—N5; 7 N—R4, P—B6,** reaching a position similar

to that in the main line. After **8 N×P, P×N; 9 Q×P, Q—K2**, it is not quite clear whether White's lead in development and his attack add up to sufficient compensation for the sacrificed material.

7...B—K3

7...B—K3. This move is not an uncommon defence in some of the old-fashioned open games. Black blunts the attack of White's bishop along the QR2—KB7 diagonal, and after White exchanges at K6, Black is left with pawns at K3 and Q3, hopefully keeping the white army away from his king. In this instance the "defence" does not work, because after **8 B×B, P×B; 9 Q—N3** (attacking both the KP and the QNP), **9...Q—B1**, White can build up a strong attack by force:

10 P—KR4!, P—N5; 11 N—R2.
Possible now that Black's queen is no longer watching White's KRP.

11...P—N6; 12 N—B3, P—K4; 13 P×P, P×P; 14 N—R3, N—K2; 15 N—B4, QN—B3; 16 N(B4)×P, N× N; 17 N×N, B×N; 18 B×P.
In return for the sacrificed piece White has a very strong (possibly decisive) attack.

8...B—R6

8...B—R6. This causes a certain amount of disruption in White's ranks, that is if he worries about the loss of the exchange and moves his rook. The correct move is **9 P×P!**, sacrificing the exchange so as to keep control of the situation on the K side. After **9...B×R; 10 Q×B, P×P; 11 B×P, Q—B3; 12 B—KN3**, White's material deficit is relatively unimportant, because Black has not yet completed his development. Play might continue:

12...O—O—O; 13 QN—Q2, KN— K2; 14 Q—R3 ch.
Played so as to vacate the KB1 square for his rook.

14...K—N1; 15 R—KB1, Q—N3; 16 N—R4, Q—N4; 17 N(R4)—B3, Q— N3; 18 N—R4.
A draw by repetition of position.

12...B—R6

12...B—R6. In comparison with the previous note, the threat of losing the exchange here assumes greater proportions because White has already sacrificed a piece. Judging just how much material one can afford to sacrifice is always a difficult task for the beginner. There are no hard and fast rules that can be used for guidance, as it is one of those things that comes only with experience.

In contrast with the last note, it is now advisable for White to move his rook. After **13 R—B2!**, Black's position remains difficult; e.g., **13...Q—Q2; 14 P—K5!, P×P; 15 P×P, B×N; 16 B× P ch, K—K2; 17 B—K3!.** White's attack is probably decisive.

MODERN DEFENCE

1 P—K4	P—K4
2 P—KB4	P×P
3 N—KB3	P—Q4
4 P×P	N—KB3
5 B—N5 ch	P—B3
6 P×P	N×P
7 P—Q4	B—Q3
8 Q—K2 ch	B—K3
9 N—KN5	O—O!
10 N×B	P×N
11 B×N	P×B
12 Q×P ch	K—R1
13 O—O	Q—B2

1 P—K4	P—K4
2 P—KB4	P×P
3 N—KB3	P—Q4

Black returns the pawn immediately so as to open lines for development. His

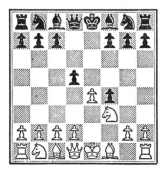

QB is now free to move and the scope of his queen has been increased.

This system has become the favourite defence of many of the world's strongest players, Spassky and Botvinnik among them.

4 P×P

White is obliged to accept this pawn.
(For 4 P—K5? see p. 52)

4 ...   N—KB3

A developing move that threatens White's forward QP.
(For 4...Q×P see p. 53)

5 B—N5 ch

This check is designed to exchange off White's attacked QP by inviting Black to reply ...P—QB3. Of course it is possible for Black to escape from the check by interposing a piece on Q2 but, as can be seen in the alternative variation (5...QN—Q2?!) this does not give Black such an active game.
(For 5 N—B3 and 5 P—B4 see p. 53)

5 ...   P—B3

(For 5...QN—Q2?! and 5...B—Q2 see p. 54)

6 P×P   N×P

This move was taken up by Spassky after he had faced it a few times in games from simultaneous exhibitions. The square QB3 is, after all, the natural one for Black's QN, and there is no reason for Black to fear the exchange B×N ch.

(For 6...P×P see p. 54)

7 P—Q4

White cannot castle at once because of (7 O—O?), Q—N3 ch, winning the bishop. He therefore blocks the KN1—QR7 diagonal and at the same time introduces an attack on Black's forward KBP.

(For 7 Q—K2 ch see p. 54)

7 ...   B—Q3

Defending the attacked pawn.

(For 7...Q—R4 ch see p. 55)

8 Q—K2 ch

Will White be able to take advantage of the coming pin on the K file?

(For 8 O—O see p. 55)

8 ...   B—K3
9 N—KN5

It certainly looks as though Black is in trouble! Now White threatens to win a pawn.

Note that 9 P—B4?, O—O; 10 P—Q5, allows Black to take full advantage of the relative positions of White's queen and king by 9...B—KN5! (10 P×N?, R—K1).

(For 9 N—K5 see p. 55)

9 ...   O—O!

Sacrificing the pawn in the interests of speedy development and the opening of an important line (the K file) for his counterattack.

10 N×B	P×N
11 B×N	P×B
12 Q×P ch	K—R1

Now Black, threatens to win the queen by 12...R—K1. His minor pieces are developed on active squares, whereas the whole of White's Q side is underdeveloped. In an open position such as this, the lead in development and the associated attacking chances provide ample compensation for the sacrificed pawn.

13 O—O	Q—B2

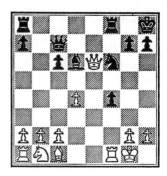

The game BHEND–MEDINA, Lugano 1970 continued:

14 Q—R3, Q—N3; 15 Q—Q3, QR—K1; 16 N—B3, Q—N1.

Threatening 17...P—B6; 18 Q×BP (not 18 P—KN3?, B×P!; 19 P×B, Q×KNP ch; 20 K—R1, Q—N7 mate), 18...B×P ch; 19 K—R1, N—R4, with a won game.

17 Q—KB3, P—B4; 18 P—Q5, P—N4!; 19 P—KR3, P—KR4; 20 Q—Q3, P—N5.

Black had a very strong attack but because he was in severe time trouble (only a little over one minute for the next twenty moves) he was unable to press his advantage home and the game was soon agreed drawn.

---

4 P—K5?

4 P—K5?. Black can now play 4...P—KN4, as in the previous variation of the King's Gambit Accepted, but with the important difference that White no longer has the use of his QB4 square for his KB, and Black will not, therefore,

find his KB2 square subjected to attack. Play might continue: **5 P—KR3, N—KR3; 6 P—Q4, N—B4,** when Black has a safe extra pawn and a fine position.

4...Q×P

4...Q×P. This brings the queen out too soon, allowing White to gain the initiative by attacking her: **5 N—B3, Q—K3 ch; 6 K—B2!** (threatening 7 B—N5 ch, followed by 8 R—K1 winning the queen), **6...Q—QN3 ch; 7 P—Q4.** White has the advantage because his king is much safer than it looks and Black is far behind in development.

---

5 N—B3

5 N—B3. After **5...N×P; 6 N×N, Q×N,** the position is not unfavourable for Black, because there is no way in which his queen can be made to suffer for her early journey into the middle of the board. Play might continue:

7 P—Q4, B—K2.

7...B—KN5; 8 B×P, N—B3, appears to put White's QP under pressure, but,

after 9 B×P!, B×N; 10 Q×B, Q×Q; 11 P×Q, R—QB1; 12 B—KB4, N×P; 13 O—O—O!, it is Black who is in dire straits, because his king is about to come under fire from moves such as B—QN5 ch, and KR—K1 at an opportune moment.

8 P—B4, Q—K5 ch.

8...Q—Q3 is not so good. After 9 Q—K2!, O—O; 10 P—B5, Q—KB3; 11 Q—K4, R—K1; 12 B—Q3, P—KN3; 13 O—O, Black cannot develop his QB without allowing his QNP to fall.

9 B—K2.

9 K—B2 used to be the popular move, but it was found that, after 9...B—KB4; 10 P—B5, N—B3; 11 B—N5, Q—Q4!, White has no active continuation, whereas Black can play ...B—K5 followed by ...O—O—O, intensifying the pressure on White's blockaded QP.

9...N—B3; 10 O—O, B—KB4; 11 R—K1, O—O—O.

The position is equal.

---

5 P—B4

5 P—B4. This is not the start of an attempt to save the attacked QP. After 5...P—B3; 6 P×P, N×P; 7 P—Q4, B—KN5, Black has the advantage by virtue of his pressure on the QP and his superior development; e.g., 8 P—Q5, B—N5 ch; 9 B—Q2, O—O!; 10 P×N, R—K1 ch; 11 B—K2, N—K5, with a strong attack.

White should therefore reply to

5...P—B3 with **6 P—Q4,** e.g.

6...B—N5 ch.

Not 6...P×P; 7 P—B5!, when Black's position is slightly cramped.

7 N—B3, P×P; 8 B×P, O—O; 9

B—Q3, R—K1 ch; 10 B—K5, N—B3; 11 O—O, N×B; 12 N×N, P×P; 13 B×BP, B—K3.

There are equal chances for both White and Black.

Black can also meet 5 P—B4 with 5...P—QN4, undermining the support of White's forward QP: e.g. 6 N—B3, P×P; 7 B×P, B—Q3; 8 P—Q4, QN—Q2; 9 N—K2, O—O; 10 B×P, N—N3, winning back the pawn with a level game.

5...QN—Q2?!

5...QN—Q2?!. 6 O—O, N×P; 7 P—B4, N—B3; 8 P—Q4, B—K2.

Or 8...P—B3; 9 B—R4, B—Q3; 10 R—K1 ch, K—B1; 11 N—B3, when White's active position gives him ample compensation for the sacrificed pawn.

9 B×P, O—O; 10 B—R4, N—N3; 11 B—QN3.

White has the advantage because of his more active development and better central control.

5...B—Q2

5...B—Q2. This is also not entirely satisfactory for Black. After 6 Q—K2 ch, B—K2; 7 B—B4, White has the more active development and Black must expend much effort in the hunt for his lost pawn.

6...P×P

6...P×P. 7 B—B4, N—Q4!.

After 7...B—Q3, White can exchange queens and take advantage of Black's poor pawn structure: 8 Q—K2 ch, Q—K2; 9 Q×Q ch, K×Q; 10 O—O, B—K3; 11 R—K1, QN—Q2; 12 P—Q4, KR—K1; 13 B×B, P×B; 14 QN—Q2, with a slight advantage to White.

8 O—O.

Now 8 Q—K2 ch is met by 8...B—K2, followed by ...O—O and ...R—K1, with a good game for Black.

8...B—Q3; 9 N—B3, B—K3.

Not 9...N×N, because of 10 R—K1 ch!.

10 N—K4, B—B2; 11 B—N3, O—O; 12 P—Q4, QN—Q2.

The chances are roughly equal. Black's forward KBP is well protected and his pieces harmoniously developed. 13 P—B4 can be met by 13...N—K6; 14 B×N, P×B.

7 Q—K2 ch

7 Q—K2 ch. This gives White only a temporary initiative: 7...B—K2 (not 7...B—K3; 8 N—N5); 8 P—Q4, O—O; 9 B×N, P×B; 10 O—O, B—Q3. Black's pieces are the more active, his

two bishops have ample scope, and he has excellent prospects of play along the K file after ...R—K1, ...N—Q4 (or KN5), and ...N—K6.

7...Q—R4 ch

7...Q—R4 ch. This looks strong, since after **8 N—B3, B—QN5,** Black threatens to win White's stray bishop by ...B× N ch, but White can avoid material loss and calmly complete his development by **9 O—O!,** and if 9...B×N, then 10 Q—K2 ch, B—K3; 11 P×B, when White's pieces are actively placed.

---

8 O—O

8 O—O. More logical than the text in the sense that White's queen tends to become exposed on K2, because Black

soon plays ...R—K1. But after **8...O—O,** White still has trouble in completing his development in a satisfactory manner: e.g., 9 P—B3, N—Q4. Better than 9...N—KN5, because White can then play 10 N—R3!, e.g., 10...B× N; 11 P×B, Q—Q3; 12 Q—Q3. Now White threatens 13 N—N5. If Black guards against the threat with 12...P— KR3, then 13 N—R4 is strong.

10 Q—Q3, R—K1.
Black's game is the more active.

---

9 N—K5

9 N—K5. Blocking the diagonal through which Black's KB defends his forward KBP, but after **9...O—O; 10 B×N, P×B; 11 B×P,** Black can get very active play for his pawn with **11...N— Q4; 12 B—N3, P—B3; 13 N—KB3, B×B ch; 14 P×B, R—K1.** In this variation the roles of the players have been reversed – Black is the one who has sacrificed the pawn for an active game!

FALKBEER COUNTER GAMBIT

1 P—K4	P—K4
2 P—KB4	P—Q4
3 KP×P	P—K5
4 P—Q3	N—KB3
5 P×P	N×P
6 N—KB3	B—QB4
7 Q—K2	B—B4
8 N—B3	Q—K2
9 B—K3	B×B
10 Q×B	N×N
11 Q×Q ch	K×Q
12 P×N	B×P
13 K—Q2	

---

1 P—K4	P—K4
2 P—KB4	P—Q4

Black ignores White's offer of a pawn, preferring to (temporarily) sacrifice a pawn himself in the interests of speeding up his development. After his second move, Black's bishops both have freedom of action and he should not be faced with any development problems.

3 KP×P

Naturally not 3 BP×P??, Q—R5 ch, winning.

(For 3 N—KB3 see p. 57)

3 . . .   **P—K5**

The secondary point of the counter gambit. Not only has Black eased his own development (by 2...P—Q4) but he also cramps White by preventing an early N—KB3.

(For 3...P×P see p. 57)

4 P—Q3

Giving his QB some scope and attacking Black's KP. As with the similar position in the Modern Defence to the King's Gambit Accepted (i.e. after Black's fourth move), White's 5 P—B4 is not an attempt to hang on to the forward QP, but the start of a plan to gain control of the Q5 square. After 4...P—QB3; 5 N—QB3, N—B3; 6 P—Q4, BP×P, however, Black has a better game than in the corresponding line of the Modern Defence, because of his strong pawn at K5; e.g., 7 Q—N3, B—K2; 8 P×P, O—O; 9 KN—K2, QN—Q2; 10 N—N3, N—N3, with a good game for Black.

(For 4 B—N5 ch see p. 57)

4 . . .   **N—KB3**

Black cannot afford to win back the pawn at once by 4...Q×P, because of 5 Q—K2, P—KB4; 6 N—QB3, B—QN5; 7 B—Q2, B×N (the only way to keep the pawn); 8 B×B, N—KB3; 9 O—O—O!, Q×RP; 10 P×P, N×P (10...Q—R8 ch?; 11 K—Q2, N×P ch?? loses a piece to 12 Q×N ch); 11 P—QN3, O—O; 12 Q—B4 ch, K—R1; 13 B—N2, and with Black's queen out of play White has a strong attack.

5 P×P

(For 5 N—Q2 see p. 58)

5 . . .   **N×KP**

Now Black is threatening 6...Q—R5 ch; 7 P—N3, N×P!.

6 N—KB3   **B—QB4**

The natural square for the bishop, hitting White's weak spot at KB2.

7 Q—K2

With this move, putting pressure on the K file, White assures himself of the advantage.

7 ...   **B—B4**

There are other ways of supporting the knight but none of them is satisfactory for Black: (*a*) 7...Q—K2; 8 B—K3!; (*b*) 7...P—KB4; 8 B—K3, Q×P; 9 B×B, Q×B; 10 N—B3; (*c*) 7...Q×P; 8 N(B3)—Q2, P—KB4; 9 N—QB3; (*d*) 7...B—B7 ch; 8 K—Q1, Q×P ch; 9 N(B3)—Q2!, P—KB4; 10 N—B3. In each case White has an advantage.

8 N—B3

Increasing the pressure on the K file. 8 P—KN4 looks at first sight as though it wins a piece, but Black can leave his bishop to be captured: 8...O—O!; 9 P×B, R—K1, and White is lost, now that Black has taken over control of the K file.

8 ...   **Q—K2**

Not 8...B—QN5?; 9 Q—N5 ch.

9 B—K3   **B×B**

It is possible for Black to win a pawn by 9...N×N; 10 B×B, N×Q; 11 B×Q, N×P; 12 B—KN5, N×QP, but, after 13 O—O—O, White has a useful initiative as compensation.

10 **Q×B**	**N×N**
11 **Q×Q ch**	**K×Q**
12 **P×N**	**B×P**
13 **K—Q2**	

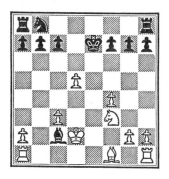

White has the initiative; e.g., 13...B—R4; 14 R—K1 ch, K—Q1; 15 R—K4.

3 N—KB3

3 N—KB3. This allows Black to take the initiative: 3...QP×P; 4 N×P, B—Q3; 5 Q—K2 (other moves also fail to stem Black's easy development; e.g., 5 B—B4, B×N; 6 P×B, N—QB3); 5...N—KB3; 6 P—Q4, P×P e.p.; 7 N×QP dis ch, B—K2. Black will follow up with 8...O—O and an excellent game.

3...P×P

3...P×P. This is also satisfactory for Black. It may even be his best defence. After 4 Q—B3, N—KB3; 5 B—N5 ch (5 N—QB3, B—Q3, gives Black an easy game), 5...P—B3!; 6 P×P, N×P, Black has an active game. The alternative, 4 N—KB3, transposes to the Modern Defence.

4 B—N5 ch

4 B—N5 ch. Winning a pawn at the cost of getting temporarily tied up by Black's

bishops, which soon become active:
4...P—B3; 5 P×P, N×P; 6 P—Q3
(6 P—Q4, Q—R4 ch; 7 N—B3, B—
QN5 is also not pleasant for White),
**6...N—B3; 7 N—QB3, B—QN5; 8
B—Q2, B—N5; 9 KN—K2, O—O.**
Black is fully developed. He exercises
pressure on White's position from both
sides (by means of the pins) and in the
centre. If 10 P×P, then Q—N3! is
strong, while 10 P—KR3, B×N(K7);
11 N×B, B×B ch; 12 Q×B, P—K6 is
good for Black. But White is able to
relieve the tension by **10 P—QR3, P×P;
11 B×P, B×N(B6); 12 B×B, N—Q4;**

13 Q—Q2, when it is not clear that
Black's open lines provide sufficient
compensation for the sacrificed pawn.
Probably White has the better chances.

5 N—Q2

5 N—Q2. This move is more popular
than the text, but less likely to give
White a lasting advantage. After
**5...P×P; 6 B×P, N×P; 7 Q—K2 ch,
B—K2,** the chances are roughly equal.

CLASSICAL DEFENCE

1 P—K4	P—K4	
2 P—KB4	B—B4	
3 N—KB3	P—Q3	
4 N—B3	N—KB3	
5 B—B4	N—B3	
6 P—Q3	B—KN5	
7 N—QR4	N—Q5	
8 N×B	P×N	
9 P—B3	N×N ch	
10 P×N	B—R4	

1 P—K4	P—K4
2 P—KB4	B—B4

This move introduces the Classical
Defence, which was the first popular

method of declining the King's Gambit.
Black takes immediate advantage of
White's vulnerability along the KN1—
QR7 diagonal. The idea is to delay
White's K-side castling for some time
and thus limit the pressure which he can
bring to bear on Black's KB2.

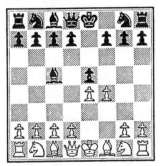

3 N—KB3

This developing move attacks Black's KP for the second time. Note that to capture this pawn immediately costs White a rook: 3 P×P??, Q—R5 ch; 4 P—N3, Q×KP ch; and 5...Q×R.

3 ...   P—Q3

Defending the KP and opening the way for the development of the QB.

(For 3...N—QB3?! see next col.)

4 N—B3

A natural developing move which prepares for the possibility of playing N—QR4 and exchanging off the irritating bishop.

(For 4 P—QN4, 4 B—B4,
4 P—B3 see p. 60)

4 ...   N—KB3

The most natural developing move.

5 B—B4

Again a normal move in keeping with White's general strategy of pressure against KB7. If 5 P×P, P×P; 6 N×P, Black can put White in a terrible bind by 6...Q—Q5; 7 N—Q3, B—N3.

5 ...   N—B3

After 5...B—K3; 6 B×B, P×B; 7 P×P, P×P; 8 N×P, Q—Q5; 9 N—Q3, N×P; 10 N×N, Q×N ch; 11 Q—K2, Q×Q ch; 12 K×Q, White has the better ending because of Black's isolated KP.

6 P—Q3   B—KN5

The most usual move but not the best. Black's idea is to weaken White's K side by ...N—Q5 followed by exchanging on KB6, doubling White's KBPs.

(For 6...O—O see p. 60)

7 N—QR4   N—Q5

Consistent with his last move.

8 N×B   P×N
9 P—B3

9 P×P is dangerous because of 9...N—Q2 (threatening 10...N×KP,

with an overwhelming game because of the effect of the pin); 10 B—B4, Q—K2; 11 O—O, O—O—O, when Black has a very active game.

9 ...   N×N ch
10 P×N   B—R4

10...N×P is interesting but unsound because of 11 O—O!, when Black has two pieces en prise.

White has the advantage because of his pair of bishops and the great influence which his pawns exert on the centre.

3...N—QB3?!

3...N—QB3?!. An inferior method of defending the KP: **4 N×P, N×N; 5 P—Q4** (the fork trick! Clearly 5 P×N is not possible because of 5...Q—R5 ch; 6 P—N3, Q×KP ch, winning a rook), **5...B×P; 6 Q×B, Q—R5 ch; 7 Q—B2, Q×Q ch; 8 K×Q,** with the better game for White, who has much the easier development and the advantage of the two bishops.

4 P—QN4 and 4 B—B4

4 P—QN4. This is only justified if Black accepts the offer: 4...B×P; 5 P—B3, B—R4; 6 B—B4, and White will continue with O—O and Q—N3, with good attacking prospects against Black's KB2 square to compensate for the sacrificed pawn.

The correct reply is **4...B—N3,** when **5 B—N2, N—KB3; 6 N—B3, O—O; 7 B—B4, N—B3** leaves Black with the advantage – White still cannot castle, his QNP is weak, and he has no real attacking chances. Note that **4 B—B4** is not correct, because, after **4...N—KB3; 5 P—Q3, B—K3; 6 B×B, P×B,** Black's doubled KPs control some important squares.

4 P—B3

4 P—B3. The main alternative. White

prepares to occupy the centre with P—Q4:
4...N—KB3.
4...P—B4 is too risky. White gains the initiative, e.g., 5 BP×P, QP×P; 6 P—Q4, P×P; 7 B—QB4, N—QB3; 8 P—QN4, B—N3; 9 Q—N3, N—R3 (9...N—B3, allows 10 P—N5, N—QR4; 11 B—B7 ch and 12 B—R3 ch); 10 O—O, BP×P; 11 B—KN5, Q—Q3; 12 N—R3, P×P dis ch; 13 K—R1, Q×P; 14 QR—K1, and White has a terrific attack to compensate for the sacrificed pawns.
5 P×P.
5 P—Q4, P×QP; 6 P×P, B—N3, leaves White's impressive looking pawn centre vulnerable to attack by Black's pieces.
5...P×P; 6 P—Q4.
6 N×P, Q—K2; 7 P—Q4, B—Q3; 8 N—B4 might possibly be slightly better for White.
6...P×P; 7 P×P, B—N3.
White has achieved his aim of establishing pawns at K4 and Q4 but, as in the note to White's fifth move, it is possible that these pawns may later come under attack from Black's pieces.

6...O—O

6...O—O. This modest developing move is Black's safest course. 7 N—QR4, B—N3; 8 N×B, RP×N; 9 O—O, N—QR4. Black will exchange off White's strong bishop and the position will be level.

5

GIUOCO PIANO AND TWO KNIGHTS DEFENCE

1 P—K4, P—K4; 2 N—KB3, N—QB3; 3 B—B4

All the openings considered in this section arise after White's move 3 B—B4. In the chapter on the Ruy Lopez, we remark that the bishop move (3 B—N5), represents the logical continuation of White's positional pressure against the Black KP, so what can be said in favour of this alternative development of the bishop? Certainly the bishop on QB4 is not badly placed, for it helps control the central square Q5, and also threatens Black's weak square KB2. But the general feeling amongst modern masters is that this is not enough. Black's defensive resources are well-known, and all too often he is able to achieve equality through some simple tactical possibility involving the placement of the bishop on QB4 (the "fork trick," for instance, or the chance of exchanging knight for bishop with ...N—QR4). The openings treated in this section are quite interesting both historically (they were great favourites in the nineteenth century), and tactically (the bishop hitting Black's KB2 often gives rise to interesting combinations), but they are not very likely to give White much advantage against reasonably experienced players.

GIUOCO PIANO

1 P—K4	P—K4
2 N—KB3	N—QB3
3 B—B4	B—B4
4 P—Q3	N—B3
5 N—B3	P—Q3
6 B—KN5	P—KR3
7 B×N	Q×B
8 N—Q5	Q—Q1
9 P—B3	N—K2
10 P—QN4	B—N3
11 N×B	RP×N
12 P—Q4!	P×P
13 N×P	O—O
14 O—O	

1 P—K4	P—K4
2 N—KB3	N—QB3
3 B—B4	B—B4

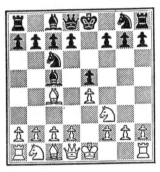

By developing his KB on move three instead of his KN, Black avoids some of the tactical possibilities arising after 3...N—KB3; e.g., in reply to 3...B—B4, White cannot consider playing 4 N—N5, because Black's queen still covers that square. Having decided that moving the KB is a sensible plan, we should ask whether QB4 is the correct square for it? The answer is clearly "yes," because any other square would entail a disadvantage for Black – developing the bishop on K2 is unnecessarily passive, on Q3 it prevents Black from subsequently mov- ing the QP, and on QN5 it only helps White to form a strong pawn centre. (White would reply to 3...B—N5? with 4 P—B3, attacking the bishop and preparing P—Q4.) In addition, the bishop on QB4 is well-placed, for it guards the central square Q5 and strikes at White's weak square KB2.

4 P—Q3

After this move the opening is often called "Giuoco Pianissimo" ("The Quietest Game"). Presumably, it was so named by those who consider 4 P—B3 a more challenging continuation than the text move. Let us merely comment here that 4 P—Q3 opens lines for the QB, and leaves the square QB3 free for occupation by a knight. Thus, we see that White's guiding strategy in this opening is to try to achieve an advantage by rapid, active, and harmonious development of his forces.

(For 4 P—B3 see p. 63)

4 ... N—B3

Black, too, wishes to bring his pieces into play quickly. He need no longer worry about threats directed against his KB2 square; e.g., after 5 N—N5?, O—O; 6 B×P ch?, R×B; 7 N×R, K×N, he has two pieces for a rook and pawn (which, in itself, is a slightly favourable material situation), and all of White's developed pieces have disappeared from the board, leaving Black with a big advantage.

5 N—B3

Another simple developing move. The knight clearly belongs on QB3, where it prevents Black from ever playing the freeing pawn advance ...P—Q4 and threatens, itself, to occupy the useful outpost square Q5 at some later time.

5 ... P—Q3

The position is now symmetrical. We can hardly say yet that Black has equalized, because White still has the advantage of moving first!

6 B—KN5

White's most aggressive continuation, pinning Black's KN. This pin is a little unpleasant for Black, for White threatens to play N—Q5 followed by N×N ch damaging Black's K-side pawn structure.

(For 6 B—K3 see p. 64)

6 ...   **P—KR3**

Trying to break the pin immediately. If White now plays 7 B—R4, Black would continue pin-breaking operations with 7...P—KN4. Normally, this advance of the K-side pawns would create serious weaknesses in front of the king, but as Black has not played ...O—O he can probably get away with it.

(For 6...N—QR4 see p. 64)

7 B×N   **Q×B**
8 N—Q5

White moves his knight to a dominating square. Black must now defend against both 9 N×Q and 9 N×BP ch forking king and rook.

8 ...   **Q—Q1**

(For 8...Q—N3!? see p. 65)

9 P—B3

White uses his initiative to strengthen his centre and to gain space on the Q side. This move keeps Black's pieces away from White's Q4 square and prepares the advance P—QN4.

9 ...   **N—K2**

Naturally Black wishes to exchange White's troublesome knight.

10 P—QN4

Attacking Black's bishop.

10 ...   **B—N3**
11 N×B   **RP×N**
12 P—Q4!

The thematic advance in the centre.

12 ...   **P×P**

After this move White gains the advantage in the centre, but there was no reasonable alternative. Black's KP is attacked twice, and attempts to defend it fail; e.g., 12...N—N3?; 13 P×P, N×P; 14 N×N, P×N; 15 Q×Q ch,

K×Q; 16 B×P; or 12...B—N5?; 13 P×P, P×P; 14 B×P ch, K×B; 15 N× P ch, winning material in each case.

13 N×P

After 13 P×P Black could reply 13...P—Q4, attacking White's centre. The best plan for White is to secure active posts for his pieces, rather than to try to set up a pawn centre which he cannot comfortably maintain.

13 ...   **O—O**
14 O—O

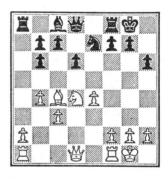

White's game is slightly superior, since his pieces are better posted. Black's best plan is to continue 14...N—B3, trying to exchange pieces and reach a drawn ending. The continuation 14... P—Q4 is a little doubtful, because, after 15 P×P, N×P; 16 Q—B3, White has a great deal of pressure.

---

4 P—B3

4 P—B3. This is much more popular

than the text move. With 4 P—B3 White prepares for P—Q4, which would give him a very strong pawn centre. If Black plays passively, this centre can become a dominant force; e.g.,

4...P—Q3; 5 P—Q4, P×P.

Forced, since after 5...B—N3?; 6 P×P, P×P; 7 Q×Q ch, Black loses material either by 7...N×Q; 8 N×P; or 7... K×Q; 8 B×P.

6 P×P, B—N3; 7 N—B3, N—B3; 8 B—K3, B—N5.

The "fork trick," 8...N×KP, does not work in this position because of the weakness of Black's KB2: 9 N×N, P—Q4; 10 B—N3, P×N; 11 N—KN5, and if 11...O—O, then 12 Q—R5, threatening both 13 Q×RP mate, and 13 N×BP. After 8...B—N5, however, Black *is* threatening the "fork trick."

9 B—N3.

To prevent 9...N×KP.

9...O—O; 10 Q—Q3.

Intending later to play B—B2 and produce mating threats along the QN1—KR7 diagonal.

10...R—K1; 11 O—O.

White, with complete control of the centre, has much the better game.

The best reply to 4 P—B3 is probably **4...N—KB3**, developing a piece and hitting White's KP. For instance, after:

5 P—Q4, P×P; 6 P×P, B—N5 ch; 7 B—Q2.

The pawn sacrifice 7 N—QB3, N×KP, is sharp and tactical, but Black can hold his own.

7...B×B ch; 8 QN×B.

Black can now play **8...P—Q4!**, demolishing White's centre before it can do him any harm.

---

6 B—K3

6 B—K3. Another developing move for the bishop, threatening 7 B×B, which would weaken Black's central pawns. Black should not play 6...B×B (which opens the KB file for White), but 6... B—N3, after which White has no important threat and will find it very difficult to make progress.

As we mentioned in Chapter 1 (cf.

p. 14), the alternative 6 O—O would be a serious mistake, because of the reply 6...B—KN5!, after which White has nothing better than 7 B—K3 (to meet 7...N—Q5 with 8 B×N), and Black secures the initiative.

6...N—QR4

6...N—QR4. This is certainly more aggressive than (and probably superior to) the text move. Black's idea is to exchange on QB5 weakening White's central pawns. An important subsidiary point is that now that the knight has moved, Black threatens 7...P—B3, keeping White's knight away from Black's Q4 square. In reply White should play 7 B—N3 or 7 B×N; the natural but over-ambitious 7 N—Q5 is an instructive error – after 7...N×B; 8 P×N, P—B3!; 9 N×N ch, P×N; 10 B—R4, KR—N1, the position actually favours Black, who can use the open KN file for attacking operations later in the game. The lesson to be drawn is that until Black has committed his king to the K side by playing ...O—O, White cannot be sure that the doubled KB pawns will be a weakness.

The reader should look closely at an

interesting combination arising in the above line. After 7 N—Q5, N×B; 8 P×N, why can Black not play 8...B× P ch?. The variation 9 K×B?, N×P ch; 10 K—B1, N×B; 11 N×N, Q×N; 12 N×P ch, K—K2; 13 N×R, B—N5 certainly favours Black. White's knight and queen are attacked and once Black has won the knight he will only be the exchange down, for which he has excellent compensation (a pawn plus a raging attack). However, White refutes 8...B×P ch by 9 K—K2!, followed by 10 R—KB1. Now it is White who has the strong attack along the open KB file. The move 8...P—B3 is undoubtedly better, since it drives White's knight from its dominating post. Of course, after 8...P—B3, White can simply retreat 9 N—QB3, but that would be an admission of total failure amounting to the loss of two tempi.

(threatening both 10...Q×R and 10...Q×BP mate); 11 R—KB1, B—KN5, White's KN cannot be defended and his QN is trapped in the corner. White should better play **9 Q—K2!** protecting his KBP and maintaining the pressure. If Black replies 9...Q×NP, then 10 R—KN1, Q—R6; 11 N×P ch wins for White. Black could however play 9...B—KN5, after which 10 N×P ch, K—Q2; 11 N×R is not good for White, because of 11...N—Q5; 12 Q—Q1 (12 Q—Q2? also defends QB2, but after 12...B×N White cannot recapture because of the forking threat to king and queen); 12...B×N; 13 P×B, Q—N7, when Black's attack seems to be breaking through. But after **10 P—QB3** (preventing 10...N—Q5 and threatening 11 N×P ch), **10...B—N3; 11 P—QR4**, White probably has a slight edge.

8...Q—N3!?

8...Q—N3!?. An interesting tactical alternative to the rather defensive text move. Now 9 N×P ch? is a blunder, for after 9...K—Q1; 10 N×R, Q×NP

EVANS GAMBIT

1 P—K4	P—K4		12 Q—R4 ch	Q—Q2
2 N—KB3	N—QB3		13 Q×N	Q—B2
3 B—B4	B—B4		14 N—Q5	
4 P—QN4!?				

4 ...	B×NP
5 P—B3	B—R4
6 P—Q4	P×P
7 O—O!	P—Q3
8 P×P	B—N3
9 N—B3	N—R4
10 B—KN5	P—KB3
11 B—B4	N×B

---

1 P—K4	P—K4
2 N—KB3	N—QB3
3 B—B4	B—B4
4 P—QN4!?	

As we saw in the section on the Giuoco Piano proper, it does not seem likely that White will be able to obtain much advantage after either 4 P—Q3 or 4 P—B3. The text represents an important attempt to inject life into the system. At the cost of a pawn, White hopes to get the extra tempo he needs to build a really powerful and dominating pawn centre. He also opens up the possibility of developing his QB to QN2 or QR3.

| 4 ... | B×NP |

"The refutation of a gambit frequently lies in its acceptance" – Steinitz.
(For 4...B—N3 see p. 67)

5 P—B3

The main point of the gambit is that now White can play this move with gain of tempo since Black's bishop is attacked. White hopes to gain control of the centre by establishing pawns on Q4 and K4.

| 5 ... | B—R4 |

This looks the most logical retreat for the bishop, since after 6 P—Q4, P×P, the White QBP is pinned. However White has no reason to fear this pin.
(For 5...B—B4 see p. 67)

| 6 P—Q4 | P×P |
| 7 O—O! | |

White cheerfully offers a second pawn.

| 7 ... | P—Q3 |

Grabbing the second pawn with 7...P×P?! is a little greedy. The text is a useful defensive move, which blocks the weak KB1—QR6 diagonal, opens lines for the QB, and helps control Black's K4 square, thus keeping White's pawn centre under control.
(For 7...P×P?! see p. 67)

8 P×P

White has achieved his first objective – the establishment of pawns on Q4 and K4. He now threatens to dislodge the black knight with P—Q5, after which Q—R4 ch would win the bishop.

| 8 ... | B—N3 |

Defending against White's threat. We have now reached the so-called "normal position" of the Evans Gambit, which has been discussed and analysed for close on 150 years!

9 N—B3

White can continue his attack in a variety of ways but this simple developing move is now considered best.
(For 9 P—Q5 see p. 68)

| 9 ... | N—R4 |

Played with the idea of exchanging White's KB or forcing it to retreat, so that it no longer attacks Black's weak square KB2. This move seems to neglect Black's development, but in fact it is quite difficult for Black to develop normally in this position; e.g., after 9...N—B3, there would follow the line-opening sacrifice 10 P—K5!, P×P; 11 B—R3!, and White's attack is very strong (probably winning, since Black's king is left exposed in the centre).

Black is not actually threatening to win White's KB, for after ...N×B, White can always regain the piece by Q—R4 ch.
(For 9...B—N5 see p. 68)

10 B—KN5

Attacking Black's queen with a developing move.

| 10 ... | P—KB3 |

Black accepts a weakness on the K side in order to force the exchange of White's KB.
(For 10...N—K2!? see p. 68)

| 11 B—B4 | N×B |
| 12 Q—R4 ch | Q—Q2 |

This is played in preference to 12...B—Q2, because Black wishes to be able to cover the weak KN1—QR7 diagonal with his queen.

13 Q×N   Q—B2

Challenging the actively-posted White queen.

14 N—Q5

Naturally White should not permit the exchange of queens. In this position White has the advantage. His strong centre and very active pieces generate enough attacking chances to provide ample compensation for the sacrificed pawn.

4...B—N3

4...B—N3. Declining the gambit pawn.
5 P—QR4!.
Threatening to win Black's bishop with 6 P—R5, B—Q5; 7 P—B3.
    5...P—QR3; 6 N—B3, N—B3.
6...N×P; 7 N×P is good for White.
    7 N—Q5, N×N.
7...N×KP?! allows White a strong attack after 8 O—O, O—O; 9 P—Q3, N—B3; 10 B—N5, with a powerful pin.
    8 P×N, P—K5!.

Retreating, 8...N—K2, or 8...N—Q5, allows White to play 9 N×KP winning a pawn with the better game, while after 8...N×P; 9 B—R3, Black's king may get stuck in the centre.
    9 P×N, O—O!.
Best – White does not have time to save the knight, because of the threat of ...Q—B3, attacking White's KBP and QR.
    10 B—N2!, P×N; 11 Q×P.
White has a slight pull. Black cannot profit from the check with either piece – 11...R—K1 ch; 12 K—B1 leaves White threatening both 13 P×NP, and 13 Q×P ch, while, after 11...Q—K2 ch; 12 K—B1, Q×P?; 13 B—N3, White has the double threats 14 P×NP, and 14 B—R3. Black's best in this position is to play simply **11...QP×P.**

5...B—B4

5...B—B4. This looks less natural than 5...B—R4, but it will actually come to the same thing. After **6 P—Q4, P×P; 7 O—O, P—Q3** (7...P×P fails to 8 B×P ch, K×B; 9 Q—Q5 ch, followed by 10 Q×B); **8 P×P, B—N3,** we are back in the "normal position."

7...P×P?!

7...P×P?!. (The "Compromised Defence" to the Evans Gambit). **8 Q—N3** (attacking KB7), **8...Q—B3** (the only real defence, since 8...N—R3 would be answered by 9 B×N; and 8...Q—K2 would allow simply 9 N×P, followed by

10 N—Q5); **9 P—K5, Q—N3; 10 N×P, KN—K2** (preventing N—Q5); **11 B—R3!** White has a very powerful attack.

---

9 P—Q5

9 P—Q5. An old continuation, now held to be less promising than 9 N—B3. After the rather passive **9...QN—K2**, White can open up the position to his advantage with **10 P—K5!**; so Black should instead play the active **9...N—R4**. Now, after 10 B—N2 or 10 N—B3, Black should emerge on top, e.g.:

(a) **10 B—N2** (attacking the KNP), **10...N—K2!; 11 B×P?!** (11 B—Q3 is stronger), **11...KR—N1; 12 B—B6** (no other retreat is any better); **12...N×B; 13 Q—R4 ch, Q—Q2; 14 Q×N**, and now Black has the winning counter-punch: **14...R×P ch!; 15 K×R, Q—R6 ch; 16 K—N1, Q—N5 ch; 17 K—R1, Q×N ch; 18 K—N1, B—R6**, with an unstoppable mate.

(b) **10 N—B3, N×B; 11 Q—R4 ch, B—Q2; 12 Q×N, P—KB3**; and now White will find it difficult to play his thematic line-opening move P—K5; e.g., **13 R—K1, N—K2; 14 P—K5, BP×P; 15 N×P** (hoping for 15...P×N?; 16 R×P, O—O; 17 P—Q6 dis ch, winning);

15...O—O!, and Black stands better. WINAWER–TCHIGORIN, Warsaw 1882.

9...B—N5

9...B—N5. This is about as frequently seen as the text move in practical play. It develops a piece but leaves Black open to the unpleasant pin **10 B—QN5** (threatening 11 P—Q5, winning the knight), when Black's best defence is **10...K—B1** (10...B—Q2 would be answered by 11 P—K5!, opening lines against Black's king), when **11 B—K3** leaves White with ample compensation for his pawn in the form of a strong centre and better development.

10...N—K2!?

10...N—K2!?. This may well be Black's best move. In the game TCHIGORIN–GUNSBERG, Match 1890, White tried this enterprising sacrifice:
11 B×P ch!?, K×B; 12 N—Q5.
Attacking the pinned knight.
12...N(R4)—B3; 13 B×N, N×B; 14 N—N5 ch, K—N3.

14...K—N1; 15 Q—N3 is fatal for Black; and 14...K—K1 is just as bad; e.g., 15 Q—R5 ch, P—N3; 16 N—B6 ch, K—B1; 17 Q—R6 mate; or 15...N—N3; 16 N×RP.

15 N—B4 ch!, K—B3.

After 15...K×N; 16 Q—R5 ch, the Black king dies a speedy death.

16 P—K5 ch.

White had a winning position. After the game, however, Tchigorin pointed out the better defence, 12...R—K1!, Now White has nothing better than:

13 B×N, R×B; 14 N—N5 ch, K—N1; 15 Q—R5.

Threatening 16 Q×P with mate next move.

15...P—KR3!.

After 15...P—N3, White is still winning: 16 N—B6 ch, K—N2; 17 Q×RP ch, K×N; 18 P—K5 ch, K×N; 19 P—B4 ch, K—B4; 20 Q—R3 ch, etc.

16 Q—N6.

Threatening 17 N—B6 ch, K—B1; 18 N(N5)—R7 mate.

16...P×N; 17 N—B6 ch, K—B1.

Not 17...K—R1??; 18 Q—R7 mate.

18 N—R7 ch, K—N1; 19 N—B6 ch, with perpetual check.

TWO KNIGHTS DEFENCE

1 P—K4	P—K4
2 N—KB3	N—QB3
3 B—B4	N—B3
4 N—N5	P—Q4
5 P×P	N—QR4
6 B—N5 ch	P—B3
7 P×P	P×P
8 B—K2	P—KR3
9 N—B3	P—K5
10 N—K5	B—Q3
11 P—KB4	Q—B2
12 O—O	O—O
13 N—B3	B×N
14 P×B	Q×P
15 P—Q4	P×P e.p.
16 Q×P	

1 P—K4	P—K4
2 N—KB3	N—QB3
3 B—B4	N—B3

With this move Black inaugurates the tricky and tactical Two Knights Defence. After the obvious 4 N—N5 White will have very strong pressure against Black's weak KB2 square. On the other hand,

White will have moved his KN twice, falling behind in development. Black hopes to profit from this (usually at the cost of a pawn), by counter-attacking and forcing White on the defensive.

4 N—N5

White accepts the challenge.
(For 4 P—Q4 see p. 71)

4 . . .   P—Q4

Defending KB2 by cutting off the line of the bishop. The alternative Wilkes Barre Variation (4...B—B4!?), is discussed in a separate section. No other Black fourth moves are worth considering for very long; 4...N×P? has been seen once or twice but it should lose quickly after 5 B×P ch (but not 5 N×N?, P—Q4!), K—K2; 6 P—Q4! (a developing move which prevents 6... N×N).

5 P×P

White cannot, of course, play 5 B×P?, because 5...N×B; 6 P×N, Q×N; 7 P×N, Q×NP wins for Black.

5 ...   N—QR4

Moving the attacked knight and threatening in turn the unprotected White's KB.

(For 5...N×P?! see p. 72)

6 B—N5 ch

The most logical continuation and one by which White ensures that he will remain a pawn to the good. After a retreat such as 6 B—N3?, Black could simply play 6...N×B and then regain his pawn.

6 ...   P—B3

Virtually forced, as after 6...B—Q2; 7 Q—K2 (protecting the bishop and attacking Black's KP); 7...B—Q3; 8 O—O, O—O; 9 QN—B3, White is a pawn up and Black has few attacking chances. Note that 7...B×B??; 8 Q×B ch loses Black a piece, and 7...N×P; 8 B×B ch, Q×B; 9 P—Q4 loses the pinned KP.

7 P×P   P×P

7...N×P? preserves the Q-side pawn structure but is hopelessly out of keeping with the character of the opening, since it self-pins Black's knight and gives White a free tempo for a developing move. Black is, after all, a pawn down, and to justify his material deficit he must strive to open lines and use his better development to attack. After the text White must waste another tempo moving the bishop yet again.

8 B—K2

This retreat is safer than 8 B—R4?!, which leaves the bishop unprotected and may expose it later to further threats if Black can find a useful opportunity to play...Q—Q5; e.g., 8 B—R4, P—KR3;

9 N—KB3, P—K5; 10 N—K5, Q—Q5 (attacking both bishop and knight); 11 B×P ch, N×B; 12 N×N, Q—B4!, when White's knight is trapped.

(For 8 Q—B3!? see p. 72)

8 ...   P—KR3

Driving back White's aggressive knight.

9 N—B3   P—K5

Again the knight is forced to move. Now, since 10 N—N1? ("undeveloping" a piece) would leave Black with an overwhelming lead in development, the knight must venture alone, and unprotected, into the centre of the board.

10 N—K5

At first sight this position looks good for Black, who seems to have ample compensation for his pawn in the form of better development and attacking chances. Rather surprisingly, there is no known way for Black to secure an equal game.

10 ...   B—Q3

A logical continuation, attacking Black's knight with a developing move.

(For 10...Q—Q5 see p. 72)

11 P—KB4

White would like to maintain his knight on K5. The text is better than 11 P—Q4, because White wants to castle as quickly as possible. To do so with safety he either needs the knight on K5 (where it blocks the vital KR2—QN8 diagonal) or on KB3 (where it covers the weak point KR2). Thus 11 P—KB4, P×P e.p.; 12 N×P(B3), Q—B2; 13 O—O is playable, because the knight guards the KRP; but after 11 P—Q4, P×P e.p.; 12 N×P(Q3), the knight is badly placed for the defence of the K side.

11 ...   Q—B2

White's supported knight at K5 is a thorn in Black's side. Black hopes to force it to move away by threatening to regain his sacrificed pawn.

12 O—O

White continues his development. He is quite happy to return the material, if in so doing he can blunt Black's attack, for Black has numerous pawn weaknesses on the Q side.

12 ...   O—O

Black brings his king to safety and develops a rook, hoping to continue the attack.

13 N—B3

Another good, developing move.

13 ...   B×N

Black has nothing better. This move restores material equality, but with the exchange of Black's KB most of his attacking prospects also disappear.

14 P×B   Q×P
15 P—Q4

White plays very actively: opening lines for his QB to enter the game.

15 ...   P×P e.p.
16 Q×P

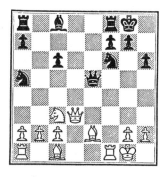

16 B×P is less accurate for Black could carry on the attack with 16...N—N5.

The position has now clarified and is favourable to White. In the game FINE-RESHEVSKY, New York 1940, Black continued with 16...N—N5 which creates two threats – the obvious 17... Q×P mate, and the more subtle 17 ...Q—B4 ch; 18 K—R1, N—B7ch. But 16...N—N5 can be met advantageously by 17 R—B4!, and if 17 ...Q—B4 ch, then 18 Q—Q4!, forcing

Black into an ending which White will surely win because of his two bishops and Black's weak isolated pawns.

---

4 P—Q4

4 P—Q4. White can decline the invitation to play an immediate N—N5 in several ways, but the alternative 4 P—Q4, which we now consider, is the only method which gives him any real chance of keeping an advantage; e.g., after the quiet 4 P—Q3, Black can choose between 4...B—B4 (transposing into the Giuoco Piano), and 4...P—Q4 (liquidating the centre), while, after 4 N—B3, Black gets immediate equality from the "fork trick" continuation 4...N×P!; 5 N×N, P—Q4.

After 4 P—Q4, the move 4...N× KP?! is a mistake, because after 5 P×P White is threatening 6 Q—Q5, with a double attack on knight and KBP, and Black must then waste a tempo saving his knight with 5...N—B4, thus falling behind in development.

Black must, however, do something about his attacked KP and, since 4...P—Q3 is rather passive (it shuts in the KB), his best reply is 4...P×P. We give some sample continuations:

(a) 5 N×P, N×P! Black does not fear the line 6 B×P ch, K×B; 7 Q—R5 ch, P—N3; 8 Q—Q5 ch, K—N2; 9 N×N, NP×N; 10 Q×N, Q—K1!!; 11 Q×Q, B—N5 ch (to be followed by 12...R×Q).

(b) 5 O—O, N×P (probably the best plan. After 5...B—B4, White could play the tricky **Max Lange Attack**, 6 P—K5!?, which gives him good practical

chances); **6 R—K1** (if 6 N—B3, Black should not be tempted by 6...P×N?; 7 B×P ch, K×B; 8 Q—Q5 ch, K—K1; 9 R—K1, when White has a winning attack. Black should simply play 6... N×N; 7 P×N, P—Q4, which leads to equality), **6...P—Q4; 7 B×P!, Q×B; 8 N—B3** (taking advantage of the fact that the QP is pinned on the queen), **8...Q—QR4; 9 N×N, B—K3** (the best move, even though White now wins back his pawn. After 9...B—K2, White could play 10 B—N5, with good attacking chances); **10 N(K4)—N5** (attacking the pinned bishop), **10... O—O—O; 11 N×B, P×N; 12 R×P, B—Q3,** with an equal position.

(*c*) **5 P—K5, P—Q4; 6 B—QN5** (6 P×N, P×B; 7 P×P, B×P, leaves, Black a pawn up with a good game) **6...N—K5; 7 N×P, B—Q2** (breaking the pin); **8 B×N, P×B; 9 O—O, B—QB4** (Black's pawns become very weak after 9...P—QB4; 10 N—N3, hitting the QP; 10...P—QB3; 11 P—QB4, P×P; 12 N(N3)—Q2, N×N; 13 N×N); **10 P—KB3, N—N4** (10...B×N?; 11 Q×B, N—N4; 12 P—K6!, B×P; 13 Q×NP wins for White); **11 B—K3, O—O,** and White has a slight edge.

5...N×P?!

5...N×P?!. This move recovers the pawn, but gives White the possibility of a very tempting sacrifice **6 N×BP!?** (exploiting the weakness of Black's KB2). After **6...K×N; 7 Q—B3 ch,** the only way for Black to keep his extra piece is to march his king into the centre of the board with **7...K—K3.** Then, however **8 N—B3** gives White a ferocious attack;

e.g., **8...N—N5** (defending, and counterattacking against White's QB2); **9 Q—K4** (defending QB2 and preparing P—Q4), **9...P—B3** (necessary to protect the knight on Q4 – for the knight on N5 will soon be dislodged); **10 P—QR3, N—R3; 11 P—Q4,** and it is doubtful if Black can survive.

---

8 Q—B3!?

8 Q—B3!?. An interesting idea, but Black's attacking chances seem to be greater after this move than in the main line. One example is **8...R—QN1; 9 B×P ch?!** (retreating the bishop may be better), **9...N×B; 10 Q×N ch, N—Q2** (threatening 11...Q×N); **11 P—Q3, B—K2** (reviving the threat against the knight), **12 N—KB3, O—O; 13 Q—K4** (Black was threatening 13...B—N2, followed by 14...B×N. White wishes to be able to recapture with the queen), **13...R—N5; 14 Q—K2, P—K5!; 15 P×P, N—B4,** with advantage to Black, who threatens...R×KP and...B—R3.

10...Q—Q5

10...Q—Q5. With this move Black puts pressure on the KBP while attacking the knight. But after **11 P—KB4, B—B4; 12 R—B1,** it is not clear how Black should continue. The usual try is **12...Q—Q1** (hoping to redeploy the queen on KR5 after the knight on KB3 has moved), to which White can reply **13 P—QB3** (opening up possibilities of P—Q4, P—QN4, or Q—R4 to follow). Now **13... N—Q4; 14 P—QN4?, Q—R4 ch** is good for Black; but after **14 Q—R4!,** attacking the Black KP and creating a nice hole for the king on Q1, Black does not seem to have enough compensation for his material deficit.

WILKES BARRE VARIATION

1	P—K4	P—K4
2	N—KB3	N—QB3
3	B—B4	N—B3
4	N—N5	B—B4
5	N×P	B×P ch
6	K×B	N×P ch
7	K—N1	Q—R5
8	P—KN3	N×NP
9	N×R	N×R
10	Q—B1	Q—N5 ch
11	K×N	Q—K5 ch
12	K—N1	Q—N5 ch
13	K—B2	Q—R5 ch
14	K—N1	

1	P—K4	P—K4
2	N—KB3	N—QB3
3	B—B4	N—B3
4	N—N5	B—B4

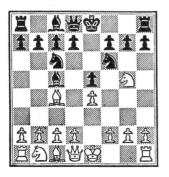

Black ignores the threat to his KB2 in order to develop a piece and counter-attack immediately against White's KB2 square. The reader, if he is seeing this line for the first time, may well be impressed by the complexity of the tactical operations that follow. But all the fireworks seem to lead only to a draw.

5 N×P

The natural reply – winning a pawn, forking Black's queen and rook, and daring Black to do his worst.

(For 5 B×P ch see p. 74)

5 ... B×P ch!

The fact that this move is playable is the whole point of 4...B—B4.

6 K×B

(For 6 K—B1 see p. 75)

6 ... N×P ch
7 K—N1!

This is the only good flight square. After 7 K—K3, Black gets a strong attack with 7...Q—R5; e.g., 8 Q—B3 (to stop the threatened ... Q—B7 ch); 8...N—B4; 9 N×R (now White threatens mate – but Black gets in first), 9...Q—Q5 ch; 10 K—K2, Q×B ch; 11 K—K1, N—Q5 (now Black has threats of ...N×Q and ...N×BP ch); 12 Q—B7 ch, Q×Q; 13 N×Q, N×P ch; 14 K—Q1, N×R; 15 N×P, P—Q3; 16 N—B4 (threatening to play N—K3, keeping

Black's knight trapped); 16...N—B7!; 17 K×N, B—B4 ch, to be followed by ...B×N, when Black emerges a pawn ahead.

7 ...   **Q—R5**

Threatening 8...Q—B7 mate.

8 P—KN3

Again best. If 8 Q—B3, 8...N—Q5 is strong, while 8 Q—B1 is answered by 8...R—B1; e.g., 9 P—Q3 (driving the menacing knight away); 9...N—Q3 (threatening to win back the piece with 10...N×N); 10 N×N ch, P×N; 11 Q—K2, N—Q5; 12 Q—Q2, Q—N5, and Black wins on account of the double threats of 13...N—B6 ch, and 13...N—K7 ch. We note en passant that 12... Q—N4!! also wins, and is much prettier (13 Q—Q1, Q×B!).

8 ...   **N×NP**

A second sacrifice to break open White's king position

9 N×R

The move 9 P×N? is dubious, but leads to some exquisite play: 9...Q× P ch; 10 K—B1, R—B1!; 11 Q—R5!, and the Czech analyst, Rohlicek, shows that Black can now win after 11...P— Q4! (the start of a combination designed to cut off White's bishop from the defence of the knight at KB7); 12 B×P, N—N5; 13 B—B4 (if 13 B—N3, then 13...N×BP), 13...P—QN4; 14 B× P ch, P—B3; 15 B—B4, N—Q4, and Black's KR will soon enter the game with devastating effect.

9 ...   **N×R**
10 Q—B1

After 10 K×N, Q×B, Black would win White's trapped knight and come out two pawns to the good. 10 B—B7 ch, K—K2; 11 K×N, Q—K5 ch; 12 K— N1, allows Black time to add another piece to the attack with 12...N—Q5. The text move protects the QB and threatens mate, but Black still has a draw in hand.

10 ...   **Q—N5 ch**
11 K×N   **Q—K5 ch**

12 K—N1	Q—N5 ch
13 K—B2	Q—R5 ch
14 K—N1	

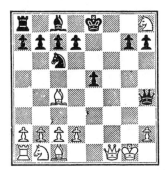

White has no good way of escaping the perpetual check. Moves like 13 Q— N2 do not help; e.g., 13...Q—Q5 ch; 14 K—R1 (14 K—B1?, Q×B ch), Q× B; 15 Q×P, Q—B8 ch; 16 Q—N1, Q— B6 ch; 17 Q—N2, Q—Q8 ch, etc.

---

5 B×P ch

5 B×P ch. This move seems to waste too much time, for, after 5...K—K2, Black threatens to win a piece by playing 6...P—KR3, and White must therefore move his bishop again. After 6 B—N3, R—B1; 7 P—Q3, P—Q3, Black is threatening to mount a decisive attack with 8...N—N5, so White must play another non-developing move, 8 P—KR3. However, after 6 B—Q5!, R—B1; 7 O—O, P—Q3; 8 P—QB3, White has the better chances.

Another possibility for White is 5 P—

Q4, trying to open some lines for his pieces before taking on KB7, but this has been refuted by Fine's move 5...P—Q4!. The complications after 6 B×P, N×QP, seem to favour Black, which is not surprising since he is better developed. Relatively best for White would appear to be 6 P×B, P×B; 7 Q×Q ch, N×Q, when the ending favours Black; but White has some prospects of a draw because of opposite-coloured bishops. A possible continuation is 8 N—QR3 (to attack Black's advanced QBP quickly), 8...P—KR3 (removing the guard from the KP); 9 N—B3, P—B6!, and White's QB pawns will make good targets for attack.

---

6 K—B1

---

6 K—B1. Declining the sacrifice does not help White, for this too seems to be a drawing line. The main variation runs:

6...Q—K2; 7 N×R, P—Q4; 8 P×P. After 8 B—K2, B—N3, Black can win the trapped knight in the corner and will have some good counter-play for the sacrificed exchange.

8...N—Q5.
Black now threatens to win the queen with 9...B—N5.

9 P—KR3!, B—R5; 10 P—B3.
Trying to chase away the knight.

10...N—B4.
With the threat of 11...Q—B4, attacking KB7 and White's bishop on QB4.

11 P—Q4, P—K5; 12 B—Q2.
Planning to use this bishop for defence along the K1—KR4 diagonal.

12...N—N6 ch; 13 K—N1, P—K6; 14 B—K1, N(B3)—K5!; 15 B×N, B×B; 16 Q—R5 ch.
Trying to extricate the trapped knight.

16...P—N3; 17 N×P.
Now it is best for Black to take the perpetual check by:

17...B—B7 ch; 18 K—R2 (18 K—B1??, N—N6 mate), 18...B—N6 ch.

6

RUY LOPEZ

1 P—K4, P—K4; 2 N—KB3, N—QB3; 3 B—N5

This is the strongest of White's third move alternatives. White speedily develops his K side and continues the plan inaugurated by move two of attacking Black's KP, this time by undermining its defence. This basic idea is logical, simple and surprisingly difficult to counter. White usually gets at least a slight initiative persisting well into the middle game.

The Ruy Lopez is one of the oldest chess openings. Ruy Lopez himself was a Spanish priest who wrote about the opening in his book *Libro del Ajedrez* in 1561. This book is usually considered the first scientific attempt to study opening theory. Since then, nearly every famous player has had a hand in enriching the theory which Ruy Lopez started, not least the 1972 World Champion, Bobby Fischer, who thinks so highly of the Lopez for White that he almost never replies to 1 P—K4 with 1...P—K4 in serious games.

The Ruy Lopez has many different variations, each with its own special characteristics. Some are quiet, positional lines in which White closes the centre and manoeuvres for a K-side attack, while Black reacts on the Q wing. Other variations are sharp and complex.

The early struggle of the opening usually revolves around the strengths and weaknesses of both KP's. White's early pressure is directed at Black's KP and on the task of preparing P—Q4. Black devotes his attention to the job of developing his pieces in such a way as to be prepared to meet White's P—Q4 when it comes. Some of the motifs of the Ruy Lopez may be somewhat difficult for the novice to grasp but an understanding of its basic features will pave the way for further study of this most tested opening.

In this section we shall look at four branches of the Lopez tree: the Closed variation, in which Black strives to maintain his KP on K4 as a strong point in the centre; the Open variation, in which Black opens the centre at move five (when White gives him the opportunity to do so); the Exchange variation, in which White gains the better pawn structure at the cost of surrendering the bishop pair; and the Schliemann Defence a lively counter-gambit try for Black.

CLOSED DEFENCE

1 P—K4	P—K4
2 N—KB3	N—QB3
3 B—N5	

3 ...	P—QR3
4 B—R4	N—B3
5 O—O	B—K2
6 R—K1	P—QN4
7 B—N3	P—Q3
8 P—B3	O—O
9 P—KR3	N—QR4
10 B—B2	P—QB4
11 P—Q4	Q—B2

1 P—K4	P—K4
2 N—KB3	N—QB3
3 B—N5	

Positionally the most logical of White's third move alternatives. With this move White speedily develops his K side and indirectly brings pressure to bear on Black's KP by attacking the knight which is guarding it.

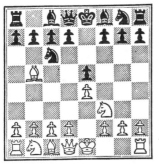

3 ...   **P—QR3!**

It has been known since the time of Morphy that this is Black's best reply. The justification is that once Black has advanced his QP (as he must do sooner or later in order to protect his KP and develop his QB), the Black QN will become pinned. The move 3...P—QR3 lessens the effect of this pin in advance.

(For 3...N—B3 see p. 79)

4 B—R4

We shall deal with the Exchange Variation (4 B×N) in a separate section in detail, but we should perhaps comment here that 4 B×N does not win a pawn for White, because, after 4... QP×B, 5 N×P, Black has 5...Q—Q5, regaining the pawn with an easy game.

4 ...   **N—B3**

A plausible move which develops a piece with a counter-attack against White's KP. Black's later plans do include the move ...P—QN4, driving away White's bishop and gaining space on the Q side, but it would be wrong for him to play 4...P—QN4, because he would be insufficiently developed to deal with an immediate White attack against his Q-side pawns by, for example, an early P—QR4.

5 O—O

White brings his king to safety in preparation for an advance in the centre. The implied sacrifice of the KP is only a pseudo-sacrifice, as we shall see in the section on the Open Defence.

5 ...   **B—K2**

The Open Defence, which starts with the move 5...N×P, will be discussed in another section. With 5...B—K2 Black opts for the more popular Closed Defence, in which he tries to maintain a pawn on K4, so that White's centre does not become too strong. With this end in view, Black's KB is better placed on K2 than (say) QB4; for on the latter square it will be attacked when White plays, after due preparation, P—Q4.

6 R—K1

White's plans are directed towards playing P—Q4 under favourable circumstances. Most of all, he would like to be able to set up and support a full pawn centre (pawns on K4 and Q4). Thus, the natural preparations for P—Q4 are the moves R—K1 (defending the KP), and P—QB3 (intending, after P—Q4, to meet . . .P × P with a pawn recapture).

6 . . .   P—QN4

Now that Black has developed his K side, the time has come to drive away White's KB. If Black delays this now and plays 6. . .P—Q3 first, White replies 7 P—B3 so that 7. . .P—QN4 can be met by 8 B—B2, saving a tempo.

7 B—N3   P—Q3

Opening lines for the QB and supporting the KP.

(For 7. . .O—O see p. 80)

8 P—B3   O—O

The move 8. . .B—N5 is less accurate, because White has an effective method of breaking the pin and increasing his own positional advantage, namely the sequence of moves P—Q3, followed by QN—Q2—B1—K3. The knight will be well placed when it gets to K3, for it would attack Black's weak Q4 and KB4 squares. If White's QP has already reached Q4, this manoeuvre is impossible, for a knight on K3 would cut off the White KR from the defence of the KP, which Black could then threaten to win. Thus, Black's best policy is to delay developing his QB until White has definitely committed himself with P—Q4.

9 P—KR3

As the reader will no doubt have guessed from our previous comment, the alternative 9 P—Q4 would have been answered by 9. . .B—N5! with a powerful pin on White's KN. The text is designed to prevent this. However, since 9 P—KR3 is essentially a non-developing prophylactic move, Black has been given a tempo to start operations on the Q side.

9 . . .   N—QR4

Black wishes to expand on the Q side by playing . . .P—QB4, so he must first move the knight which blocks the path of the QBP. He chooses QR4 because on that square the knight threatens the exchange of White's valuable KB.

(For 9. . .N—N1 and 9. . . P—KR3 see pp. 80–81)

10 B—B2

Naturally, White will not willingly surrender the advantage of the two bishops. The move B—B2 looks at first sight like yet another loss of time for White, but this is not really so, for once White's bishop has moved out of range, Black's knight is rather badly placed on the edge of the board. Black will soon have to expend a move in returning the knight to a more central position.

10 . . .   P—QB4
11 P—Q4

The long expected advance in the centre. Now White has immediate threats against Black's KP.

11 . . .   Q—B2

Defending the KP and clearing Q1 for later occupation by a rook.

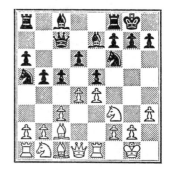

This position has been seen literally thousands of times in master play, and several grandmasters play this line both as White and as Black. The resulting middle games are often struggles of great positional and tactical subtlety. Black has not yet completely equalized but neither has he allowed his disadvantage in the opening phase of the game to increase. White stands a little better in the centre, but, so long as Black maintains a pawn on K4, White will find it difficult to break through in that part of the board. White's prospects are distinctly superior on the K side, and with careful play he may be able to build up a strong attack. He should develop his QN via Q2 and KB1, either to K3 or KN3, to assist in this attack.

In contrast, Black has the better chances on the Q wing, but he must beware of attacking too rashly, as this would probably lead only to the weakening of his advanced pawns (the counterpunch P—QR4 is one of White's thematic ideas in the Ruy Lopez).

The game FISCHER–SHOCRON, Mar del Plata 1959, continued:

12 QN—Q2, B—Q2; 13 N—B1, KR—K1.

Black is biding his time and strengthening his position. He will not undertake active operations until he knows what White plans to do.

14 N—K3, P—N3.

Played to prevent White's knights invading via Black's KB4 square. It also prepares to redeploy the bishop via KB1 to KR3 or KN2 in some lines.

15 P×KP.

White releases some of the central tension in order to increase the pressure on Black's Q4 square, which is a "hole" in Black's position.

15...P×P; 16 N—R2.

Preparing to exchange off Black's KN, a useful defensive piece.

16...QR—Q1; 17 Q—B3.

Black threatened 17...B×P, exposing an attack on the queen.

17...B—K3.

17...P—R4; 18 N—Q5!, N×N; 19 P×N, leaves Black's K side rather weak.

18 N(R2)—N4, N×N; 19 P×N.

White opens the KR file in the hope of using it later on for an attack.

19...Q—B3; 20 P—N5!?.

Freeing KN4 for a knight.

20...N—B5.

Returning the knight to the centre of the board. A more crucial line is 20...B×NP; 21 N—Q5, B×B (21...B×N?; 22 B×B, and Black will lose material); 22 N—B6 ch, with complications which may favour White.

21 N—N4, B×N.

Forced, since Black cannot permit N—B6 ch.

22 Q×B, N—N3.

Preventing 23 P—R4.

23 P—KN3.

Preparing to move the king and place a rook on the KR file.

23...P—B5!.

Black wishes to move his QN to the K side for defence, but he must first play this move, blocking the KN1—QR7 diagonal. After an immediate 23...N—Q2? there would follow 24 P—R4, P—N5; 25 P×P, P×P; 26 B—N3, and White's KB is beautifully posted.

24 K—N2, N—Q2; 25 R—R1, N—B1; 26 P—N4.

A shift of attack to the Q side.

26...Q—K3.

Hoping to exchange queens.

27 Q—K2, P—QR4; 28 P×P, Q—R3; 29 B—K3, Q×P; 30 P—R4, R—R1.

30...Q×BP; 31 P×P, may be better for Black than what was played.

31 P×P, Q×NP; 32 KR—QN1, Q—B3; 33 R—N6!.

Black's queen is chased around, and White gains control of the QR file.

33...Q—B2; 34 R(N6)—R6, R×R; 35 R×R, R—B1.

White was threatening 36 R—R7, when the Black queen cannot defend both the bishop and the QBP.

36 Q—N4.

Threatening to play R—R7, followed by 38 R×B and 39 Q×R.

36...N—K3; 37 B—R4, R—N1; 38 R—B6, Q—Q1?.

A mistake: after 38...Q—Q2 the issue is still in doubt.

39 R×N!, Q—QB1.

39...P×R; 40 Q×P ch, K—B1; 41 Q×KP, with a winning attack.

40 B—Q7! and Black resigned since he would lose his queen after 40...Q×B; 41 R×NP ch.

3...N—B3

3...N—B3. This is the older **Steinitz Defence** to the Ruy Lopez. White gets a freer hand in the centre than in the main line; e.g., after 4 O—O, P—Q3, he can play an immediate **5 P—Q4**, because of the pin on Black's QN. The main variation runs **5...B—Q2; 6 N—B3, B—K2; 7 R—K1,** and now Black must surrender

92

the centre with **7...P×P**, because 7...
O—O? fails to the following combina-
tion: 8 B×N, B×B; 9 P×P, P×P; 10
Q×Q, QR×Q; 11 N×P, B×P; 12 N×
B, N×N; 13 N—Q3 (not 13 R×N??,
R—Q1 ch, with mate next move); 13...
P—KB4; 14 P—KB3, B—B4 ch; 15
N×B, N×N; 16 B—N5, R—Q4; 17
B—K7, and White wins the exchange
(17...R—KB2?; 18 P—QB4, winning a
piece).

7...O—O

93

7...O—O. This move can simply transpose back into the main line after 8 P—
B3, P—Q3; but it can also lead to an
interesting gambit line: **8 P—B3, P—
Q4!?** (the **Marshall Counter Gambit**),
and after **9 P×P, N×P; 10 N×P, N×N;
11 R×N**, White has won a pawn at the
cost of somewhat backward development. Black's plan is to launch a violent
counter-attack against White's king
position, which has been denuded of
protection by the exchange of White's
KN. There is considerable theory on
this line, which has been popular in
recent years, but currently the soundness
of Black's sacrifice is believed to be
doubtful. One recent game in which

White emerged on top is TAL–KROGIUS,
39th USSR Championship 1971, which
concluded:
11...P—QB3; 12 P—Q4.
After 11 B×N, P×B, Black's bishop
pair are sufficiently active to compensate
for the pawn.
**12...B—Q3; 13 R—K1, Q—R5; 14
P—N3.**
14 P—KR3?, B×P; 15 P×B, Q×RP,
and White has no defence against the
threatened 16...B—R7 ch; 17 K—R1,
B—N6 dis ch; 18 K—N1, Q—R7 ch,
etc.
14...Q—R6; 15 R—K4.
An improvement on 15 B—K3, B—
KN5, which was the older continuation
in this position.
**15...Q—Q2; 16 N—Q2, N—B3; 17
R—R4, B—N2; 18 N—B3, QR—K1;
19 B—N5, N—K5; 20 B—B2, P—
KB4?.**
Black loses the exchange after 20...
N×B; 21 N×N, P—R3; 22 N—R7, but
the text is no better.
21 B—N3 ch.
Black must have overlooked the
strength of this move; he cannot reply
21...K—R1 because of 22 N—K5!,
attacking Black's queen and clearing the
Q1—KR5 diagonal; e.g., 22...B×N;
23 R×P ch!, K×R; 24 Q—R5 mate.
21...R—B2; 22 B—B4.
Black, who is going to lose at least the
exchange anyway, resigned.

9...N—N1

94

9...N—N1. The **Breyer Variation.** The
"undevelopment" of Black's QN looks
like a gross loss of time, but in fact this is
quite a playable and popular system

with a sound positional basis. As in the main line, Black moves his QN to prepare the advance of his QB pawn. Since experience shows that the knight is not very active on QR4, he chooses instead the square QN1, in order to play ...N—Q2, where the knight will be well-posted, guarding the KP.

Later on, Black will gradually build up a Q-side attack with moves like ...P—QR4—R5 and ...N—B4, if allowed. White must play aggressively if he is to have hopes of keeping any advantage. After **10 P—Q4, N—Q2**, the usual plan of QN—Q2—B1—K3/N3 is not so strong; e.g., 11 QN—Q2, B—N2; 12 B—B2 (to protect the KP), and Black should get a comfortable game after either 12...P—B4, or 12...R—K1 (to be followed by ...KB—B1). White's most challenging plan is to try to seize a Q-side initiative himself with **11 P—B4, P—B3; 12 P—B5**, and now 12...P×BP; 13 P×KP, N—K1; 14 P—K6 gives White good attacking chances; but if Black plays 12...Q—B2 (threatening...P×BP); 13 P×QP, B×P, it is hard for White to make progress.

another popular ninth move alternative for Black. Black's plan here is to regroup his pieces with ...R—K1 and ...B—B1, strengthening the protection of his K4 square before undertaking action on the Q side. The immediate 9...R—K1? fails, of course, to 10 N—N5!, attacking Black's KB2 square; so Black must first play 9...P—KR3 to deny the White pieces the use of his KN4. Again, it is difficult for White to keep an advantage. After **10 P—Q4, R—K1; 11 QN—Q2, B—B1; 12 N—B1**, Black can play either 12...B—Q2 or 12...B—N2, with good chances of equality; e.g., 12...B—Q2 (the bishop on this diagonal keeps an eye on the weak square KB4); 13 N—N3, N—QR4; **14 B—B2, P—B4; 15 P—N3** (keeping the knight away from QB4), 15...P—N3 (stopping N—R4—B5); **16 P—Q5, N—N2**, and neither side has any weaknesses (KAVALEK–RESHEVSKY, Sousse 1967).

9...P—KR3

9...P—KR3. The **Smyslov Variation**,

OPEN DEFENCE

1 P—K4	P—K4		10 R—Q1	O—O
2 N—KB3	N—QB3		11 P—B4!	NP×P
3 B—N5	P—QR3		12 B×P	Q—Q2
4 B—R4	N—B3		13 N—B3	N×N
5 O—O	N×P		14 P×N	P—B3
			15 P×P	B×P
6 P—Q4	P—QN4			
7 B—N3	P—Q4		1 P—K4	P—K4
8 P×P	B—K3		2 N—KB3	N—QB3
9 Q—K2	B—K2			

3 B—N5	P—QR3
4 B—R4	N—B3
5 O—O	N×P

With his last move (5 O—O), White seems to have left his KP unprotected. In this section we examine what can happen if Black captures the pawn.

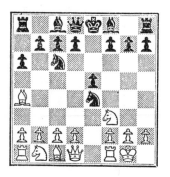

6 P—Q4

White can, of course, regain his pawn immediately with either 6 R—K1 or 6 Q—K2, but in either case Black would reply 6...N—B4, forcing the exchange of White's KB for a knight, and this should lead to equality. With 6 P—Q4 White finds a better plan – opening up the game in order to exploit his better development. Black has, after all, wasted time in capturing White's KP.

6 ...	P—QN4

Breaking the potential pin on the QN in preparation for playing...P—Q4.

(For 6...P×P?! see p. 83)

7 B—N3	P—Q4
8 P×P	

Material equality has now been restored. Black's position does not look too bad, but, as we shall see, he still has difficulties to face.

8 ...	B—K3

Protecting the QP, which was twice attacked.

9 Q—K2

Freeing he square Q1 for a rook, so that White can exert pressure along the Q file.

9 ...	B—K2

There are several alternative moves for Black to consider at this stage, but this simple development of the KB was usually considered to be Black's most solid continuation. Some recent games have, however, cast doubt on whether Black can equalize.

(For 9...N—B4 see p. 83)

10 R—Q1	O—O

(For 10...N—B4!? see p. 84)

11 P—B4!

Exploiting the pin on the QP to open the game still further. Now White threatens P×QP, winning a piece.

11 ...	NP×P
12 B×P	Q—Q2

Recommended by Larsen and considered best. Black's rooks are now connected on the back rank and can enter play more easily. Also Black can subsequently consider advancing his KBP now that his QB is protected.

13 N—B3

After 13 B×RP, N—B4!, Black gets excellent play.

13 ...	N×N
14 P×N	P—B3

Eliminating White's KP and seemingly getting good play for Black's KB on the long diagonal.

15 P×P	B×P

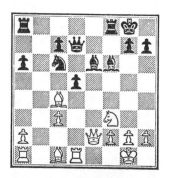

This position was formerly considered to offer equal chances to both players, but this was probably an incorrect evaluation. One strong move at White's disposal is **16 B—KN5**; e.g., **16...B×P** (16...N—R4?; 17 Q×B ch, Q×Q; 18 B×P wins a pawn); **17 QR—B1, B—B3; 18 B—N3!** (threatening B—R4, winning the knight), **18...N—Q1; 19 B×B, R×B; 20 Q—B2,** and White stands better; or **16...K—R1** (preventing tactical threats such as Q×B ch); **17 B×B, R×B; 18 N—N5** (threatening N×B, after which the QP must fall), **18...B—N1; 19 B×RP,** and White will emerge at least a pawn ahead (19...P—R3; 20 N—B3, R×B!?; 21 Q×R, N—Q5; 22 N—K5 wins for White).

The older continuation, **16 N—N5**, also gives White good chances. This is illustrated by the game SCHMID-KRISTINSSON, Siegen 1970, which concluded:

16...B×N; 17 B×B, P—R3; 18 B—K3, Q—Q3.

Preparing...N—K4.

19 B—N3, N—K4; 20 R—Q4!.

Threatening 21 B—KB4.

20...P—B4; 21 R—KB4!.

Opening up possibilities of B×BP, followed by Q×N.

21...K—R1.

Freeing KN1 as a retreat square for the bishop.

22 R—Q1, N—Q2; 23 Q—B3!.

Yet more pressure on Black's QP. The numerous pins, and threatened pins, in this game create a very pleasing effect.

23...N—B3; 24 P—B4!, QR—B1.

24...P—Q5?; 25 R×N, and White wins after either 25...R×R; 16 Q×R ch; or 25...P×R; 26 B×RP.

25 P×P, B—N1 (the only defence); **26 B—B4!.**

Black is not permitted any counterplay from his passed QBP.

26...N—Q2; 27 Q—N3, N—K4; 28 B—N3!.

The variation 28 B×RP, Q×B; 29 R×R, R×R; 30 Q×N, Q×P; 31 B×BP, Q—B7!; 32 Q—Q4, R—B5!; 33 Q—Q2, Q×Q; 34 R×Q, R—B4 leads only to a draw, after Black wins back the QP.

28...P—B5; 29 R×R, R×R; 30 B—B2, R—K1; 31 B—Q4!.

Now the knight is pinned again

because of the mating threat; so Black must prevent 32 P—B4.

31...B—R2; 32 B×B, K×B; 33 B—B3.

Black resigned because there was no defence against the final pin, 34 R—K1.

6...P×P?!

6...P×P?!. This attempt to hold on to the extra material is considered unsound. The game CAPABLANCA-ED. LASKER, New York 1915, continued:

7 R—K1, P—Q4; 8 N×P.

Threatening both 9 P—KB3, winning the knight, and 9 N×N, P×N; 10 B×P ch, winning the QR.

8...B—Q3.

A fighting defence which almost works.

9 N×N, B×P ch; 10 K—R1!.

10 K×B?, Q—R5 ch; 11 K—N1, Q×P ch, and Black draws by perpetual check.

10...Q—R5; 11 R×N ch!, P×R; 12 Q—Q8 ch!, Q×Q; 13 N×Q dis ch, K×N; 14 K×B.

White, with two minor pieces for the rook, has the better game.

9...N—B4

9...N—B4. This is an attempt to reduce the pressure on the QP by exchanging White's KB, but it represents too great a loss of time. After **10 N—Q1, N×B; 11 RP×N,** Black's plan is to play **11...Q—B1,** removing the queen from the rather dangerous Q file. However:

12 P—B4!, N—N5.
12...QP×P; 13 P×P, B×P; 14 Q—K4, N—K2; 15 N—R3 is good for White, since if the bishop retreats, White can play N×P.
13 P×NP, P×P; 14 R×R, Q×R; 15 B—Q2!.
Threatening 16 B×N, B×B; 17 Q× P ch, winning a piece.
15...P—QB3; 16 N—Q4.
Threatening 17 N×NP, P×N; 18 B×N, B×B; 19 Q×P ch, etc.

Other ninth moves that have been tried for Black are 9...B—QB4, 9... N—R4, and even 9...P—N4, but none of these seems satisfactory either.

10...N—B4!?

10...N—B4!?. After this, the play

becomes very complicated, because White can continue with **11 B×P, B×B; 12 N—B3,** and now Black's best is to boldly sacrifice his queen with **12...B—B5!.** This queen sacrifice gives rise to a collection of variations which have been analysed – in some cases as far as move thirty or beyond!

The main line runs:
13 R×Q ch, R×R; 14 Q—K3.
After 14 Q—K1?!, Black has 14...N—N5, with a forking threat on QB7.
14...P—N5; 15 P—QN3, B—K3.
15...P×N?; 16 B—R3! is good for White.
16 N—K4, R—Q8 ch; 17 N—K1, N—Q5; 18 B—N2, N×BP; 19 Q—K2, R×R; 20 B×R, N×B; 21 N×N, B×N.
It is the opinion of some theoreticians that, in spite of the strange material imbalance, the position is roughly equal.

EXCHANGE VARIATION

1 P—K4	P—K4	1 P—K4	P—K4
2 N—KB3	N—QB3	2 N—KB3	N—QB3
3 B—N5	P—QR3	3 B—N5	P—QR3
4 B×N	QP×B	4 B×N	QP×B

5 O—O	P—B3
6 P—Q4	B—KN5
7 P—B3	P×P
8 P×P	Q—Q2
9 P—KR3	B—K3
10 N—B3	O—O—O
11 B—B4!	

For the beginner, the move, 4 B×N always seems slightly paradoxical, for White voluntarily gives his opponent the advantage of the two bishops. The secret is that even as early as move four, White is trying to obtain an endgame advantage. After White has subsequently played P—Q4 and exchanged his QP for

Black's KP, a pawn formation arises which is favourable to White. White will have a pawn majority of four to three on the K side and in the ending he can use this pawn majority to create a passed pawn, which he can then try to queen. Black, of course will have a pawn majority of four to three on the Q side, but Black's pawns are crippled since his QB-pawns are doubled and, against best play by White, Black should not be able to get a passed pawn of his own.

As an experiment the reader should remove from the board White's QP, Black's KP, and all the pieces and then try playing through some sample king and pawn endgames. He will soon convince himself that White has very good chances of winning these endings. However, as a well-known chess sage once observed: "Between the opening and the ending the gods have placed the middle game." It is in the middle game that Black's salvation lies – he should seek compensation for his pawn weaknesses through active piece play (the two bishops will help here). In former times the Exchange Variation had a reputation for being very drawish and, even with Fischer's improvements, Black has no reason to fear this system.

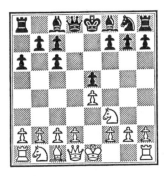

The recapture 4...QP × B, which opens lines for Black's QB, is preferable to 4...NP × B, since White stands better after 5 P—Q4, P × P; 6 Q × P. We have already noted elsewhere that the attempt to win a pawn with 5 N × P?! is faulty, because of 5...Q—Q5, when Black equalizes easily.

5 O—O

This is an old move which was reintroduced into modern practice by the Dutch master Barendregt, and then adopted by Bobby Fischer in 1966. Before that date the more usual continuations were 5 N—QB3 and 5 P—Q4 (playing for the exchange of queens: 5...P × P; 6 Q × P, Q × Q; 7 N × Q); but neither of these seems to lead to more than equality. With 5 O—O, White completes the development of his K side and revives the threat to Black's KP.

(For 5 N—B3 see p. 86)

5 ...   P—B3

The KP now needs to be defended. Defending with the queen, 5...Q—B3, allows White to gain time by attacking the queen later; e.g., 6 P—Q4, P × P; 7 B—N5, Q—N3; 8 Q × P. Defending with the bishop, 5...B—Q3, also seems inferior because of 6 P—Q4, P × P (6...P—B3; 7 P × P, P × P; 8 N × P!, and White will regain the piece by 9 Q—R5 ch); 7 Q × P (attacking the KNP); 7...P—B3; 8 QN—Q2!, to be followed by 9 N—B4, with pressure against the Black position.

(For 5...B—KN5 see p. 87)

6 P—Q4   B—KN5

6...P × P surrenders the centre and gives White too free a hand; e.g., 7 N × P, B—Q3, and now White can play 8 Q—R5 ch, P—N3; 9 Q—B3, weakening Black's K side, because 9...B × P ch; 10 K × B, Q × N; 11 R—Q1 leaves Black struggling to avoid a quick knock-out. The text move, pinning White's KN, is a much more active defence.

7 P—B3

Supporting the QP in the hope of setting up a full pawn centre. This move involves a potential pawn sacrifice which is probably too dangerous for Black to accept – after 7...P × P; 8 P × P, B × N 9 Q × B, Q × P, White can play 10 R—Q1, and Black will have to spend considerable time manoeuvring his queen to a reasonable square; e.g., 10...Q—B5; 11 B—B4 (attacking the QBP), 11...Q—KB2. White has obvious compensation for his pawn.

(For 7 P × P see p. 87)

7 . . .   P×P

Opening up the game a little. This is not played in order to accept the risky pawn sacrifice mentioned above, but rather with the idea of continuing with . . .Q—Q2 and . . .O—O—O, and applying pressure to White's centre.

(For 7. . .B—Q3 see p. 87)

8 P×P   Q—Q2
9 P—KR3

Attacking the bishop and driving it away before the pin becomes too troublesome.

9 . . .   B—K3

A natural retreat, but maintaining the pin with 9. . .B—R4 may be preferable. The ending after 9. . .B—R4; 10 N—K5, B×Q; 11 N×Q, K×N; 12 R×B is better for White, but probably not enough to win. The greedy 9. . .B×N; 10 Q×B, Q×P; 11 R—Q1 is still good for White.

10 N—B3   O—O—O
11 B—B4!

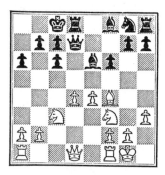

Attacking QB7, the square in front of the Black king. White now threatens 12 P—Q5!; e.g., 12. . .P×P; 13 R—B1, P×P; 14 N—QR4!, Q×Q; 15 R×P ch, K—N1; 16 R—B8 dbl ch!, K×R; 17 N—N6 mate (or 16. . .K—R2; 17 B—N8 ch, K—R1; 18 N—N6 mate). Black's best continuation is 11. . .B—Q3; 12 B×B, Q×B, which removes some of his difficulties; but even so White will retain an advantage, because his pawn centre cramps Black's game and because he can use the beautiful

square QB5, as an outpost for his QN. In FISCHER–GLIGORIC, Havana Olympiad 1966, Black continued less correctly with 11. . .N—K2 and was soon lost. The game concluded:

12 R—B1, N—N3; 13 B—N3, B—Q3;
14 N—QR4! (heading for QB5),
14. . .B×B; 15 P×B, K—N1.

Black cannot keep the knight away with 15. . .P—N3, because of 16 P—Q5, P×P; 17 N×P ch, winning the queen.

16 N—B5, Q—Q3; 17 Q—R4!.

Pressing home the attack with great vigour.

17. . .K—R2?.

A blunder, which speeds up the end – relatively best was 17. . .B—B1, to prevent White's next move.

18 N×RP!, B×KRP.

Hoping for 19 P×B, Q×NP ch, with some complications on the K side. Black cannot play 18. . .P×N, because of 19 R×P, which leads to mate or loss of queen.

19 P—K5, N×P.

All moves are hopeless now.

20 P×N, P×P; 21 N—B5 ch, K—N1;
22 P×B, P—K5; 23 N×KP, Q—K2;
24 R—B3 (threatening 25 R—R3),
24. . .P—QN4; 25 Q—B2 .

Black, who is two pieces down, decided to resign.

---

5 N—B3

5 N—B3. This is not as aggressive as the main line and should lead to equality. Black should play 5. . .P—B3 to protect his KP, and if White tries for the ending with 6 P—Q4, P×P; 7 Q×P, Q×Q; 8 N×Q, Black can continue simply with

8...B—Q3. The bishop on Q3 is well-posted, and it is difficult for White to improve his position. If White challenges this bishop with **9 N(Q4)—K2, N—K2; 10 B—B4,** Black can play **10...N—N3,** and after **11 B×B, P×B; 12 O—O—O, K—K2,** Black's pawns are undoubled and the ending is completely equal.

5...B—KN5

5...B—KN5. The most aggressive plan, for after **6 P—KR3,** Black will continue with **6...P—KR4!?.** White's best, according to Fischer, is then **7 P—Q3,** for if **7 P×B?, P×P,** White has nothing better than immediately returning the piece (moving the knight would allow **8...Q—R5** with a mating attack). Nor does White have time to support his centre with **7 P—B3,** because of the drawing variation **7 P—B3, Q—Q6!** (threatening to get the better of things with **8...B×N); 8 P×B, P×P; 9 N×P, B—Q3!; 10 N×Q, B—R7 ch.**

After **7 P—Q3** play might continue:
7...Q—B3.
Increasing the strength of the pin on White's KN.
8 QN—Q2.
8 P×B, P×P; 9 N—N5, Q—R3; 10 N—R3, Q—R5 is still good for Black.
8...N—K2.
Intending to move **N—N3—R5.**
9 R—K1, N—N3; 10 P—Q4!, B—Q3.
10...P×P; 11 P—K5, and Black's queen has no good square.
11 P×B, P×NP; 12 N—R2, R×N!.
Hoping for **13 K×R,** when Black has a winning attack.
13 Q×P!, R—R5; 14 Q—B5.
White has a small advantage.

---

7 P×P

7 P×P. Playing for the exchange of queens, but after **7...Q×Q; 8 R×Q, B×N; 9 P×B, P×P,** White's position is not noticeably superior, although Black's isolated KP may give White some chances of building up an initiative (he can play **10 B—K3,** followed by **N—Q2—B4).**

7...B—Q3

7...B—Q3. This holds the centre and is more solid than the main line **7...P×P,** which can lead Black into difficulties. Play might continue:
8 P—KR3, B—R4; 9 R—K1, Q—K2; 10 B—K3, N—R3; 11 QN—Q2.
11 B×N?, P×B, only opens the KN file for Black.
11...N—B2; 12 Q—N3, N—Q1.
If **12...O—O—O,** then **13 N—B4,** intending **N—R5,** is troublesome for Black.
13 P×P, P×P.
Chances are roughly equal Hort–Gligoric, Sousse, 1967.

SCHLIEMANN DEFENCE

1 P—K4	P—K4
2 N—KB3	N—QB3
3 B—N5	P—B4?!
4 N—B3	P×P
5 QN×P	P—Q4
6 N×P	P×N
7 N×N	P×N
8 B×P ch	B—Q2
9 Q—R5 ch	K—K2
10 Q—K5 ch	B—K3

---

1 P—K4	P—K4
2 N—KB3	N—QB3
3 B—N5	P—B4?!

The strategy behind the Schliemann Defence to the Ruy Lopez is in some ways similar to that which motivates the King's Gambit – a pawn is offered in exchange for quick, active development, and the possibility of a direct attack against the opponent's king along the open KB file. However, in this case it is Black rather than White who is offering the pawn, and Black starts a move behind! If the reader deduces that for this reason the Schliemann is likely to be a less powerful attacking weapon than the King's Gambit, he would be right. Indeed, most masters regard this defence as totally unsound.

4 N—B3

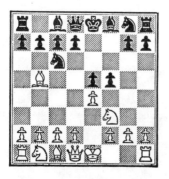

The most sensible policy for White is quick development. 4 P×P, P—K5 is less clear; e.g., 5 Q—K2, Q—K2; 6 B×N, NP×B; 7 N—Q4, N—B3; 8 O—O, P—B4, and Black's strong central pawns give him some compensation. Another plan which doesn't work is 4 B×N?!, QP×B; 5 N×P, Q—Q5; 6 Q—R5 ch?, P—N3; 7 N×NP, P×N; 8 Q×P ch, K—Q1, and White's premature attack has come to an end, leaving Black with the advantage.

4 ...	P×P

Opening the KB file. The otherwise desirable 4...N—B3; 5 P×P, B—B4, attacking White's KB2, allows the "fork trick," 6 N×P.

(For 4...N—Q5!? see p. 89)

5 QN×P	P—Q4

Hoping to profit from the exposed position of White's QN by gaining a tempo.

(For 5...N—B3 see p. 90)

6 N×P!

Exploiting the pin on Black's knight. This move probably refutes the whole variation. After the weaker 6 N—N3, B—KN5; 7 P—KR3, B×N; 8 Q×B, N—B3, White has no advantage, as Black's strong pawn centre compensates for White's two bishops. If 6...B—Q3?, then 7 N×P, B×N; 8 Q—R5 ch and White regains his piece and emerges a pawn ahead.

6 ...	P×N

6...Q—K2 would be answered simply by 7 P—Q4.

7 N×N	P×N

(For 7...Q—Q4 see p. 90)

8 B×P ch	B—Q2
9 Q—R5 ch	

This is more precise than 9 B×R, since Black's king will now be left stranded and exposed in the centre of the board.

9 ...　　　　K—K2

If 9...P—N3, then 10 Q—K5 ch, and White will win at least the exchange.

10 Q—K5 ch　　　B—K3

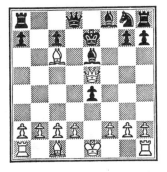

If 10...K—B2, then 11 B—Q5 ch, and Black loses immediately.

White now has a winning advantage, for, after 11 B×R, Q×B; 12 Q×BP ch, he has a rook and three pawns for two pieces and, for good measure, Black's king is very exposed.

Another interesting move at White's disposal is 11 P—KB4!?, threatening to win the pinned bishop with 12 P—B5. If Black defends with 11...N—R3, there would follow 12 P—B5!, N×P; 13 R—B1! (better than 13 O—O, Q—Q5 ch; 14 Q×Q, N×Q; 15 B×R, N×P), with a very strong attack. The game LIBERZON-A. GELLER, Leningrad 1960 concluded: 13...N—Q5?; 14 Q—B5 ch, Q—Q3; 15 Q—N5 mate. An alternative defensive try is 11...P×P e.p., but this also holds out little hope. The game ROLLAND-DUCKSTEIN, Le Havre 1966, continued:

11...P×P e.p.; 12 P—Q4.
Opening lines for the QB and threatening P—Q5.

12...N—B3; 13 P—Q5?!.
White wishes to bring his QB and QR into play quickly but this move is incorrect: Black could now get counterplay with 13...P—B7 ch!, after which White's king is also stranded in the centre. More precise is 13 O—O; e.g., 13...R—N1; 14 P—Q5, Q—Q3; 15 Q×B ch, when White retains a big plus.

13...N×P?.
Black misses his chance and now he is completely lost.

14 B—N5 ch, N—B3; 15 R—Q1, Q—B1; 16 B×R, Q×B.
Black has two pieces for a rook – a slight material advantage – but his king is so exposed that his game is hopeless.

17 O—O, K—B2.
Trying to develop his K-side pieces; 17...P×P? would be met by 18 B×N ch, P×B; 19 Q×KBP ch, K—K1; 20 Q×B ch, B—K2; 21 KR—K1.

18 R×P, B—K2; 19 B×N, P×B.
19...B×B allows 20 Q×P ch; e.g., 20...K—N1; 21 R×B, P×R; 22 R—Q8 ch, winning the queen.

20 Q—KR5 ch, K—N2; 21 R—K1, Q—B3.
21...Q—QB1? loses a piece to 22 R(B3)—K3.

22 R—B3, Q—N3 ch; 23 K—R1, R—Q1; 24 R(B3)—K3, R—Q3; 25 R—KN3 ch.
Now that the Black rook no longer guards the KRP, White can invade on the K side.

25...K—B1; 26 Q×P.
Threatening 27 Q—R8 ch, B—N1; 28 Q×B mate.

26...K—K1; 27 R—N7, B—KB1.
27...B—Q1 allows mate in two by 28 Q—R8 ch.

28 Q—N6 ch, K—Q1; 29 Q×P ch, K—B1.
Black could cheerfully have resigned.

30 Q×B (B8) ch, K—N2; 31 P—KR3.
Stopping any back rank mating threats and thus increasing the scope of his rook on K1.

31...B—Q4.
Not 31...Q×P?; 32 Q×R.

32 R—K8, K—B3; 33 R(K8)—K7, K—N4; 34 Q—B1 ch, B—B5; 35 P—QR4 ch, K—N5; 36 R—N4, R—Q5; 37 R×R, Q×R; 38 P—B3 ch.
Black, not before time, resigned.

4...N—Q5!?

4...N—Q5!?. This is a modern attempt to rehabilitate the Schliemann, but it violates the principle that the same piece should not be moved twice in the opening. White's strongest reply is simply

5 N×P!. The usual continuation is 5...Q—B3; 6 N—B3, P×P; and now White should play 7 N×N! (7 N×P, N×N ch; 8 Q×N, Q×Q; 9 P×Q, leaves White with an extra pawn, but it is doubled, isolated and practically worthless), 7...Q×N; 8 O—O, after which White is ensured of an advantage due to his superior development.

5...N—B3

5...N—B3. This is no more promising than the main line:

6 N×N ch, P×N.

6...Q×N; 7 Q—K2, P—Q3; 8 P—Q4 leaves Black with many problems, since White threatens 9 P—Q5, and 9 P×P, and 9 B—N5.

7 P—Q4, P—Q3.

7...P—K5? allows 8 N—N5!, attacking the KP and threatening 9 Q—R5 ch, Black cannot play 8...P×N? because of 9 Q—R5 ch, K—K2; 10 B×P ch, winning the queen.

8 P—Q5, P—QR3; 9 B—K2!; N—K2; 10 N—R4.

Now Black cannot prevent his king from being stranded in the centre after 11 B—R5 ch.

7...Q—Q4

7...Q—Q4. A slight improvement on the text continuation, but not good enough to improve Black's chances substantially. White should first protect the square QN5 with 8 P—B4, and after 8...Q—Q3 (best, since 8...Q—N4; 9 P—Q4, Q×P; 10 Q—R5 ch leads to sudden death), he should play: 9 N×P dis ch, B—Q2; 10 B×B ch, Q×B; 11 Q—R5 ch, P—N3; 12 Q—K5 ch, K—B2; 13 N—N5!. White has two extra pawns for which Black has little compensation. Note that 13 Q×R!? is double-edged and complicated, since Black can win the queen after 13...N—B3; 14 N—N5, R—K1, followed by 15...B—N2.

7

SICILIAN DEFENCE

1 P—K4, P—QB4

The Sicilian Defence has been analysed more than any other chess opening. Books have been written about particular variations. Over 25 per cent of all master games are Sicilians. Why this popularity?

With his first move, Black announces his intention for a fight. By attacking the centre from the QB file, he creates an imbalance which leads to sharp positions offering many interesting possibilities to both sides. In this chapter, we discuss four variations which differ fundamentally in one respect – Black's pawn structure.

The various possible pawn structures which Black may choose to adopt, each have their own strong and weak points. If Black has a pawn at K4 (e.g., the Lowenthal Variation) his Q4 square is vulnerable with the result that White will eventually be able to occupy that square with a piece. And of course, if Black has little or no control over his Q4 square, he will be unable to force the thematic advance of his QP. The advantage of Black's pawn at K4 is that it deprives White's KN of its natural post at Q4, and it paves the way for the possibility of a later . . .N—Q5.

In the Kan/Taimanov set-ups, Black has pawns at QR3 (preventing the invasion of a White knight at QN5 and preparing for the advance . . .P—QN4), and at K3 (helping the development of his KB and, in some variations, his KN, as well as supporting an eventual . . .P—Q4). Black's QP is sometimes advanced to Q3 in order to prevent the threat P—K5 by White. This kind of pawn structure tends to leave Black a little weak on the dark squares.

When Black fianchettoes his KB (e.g., the Dragon Variation) he incurs the kind of K-side weakness mentioned on page 24 but otherwise his pawn structure is in no way vulnerable.

Black has two principal aims in the Sicilian, after completing his development. The most important of these is his attack on White's KP, usually taken up by his knight at KB3 and sometimes by his QB at QN2 as well. The attack is sometimes made complete by means of the freeing move . . .P—Q4. When Black can make that move with impunity his game will inevitably be satisfactory.

The other theme of Black's set-up is the attack along the QB file, normally accomplished by developing his QR at QB1. Sometimes this rook is sacrificed for White's QN (which is defending the KP) so as to cripple the White's Q-side pawns and undermine his KP.

LOWENTHAL VARIATION

1 P—K4	P—QB4
2 N—KB3	N—QB3
3 P—Q4	P×P
4 N×P	P—K4
5 N—N5	P—QR3
6 N—Q6 ch	B×N
7 Q×B	Q—B3
8 Q—Q1	Q—N3
9 N—B3	KN—K2
10 P—KR4!	P—KR4
11 B—KN5	P—Q4
12 P×P	N—N5
13 B×N	K×B
14 B—Q3!	

---

1 P—K4	P—QB4
2 N—KB3	

The most natural developing move. It would be possible to write a whole book on White's alternative second moves but not wishing to cloud the issue we examine only one other possibility.

(For 2 N—QB3 see p. 93)

2 ...	N—QB3

Also a natural move, adding support to Black's Q5 square, which is about to become the pivot of the position.

3 P—Q4

Opening the position, improving the development possibilities of his pieces, and staking a claim in the centre.

3 ...	P×P

Otherwise White will disrupt Black's position with 4 P—Q5.

4 N×P	P—K4

This move introduces the Lowenthal Variation. Black seizes the initiative, but at the cost of landing himself with a permanently weak square at Q4. Our discussion of this variation illustrates many of the important aspects of Sicilian

positions in which Black plays an early ...P—K4.

5 N—N5

The only active move. 5 N—B5?, P—Q4!; 6 Q×P, Q×Q; 7 P×Q, B×N; 8 P×N is good for Black. In almost all Sicilian positions, White should refrain from the knight exchange N(Q4)×N, because when Black recaptures with a pawn, his Q4 square receives better protection. This position is no exception: 5 N×N, NP×N; 6 B—QB4, B—R3, with a level game. If 7 B×B?, then Q—R4 ch, followed by 8 ... Q×B, preventing White from castling K side for the time being.

5 ...	P—QR3

The logical continuation of his plan. Black plays the useful move ...P—QR3 with gain of tempo, maintaining his initiative.

6 N—Q6 ch	B×N
7 Q×B	Q—B3

Using his initiative to offer the exchange of queens.

8 Q—Q1!

It is paradoxical that after all we have written about development, this "undeveloping" move is probably the only one that gives White a lasting advantage.

(For 8 Q×Q? and 8 Q—R3 see p. 94)

8 . . .   Q—N3

Attacking White's KP and putting pressure on White's KNP, thereby preventing the development of White's KB.

9 N—B3   KN—K2

Not 9... N—B3, which seems more natural, because of 10 Q—Q6, when Black cannot castle.

10 P—KR4!

An unusual move, taking advantage of the position of Black's queen to force further dark square weaknesses. Now White assumes the initiative.

10 . . .   P—KR4

10...P—R3?, gives White the opportunity to increase his space while maintaining his initiative: 11 P—R5, Q—B3; 12 B—K3, O—O; 13 Q—Q2, P—QN4; 14 O—O—O, P—N5; 15 N—R4, and White has a clear advantage – Black's position is full of weak squares.

11 B—KN5

Cashing in on Black's weak dark squares.

11 . . .   P—Q4

Black has no better move – he must try to free his game. If 11...P—B3; 12 B—K3, P—Q4, White should capture with the knight rather than the pawn, because after 13 N×P, N×N; 14 Q×N, Black does not have the move ...B—K3 at his disposal.

12 P×P   N—N5

If 12...N—Q5, then 13 B—Q3, B—B4; 14 O—O, and Black has no compensation for the sacrificed pawn.

13 B×N   K×B

Not 13...N×BP ch?; 14 K—Q2, N×R; 15 B—KN5 when White wins the knight and emerges with two pieces for rook and pawn.

14 B—Q3!

Allowing Black to land White with doubled, isolated QP's. But White is still a pawn ahead and his forces co-

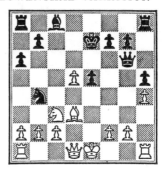

operate well in the endgame: 14...N× B ch; 15 Q×N, Q×Q; 16 P×Q, P— QN4 (otherwise 17 P—QR4 restricts Black's freedom on the Q side); 17 O—O—O! (bringing his king to the Q side, where it will be useful in the endgame), 17...R—Q1; 18 KR—K1. White, who is threatening 19 P—Q4 (undoubling his pawns), has the advantage.

---

2 N—QB3

2 N—QB3. The Closed Variation. Rather than play for an early P—Q4, White develops his forces in a manner that keeps the position closed, intending an eventual advance on the K side. The point of keeping the centre closed is that flank attacks are traditionally met by central counter-punches. If Black has no play in the centre, White may gain an advantage.

Here Black has time to launch a Q side counter-attack. If he plays this counter-attack with sufficient forcefulness, White's K-side play will not be permitted to make much progress. Play might continue:

2...P—KN3.

The fianchetto of the KB is the most effective way of building up Q-side pressure.

3 P—KN3, B—N2; 4 B—N2, N—QB3; 5 P—Q3, P—Q3; 6 B—K3, R—N1!.

Very strong, for it prepares the immediate advance...P—QN4—N5.

7 N—B3, N—B3; 8 P—KR3.

Keeping Black's pieces away from KN4.

8...P—QN4; 9 Q—Q2, P—N5; 10 N—Q1 (10 N—K2 is better), **10...B—QR3!.**

Threatening ...P—B5 – Black already has the initiative.

11 N—R4, O—O; 12 O—O, P—B5; 13 P—B4, Q—B2; 14 R—B2, KR—Q1; 15 P—Q4, P—Q4.

Black's position is very good. We have been following the game HECHT–KEENE, Teeside 1972, which now went:

16 P—K5, N—K5; 17 B×N, P—B6!.

A fine pawn sacrifice to open up game.

18 P×P, P×B.

Now all Black's pieces are superbly placed, while White's game is disorganized. White's pawn centre soon collapsed under Black's pressure.

---

8 Q×Q?

8 Q×Q?. A pointless move: **8...N×Q; 9 N—B3** (the only move that both defends the KP and prevents ...P—Q4), **9...N—QN5!; 10 B—Q3** (if 10 K—Q1, then N—N5; 11 B—K3, N×B ch; 12 P×N, with a level position), **10...N×**

B ch; **11 P×N, P—R3!** (preventing B—KN5); **12 B—K3, P—Q3.** The position is equal – both sides have weak Q4 squares.

---

8 Q—R3

8 Q—R3. This move introduces quite a logical idea. Black's dark squared bishop has been exchanged, leaving him weak on the dark squares in general and his KB1—QR6 diagonal in particular. White hopes to hold up Black's K-side castling by mounting pressure along that diagonal. It has been shown, however, that by playing actively on the Q side, Black can obtain a satisfactory position:

8...KN—K2.

8...Q—N3 appears dangerous, but White can sacrifice his KP for active piece play: 9 B—K3!, Q×KP; 10 N—B3, Q—QN5; 11 Q×Q, N×Q; 12 O—O—O, N—K2; 13 B—B5, QN—B3; 14 B—B4!. Black cannot castle, because of 15 N—Q5. 14...P—QN4 is also bad: 15 N—Q5!, N×N; 16 B×N, B—N2; 17 P—KB4, with an excellent game for White.

9 N—B3, R—QN1; 10 B—K3.

10 N—Q5, N×N; 11 P×N, N—K2; 12 P—QB4 appears to be a logical way to obtain control of the important Q5 square, but Black can react sharply with 12...P—QN4!.

10...P—QN4; 11 N—Q5, N×N; 12 P×N, P—N5.

Attacking the exposed queen.

13 Q—Q3, N—K2; 14 P—Q6, N—B4; 15 O—O—O, B—N2.

Black has the more active position. White's advanced QP in no way hinders Black's play.

RAUZER VARIATION

1 P—K4	P—QB4
2 N—KB3	P—Q3
3 P—Q4	P×P
4 N×P	N—KB3
5 N—QB3	N—B3
6 B—KN5	B—Q2
7 Q—Q2	R—B1
8 O—O—O	N×N
9 Q×N	Q—R4
10 P—B4	R×N!?
11 P×R	P—K4
12 Q—N4	Q×Q
13 P×Q	N×P

1 P—K4	P—QB4
2 N—KB3	P—Q3
3 P—Q4	P×P
4 N×P	N—KB3
5 N—QB3	N—B3

Black first puts more pressure on t he centre, inviting White to commit himself, before completing his K-side development.

6 B—KN5

By introducing the possibility of B × N at some stage, White puts indirect pressure on Black's QP. For example, 6...P—KN3; 7 B×N, P×B, leaves the QP isolated and weak – after 8 P—B4, if Black continues with his normal plan of development he is immediately put under strong pressure in the centre: 8...B—N2; 9 N(Q4)—N5, O—O; 10 Q×P, P—B4; 11 O—O—O, and White's game is better.

6 B—K3 is simply answered by 6... N—KN5 and 7 ...N×B.

(For 6 B—QB4 see p. 96)

6 ...   B—Q2

The most modern move. Black plans quick mobilization of his Q side with ...R—B1 and ...Q—R4, followed in many cases by the exchange sacrifice ...R×N, mentioned i n the introduction.

(For 6...P—K3 see p. 96)

7 Q—Q2

(For 7 B×N, NP×B; 8 N—B5 see p. 97)

7 ...   R—B1
8 O—O—O

It may seem risky to "castle into it" in view of Black's coming Q-side play, but a study of the alternatives seems to indicate that White has nothing better.

(For 8 N—N3 see p. 97)

8 ...   N×N

Openingt he QB file for his rook.

9 Q×N   Q—R4

The first part of Black's plan has been accomplished. His Q side is fully developed and he is ready for the thematic sacrifice ...R×N. Now White must do something about his attacked QB.

10 P—B4

The most natural way to defend his bishop, simultaneously increasing his centre control.

10 ...   R×N!?
·11 P×R

11 B×N? loses material to 11...R—B2; 12 B×NP (12 B—R4, Q×P is hopeless for White); 12...P—K4!.

(For 11 Q×R? see p. 97)

11 . . .   P—K4!

A bold move, considering that Black's king is still in the centre. But Black must stay active.

12 Q—N4

Other queen moves allow 12...N—N5, threatening 13. .. P—KR3, followed by 14...P×P.

12 . . .   Q×Q
13 P×Q   N×P

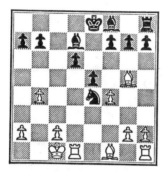

Black has one pawn for the exchange, and numerous factors which add to his compensation: his threats include 14... N—B7, forking the White rooks, and 14...N—B6, followed by 15...N×P ch and 16...N×P. Practical experience suggests that Black has a perfectly satisfactory position. The game UNZICKER-GHEORGHIU, Ljubljana 1969, continued: 14 B—R4, P—KN4!; 15 P×NP (not 15 B×P?, N—B7, when Black regains the exchange), 15...B—K2; 16 R—K1, P—Q4; 17 B—Q3, P—KR3; 18 P—B4, RP×P; 19 P×P, R×B; 20 R×N, R×R; 21 B×R, P—B4 and the game was soon agreed drawn.

This variation offers an excellent example of the power of Black's thematic exchange sacrifice in the Sicilian. See also the Dragon Variation, page 98.

6 B—QB4

6 B—QB4. This aggressive move has

long been the favourite of Bobby Fischer. The idea is to put the pressure on Black's K side in readiness for when Black castles. The complications that arise from this move are well beyond the scope of this book, but here is one sample variation:

6...P—K3.

Necessary to reduce the scope of White's KB. If 6...P—KN3?, then 7 N×N, P×N; 8 P—K5, P×P??; 9 B×P ch wins Black's queen – how weak is that KB2 square!

7 B—K3, B—K2; 8 Q—K2, O—O; 9 O—O—O.

Now the position is ripe for each player to launch an attack against the other's king. White's plans involve the thrust P—KN4 (possibly prefaced with KR—N1), followed by P—N5 and a general advance on the K side. Black counters on the Q side. Amongst his possible plans are ...B—Q2, followed by ...N×N, and an eventual ...P—QN4, ...P—QR4, ...P—N5, and ...P—R5; or the manoeuvre ...N—QR4, followed by ...P—QR3, ...P—QN4, exchanging knight for bishop and continuing with ...B—N2 and ...R—QB1.

6...P—K3

6...P—K3. The older (and more thoroughly analysed) variation. Black avoids the doubling of his KBPs, putting up with the pin on his knight, which he will soon relieve by...B—K2.

7 Q—Q2, B—K2; 8 O—O—O, O—O; 9 P—B4.

The strongest continuation, taking control of the K5 square.

9...N×N.

9...P—K4 is met by 10 N—B5, B×N; 11 P×B, when White will follow up with B—Q3, P—KN4, and a K-side attack. Note that whenever Black plays ...P—K4 in the Sicilian, attacking White's knight at Q4, the knight would like to play to the active square KB5, but this is only possible when Black cannot free his game by either...P—Q4 immediately, or...B×N followed by ...P—Q4.

10 Q×N, Q—R4.

The logical square for the queen – if White's knight can be driven from QB3, his QRP will be *en prise*. Black often follows up his...Q—R4 by bringing a rook to QB1, and sacrificing the exchange on QB6, so as to weaken White's control of his QR2.

11 B—B4, B—Q2.

If 11...R—Q1, preventing 12 P—K5, White continues with 12 KR—B1, followed by P—B5 and a K-side attack.

12 P—K5, P×P; 13 P×P, B—B3; 14 B—Q2!.

14 B×N, P×B; 15 P×P, Q—N4 ch is perfectly satisfactory for Black.

14...N—Q2; 15 N—Q5.

A common move in the Sicilian, uncovering an attack on Black's queen, while improving the position of White's QN.

15...Q—Q1; 16 N×B ch, Q×N; 17 KR—K1.

White has the advantage because of his pair of bishops and better centre control.

---

7 B×N, NP×B; 8 N—B5

---

7 B×N, NP×B; 8 N—B5. A natural idea, restricting Black's development because his KB cannot move and ...P—Q3 is impossible.

8...Q—R4!.

The most active move, threatening simply to win a pawn by 9...B×N; 10 P×B, Q×BP.

9 B—N5, P—QR3; 10 B×N, P×B; 11 Q—Q3, R—QN1.

Black has the advantage of two bishops for two knights, and although White's KN is aggressively placed, we feel that Black's long term advantage is the more significant.

---

8 N—N3

8 N—N3. Played with the intention of avoiding the coming knight exchange ...N×N. Play might continue: **8...P—KR3; 9 B×N, NP×B; 10 B—K2, P—B4** (eliminating the doubled pawns); **11 B—Q3, P×P; 12 B×P, B—N2,** when White has insufficient compensation for having presented Black with the advantage of the two bishops.

---

11 Q×R?

---

11 Q×R?. After **11...Q×Q; 12 P×Q, N×P,** Black has a pawn for the exchange, and various unpleasant threats; e.g.:

13 B—R4.
Defending the KB2 square.
13...P—KN3.
If 13...N×P, then 14 R—Q4 (threatening 15 K—N2, N—N4; 16 R—N4, P—QR3; 17 P—QR4, N—B2; 18 R×P.
14 B—K1, B—N2; 15 K—N2, O—O; 16 B—Q3, N—B4.
Threatening 17...N—R5 ch.
17 K—R3, R—B1.
A clear advantage for Black, whose active Q-side play more than outweighs the sacrificed material.

DRAGON VARIATION

1 P—K4	P—QB4
2 N—KB3	P—Q3
3 P—Q4	P×P
4 N×P	N—KB3
5 N—QB3	P—KN3
6 B—K3	B—N2
7 B—K2	N—B3
8 O—O	O—O
9 N—N3	B—K3
10 P—B4	Q—B1!
11 P—KR3	P—QR4
12 P—QR4	N—QN5
13 B—Q4	B—B5

---

1 P—K4	P—QB4
2 N—KB3	P—Q3

Opening the way for Black's QB and preventing an early P—K5 by White.

3 P—Q4	P×P
4 N×P	N—KB3

An important part of Black's opening strategy, attacking the KP in order to encourage White's next move, and thereby hold back White's QBP. If Black plays 4...P—KN3 instead, White can play 5 P—QB4, establishing what is known as a Maroczy Bind (after a famous Hungarian Master of the 1920's). The idea of the Bind is to prevent (hopefully for all time) the move ...P—Q4, by which Black seeks to free his game. If Black's thematic freeing move can indeed be held up, he will rapidly reach a passive position, offering little or no counterplay.

5 N—QB3

(For 5 P—KB3 see p. 99)

5 . . .	P—KN3

This move introduces the Dragon Variation, so named because Black's pawn structure resembles the silhouette of a dragon. Black fianchettoes his KB, putting pressure on the long (KR1—

QR8) diagonal and creating a safe area for his king.

6 B—K3

(For 6 P—B4 see p. 100)

6 ...   **B—N2**

Not 6...N—KN5?, because of 7 B—N5 ch, B—Q2; 8 Q×N, winning a piece. But now 7...N—N5 *is* a threat.

7 B—K2

(For 7 P—B3 see p. 100)

7 ...   **N—B3**
8 O—O   **O—O**

Both sides are making normal, developing moves.

9 N—N3

By vacating the Q4 square, White makes it more difficult for Black to create play based on the possibility of ...P—Q4. This move also prepares for 10 P—B4.

A quiet alternative that poses Black few problems is 9 Q—Q2 – the natural response, 9...N—KN5; 10 B×N, B×B, produces a somewhat sterile position.

(For 9 P—B4 see p. 101)

9 ...   **B—K3**

The most active square for the bishop, preparing for the eventual occupation of QB5 by the bishop or the QN. 9...B—Q2 is too passive.

10 P—B4

White also reacts vigorously. If Black does nothing he will find himself facing a strong K-side attack after P—B5, P—N4, and P—N5.

10 ...   **Q—B1!**

A triple-purpose move – preventing 11 P—B5; threatening the exchanging manoeuvre 11...N—KN5; and vacating the Q1 square for his rook, which may wish to support the advance of his QP.

11 P—KR3

To prevent 11...N—KN5.

11 ...   **P—QR4!**

Black continues in active vein – the threat now is 12...P—R5; 13 N—Q4, P—R6, weakening White along the long diagonal over which his fianchettoed bishop exerts so much influence.

12 P—QR4   N—QN5

Black has a fully satisfactory position. His Q, QN, QB, and KB all point towards the Q side, where he has sufficient chances to off-set White's slightly better control of the centre. Black's immediate threat is 13...N×KP!; 14 N×N, N×P.

13 B—Q4   B—B5

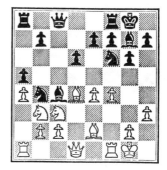

In this lively position the chances are about equal.

---

5 P—KB3

5 P—KB3. By defending his KP, White leaves his QBP free to advance. If Black plays a quiet developing move, White will continue with 6 P—QB4, establishing the dreaded Maroczy Bind. So Black must hit out at once:

5...P—K4!.
Apparently unthematic, since it creates a weak square at Q4 and leaves the QP backward. But these factors are both dispelled by dynamic play.
6 B—N5 ch.
Gaining a tempo for his development. 6 N—N3 is met by 6...P—Q4!; 7 B—KN5, P—Q5.
6...B—Q2; 7 B×B ch, QN×B; 8 N—B5, P—Q4!.
A temporary pawn sacrifice that frees Black's game.
9 P×P, Q—R4 ch; 10 N—B3, N—N3.
Already preparing to regain the pawn.
11 Q—K2.
If 11 N—K3, N(N3)×P; 12 N(K3)×N, O—O—O, Black wins back the piece.
11...O—O—O; 12 O—O, N(N3)×P; 13 N×N, R×N.
Black has no more problems in the centre. The chances are equal.

---

6 P—B4

6 P—B4. This move is designed to prevent an immediate 6...B—N2, because of 7 P—K5, upon which, Black's position can quickly become totally disorganized if he is not careful. But it has recently been found that Black can meet **7 P—K5** with **7...N—R4!; 8 B—N5 ch** (or 8 B—K2, N×P; 9 B×N, P—K4), **8...B—Q2; 9 P—K6, P×P; 10 N×P, B×N ch; 11 P×B, Q—B1,** and Black has sufficient counterplay to maintain the balance.

Black's best counter to 6 P—B4 is **6...QN—Q2,** followed by ...B—N2, ...O—O, ...N—N3 and, if possible, ...P—K4.

---

7 P—B3

7 P—B3. The most aggressive and modern way to meet Black's Dragon set-up. White supports his KP, protects his KN4 square, and prepares for a K-side attack. The following variation is only a sample of what can happen in this system:
7...N—B3; 8 Q—Q2, O—O; 9 B—QB4.
The main point of this move will become apparent later.
9...B—Q2; 10 P—KR4.
The start of an all-out assault against Black's king.
10...Q—R4; 11 O—O—O, KR—B1.
A typical counter-attacking idea. The immediate threat is 12...N×N; 13 Q×N, N—N5; 14 Q—Q3, N×B; 15 Q×N, R×B, winning a piece.
12 B—N3, N—K4; 13 P—R5.
Now we see why B—QB4 was so important – White intends to exchange pawns by 14 P×P, when Black must recapture with the RP, leaving the KR file open for a later attack by White's queen (after B—KR6 and B×B), and rook. So Black does not wait for 14 P×P.
13...N×RP; 14 B—R6.
Threatening 15 R×N, P×R; 16 Q—N5, N—Q6 ch (forced); 17 R×N, Q×Q; 18 B×Q, and White's two minor pieces will win against Black's rook.
14...B×B; 15 Q×B, R×N!.
Now that White's queen has been lured away from the centre, this thematic sacrifice gives Black sufficient play to maintain the balance. Play might continue:
16 P×R, R—QB1; 17 R×N!?.
Giving back the sacrificed material in

the hope of breaking through on the K side.

17...P×R; 18 K—N1.
18 Q×P(R5)??, N—Q6 ch!.
18...N—B5; 19 P—N4, Q×BP; 20 B×N, Q×B; 21 P×P, K—R1.
Black's attack is stronger than White's.

---

9 P—B4

---

9 P—B4. This move allows Black to take the initiative with **9...Q—N3** (threatening 10...N×KP; 11 N×N (K4), B×N, winning a pawn). White normally replies with **10 Q—Q3**, when play should continue:
10...N—KN5.
Not 10...Q×P?; 11 P—QR3!.

11 N—Q5, B×N!; 12 B×N.
After 12 N×Q, B×B ch; 13 K—R1, B×N; 14 B×N, B×B, Black's three pieces are of more use than White's queen, which has no way of breaking through the Dragon pawn formation.
12...B×B ch; 13 Q×B, Q×Q ch; 14 N×Q, B×B; 15 N×B.
A very drawish position.

KAN/TAIMANOV VARIATION

1 P—K4	P—QB4
2 N—KB3	P—K3
3 P—Q4	P×P
4 N×P	P—QR3
5 N—QB3	Q—B2
6 B—Q3	N—QB3
7 B—K3	N—B3
8 O—O	B—Q3
9 P—KR3	P—QN4
10 N×N	Q×N
11 B—Q4	B—N2
12 P—R3	P—K4!
13 B—K3	B—B4

---

1 P—K4	P—QB4
2 N—KB3	P—K3

Having discussed the importance of Black's Q4 square more than once, we now turn our attention to a variation in

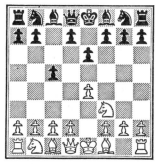

which Black's pawn structure is built around the control of that square.

The text opens the way for Black's KB to be brought into the game at Q3 or QB4 (or even QN5 in some variations). The reader should observe carefully the manoeuverings of this useful piece, as it plays an active role on more than one square.

3 P—Q4   **P×P**

4 N×P   P—QR3

Black's play so far fails to conform to all we have written concerning the importance of speedy development. The logic behind this "pawns first" strategy is that Black is building an impregnable pawn structure, waiting for White to commit his pieces before developing his own pieces at their optimum posts.

5 N—QB3

Already White is two tempi ahead in development.

(For 5 P—QB4 see p. 103)

5 . . .   Q—B2

5...P—QN4 is also sometimes seen in master games, but it seems that after 6 B—Q3, B—N2; 7 O—O, White's lead in development gives him a fine, active position.

6 B—Q3

(For 6 P—KN3 see p. 103)

6 . . .   N—QB3

A natural developing move, attacking White's QN.

7 B—K3

7 N×N, as usual in the Sicilian, serves only to strengthen Black's control of his Q4 square: 7...NP×N; 8 O—O, N—B3, and the chances are roughly equal.

(For 7 N—N3 see p. 104)

7 . . .   N—B3

In this type of variation (i.e., with ...P—K3), Black sometimes plays to relieve the tension by ...N×N, followed by ...N—K2 and ...N—B3. Such tactics, however, have the disadvantage that Black's K side is left unprotected; e.g., 7...N×N; 8 B×N, N—K2; 9 O—O, N—B3; 10 B—K3, P—QN4; 11 P—B4, B—N2; 12 Q—R5. White has the initiative and attacking chances on the K side.

(For 7...P—QN4 see p. 105)

8 O—O

After 8 Q—K2, B—Q3, Black's active bishop guarantees him equal chances. White should continue with 9 P—KN3 (to prevent the exchanging manoeuvre 9...B—B5 and 10...B×B), 9...B—K4! (putting the bishop on its most versatile square); 10 N—N3, B×N ch; 11 P×B, P—Q4; 12 P×P, N×P; 13 B—Q2, when the chances are roughly equal.

The text is a more natural move, offering White greater chances of retaining some advantage.

8 . . .   B—Q3

Threatening the KRP and controlling the useful squares K4 and KB5. White's first task is to save his attacked pawn.

(For 8...N—K4 see p. 105)

9 P—KR3

9 P—B4? loses a pawn to 9...N×N; 10 B×N, B×P; while 9 K—R1 is satisfactorily met by 9...B—B5; 10 B×B, Q×B; 11 QN—K2, Q—B2, with equal chances. N.B. not 9...B×P?; 10 P—KN3, B×P; 11 P×B, Q×P; 12 Q—B3, when White's extra piece is worth more than Black's three pawns.

9 . . .   P—QN4

The most active move, preparing to develop his QB at QN2, thereby increasing the pressure on White's KP.

10 N×N

Since Black is intending to put his bishop on the long diagonal (QR1—KR8), White decides to save a tempo by exchanging on QB6, rather than allowing Black to exchange knights himself. When Black recaptures the knight, his queen gets in the way of his own bishop. In order to increase the scope of his bishop he must later move his queen away, losing a tempo.

10 . . .   Q×N
11 B—Q4

Putting the bishop on a more aggressive square and threatening 12 P—K5 followed by 13 B—K4.

11 . . .   B—N2

Preventing 12 P—K5 for obvious reasons.

12 P—R3

Often a useful precaution in positions in which Black has a pawn at QN4. It is now no longer possible for Black to play ...P—N5, driving the knight away and winning the KP.

12 ...   P—K4!

At first sight a surprising move, for it weakens Black's Q4 square and his KB4. But in fact there is no way that White can take advantage of these weaknesses, since he has no knight on Q4 to go to KB5, and Black's knight guards his Q4 square in case White has any ideas of playing N—Q5. The text also rules out for good the possibility of P—K5 by White.

13 B—K3   B—B4

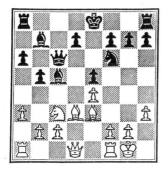

In order to exchange a pair of bishops. After 14 Q—B3, B×B; 15 Q×B, O—O; 16 QR—Q1, P—Q3, the chances are about equal.

---

5 P—QB4

5 P—QB4. Establishing the "Maroczy Bind" mentioned in the section on the Dragon Variation. White's pawns at QB4 and K4 serve to prevent Black's thematic, freeing break ...P—Q4. In addition, White's QBP hinders another of Black's thematic ideas, namely ...P—QN4. If Black develops quietly, White will build up a dominating position. By active play, however, Black can assure himself of a level game:

5...N—KB3.
Attacking White's KP.
6 N—QB3.
6 B—Q3 is met by 6...N—B3, when White may either exchange knights, strengthening Black's Q4 square, or retreat with 7 N—B2, when 7...P—Q4; 8 KP×P, P×P, gives Black an easy game.
6...B—N5.
Renewing the threat to White's KP.
7 B—Q2, O—O.
Not 7...B×N; 8 B×B, N×P?, because of 9 Q—N4!, N×B; 10 Q×NP, R—B1; 11 P×N, Q—R4; 12 N—N3!, Q—KB4; 13 Q—N3, N—B3; 14 P—B4 (preventing 14...N—K4); 14...P—N3; 15 B—Q3, Q—KR4; 16 O—O. White has the advantage because of the permanent insecurity of Black's king either in the centre or on the Q side.
8 B—Q3.
Or 8 P—K5, B×N; 9 B×B, N—K5.
8...N—B3; 9 N×N.
9 N—B2 could be met by 9...P—Q4.
9...QP×N; 10 Q—B2, P—K4.
An equal position.

---

6 P—KN3

6 P—KN3. This move has been popular

in recent years but it appears that with accurate play Black can hold his own. The idea of the fianchetto (rarely seen on the White side of the Sicilian), is to put pressure on the diagonals leading to Black's Q side, not only from the bishop at KN2, but also from the QB at KB4 or K3.

6...N—KB3; 7 B—N2, N—B3; 8 O—O, N×N; 9 Q×N, B—B4; 10 B—B4!.

A good try. If 10...B×Q; 11 B×Q, B×N; 12 P×B, P—Q4; 13 P×P, N×P; 14 B—K5, White has the better ending because of his two bishops.

10...P—Q3; 11 Q—Q3, N—Q2; 12 N—R4, P—K4.

The chances are even. After 13 B—Q2, P—QN4; 14 N×B, N×N; 15 Q—R3, B—N2, Black's active piece placement fully compensates for the weakness of his backward QP.

---

7 N—N3

7 N—N3. White wishes to avoid the exchange of knights in the centre, preferring to use them to attack on the K side. This active plan leads to sharp middle games – but Black should hold his own unless he defends carelessly:

7...N—B3; 8 O—O, P—QN4; 9 B—K3, B—K2.

Not 9...B—N2; 10 N—N5.

10 P—B4.

Threatening 11 P—K5.

10...P—Q3.

From this position the game ANDERSSON-STEIN, Reykjavik 1972, continued:

11 P—QR4.

Tempting the advance of Black's Q-side pawns still further, in the hope of block-ing the position on that side of the board and depriving Black of counter-play.

11...P—N5; 12 N—N1, P—QR4; 13 N(N1)—Q2, O—O; 14 Q—K2, P—K4; 15 P—B5, P—Q4; 16 P—N4.

Commenting on these moves in the *British Chess Magazine*, Keene made the apt remark: "All this looks out of phase. Normally the wing-thrust (P—KN4), precedes the central breakthrough (...P—Q4), in such typical situations from the Sicilian Defence. The fact that P—N4 comes only as a reaction to ...P—Q4 strongly suggests that everything is in order with Black's game."

16...P×P?!.

But now Black starts to go wrong, for White's knight gets to the strong square K4, with gain of tempo. Better is 16...B—N2.

17 N×KP, N—Q4; 18 P—B6!.

A fine pawn sacrifice which gives White's attack real force.

18...P×P.

Black cannot avoid the break-up of the K-side pawns – after 18...N×P there would follow 19 N×N ch, B×N; 20 R×B!, P×R; 21 B—R6, and 22 Q—K4.

19 B—KR6, R—Q1; 20 R—B3, N—B5?.

A losing blunder – Black should still survive after 20...K—R1!; e.g., 21 QR—KB1, B×P; 22 R—N3, B×Q; 23 B—N7 ch only draws by perpetual check.

21 R×N!, R×R.

If 21...P×R, then 22 N×P ch, B×N; 23 Q—K4, threatening mate on KR7, and Black can only stop this by giving up two pieces: 23...B—Q5 ch; 24 N×B, P—B4; 25 Q×N.

22 P×R, B—K3.

22...P×R; 23 N×P ch, B×N; 24 Q—K8 mate; or 23...K—R1; 24 Q—K4, with mate to follow.

23 N×P ch, B×N; 24 R×B, B×N.

White is now the exchange ahead and still has a crushing position.

25 R—QB1, B—Q4; 26 Q—KB2, R—K1; 27 R—QB5.

One last tactical point – not 27 R(B6)×N?, B×R; 28 Q—B6, because of 28...Q—N3 ch; 29 K—B1??, B—N7 ch, winning White's queen.

27...B—K3; 28 Q—R4, K—R1; 29 R—B2, and Black resigned, having no defence to 30 Q—B6 ch.

7...P—QN4

7...P—QN4. This move nearly always forms an important part of Black's plans, but here it is somewhat premature: **8 N×N** (this is quite successful now that Black cannot capture with the NP), **8...Q×N; 9 O—O, B—N2; 10 P—QR3** (preventing 10...P—N5); **10... N—B3; 11 Q—K2, B—K2; 12 P—B4, O—O; 13 P—K5, N—K1; 14 P—B5!, P×P; 15 B×BP**, and White has excellent attacking chances against Black's castled king.

The lesson to be learned from this variation is that Black should attend to the development of both knights (in order to exert more influence on the centre), before resorting to his thematic expansion on the Q side.

8...N—K4

8...N—K4. The idea of this move is to occupy QB5 with the knight, and force

White to exchange his KB for this knight. Also, 9...N(K4)—N5 comes into consideration and so:

9 P—KR3, P—QN4; 10 P—B4, N—B5.

10...N×B; 11 P×N gains Black the advantage of the two bishops, but at the cost of strengthening White's pawn centre and giving White play with his QR along the QB file.

11 B×N, Q×B; 12 Q—Q3, P—Q4.

The exchange of queens, 12...Q×Q, gives White a substantial endgame advantage because of his strong centre and his potential initiative on the QB file.

13 P—K5, N—Q2; 14 Q×Q, QP×Q.

14...NP×Q; 15 P—B5!.

15 P—B5, N×P; 16 P×P, B×P; 17 QR—K1.

White has an active position and Black lags behind in his development. A game between Fischer and Petrosian continued:

17...N—Q2; 18 N×B, P×N; 19 B—Q4, O—O—O; 20 R×P, N—B4; 21 R—B6 ch, K—N2; 22 R×N, R×B; 23 R(B5)—B5.

White has retained his initiative.

8

FRENCH DEFENCE

1 P—K4, P—K3; 2 P—Q4, P—Q4

This is a very old and very solid defence to 1 P—K4. With the move
1...P—K3 Black announces his willingness to accept an inferior
position in the centre in exchange for the relative safety from direct
attack which his chain of pawns provides. In addition he has the distant
prospect of a superior pawn formation in the ending. In contrast with
the Sicilian Defence, which generally produces a dynamic game, games
arising out of the French often resemble siege warfare. After a few
moves the centre usually becomes closed and two conflicting pawn
chains arise (White pawns at Q4 and K5; Black pawns at Q4 and K3).

The fight then shifts to the two bishops' files, with each player trying
to undermine and outflank the position of the other. As we shall see
when we consider the Advance Variation, White can play the thematic
advance, P—K5, as early as move three; but if he plays this move so
soon he surrenders the initiative. Most players of the White pieces
prefer to wait until Black has played ...N—KB3, so that P—K5 comes
with the threat of P × N, thereby gaining a tempo.

Any changes which come about in this blocked, central pawn
structure, are due to Black's undermining attempts ...P—QB4 and/or
...P—KB3. The flanking blow ...P—QB4 is most effective when
White has a knight at QB3, so that he is unable to support his pawn
centre by P—QB3. The move ...P—KB3 by Black is usually a less
successful try, because White can allow Black to play ...P × KP and
then recapture with his KN (from KB3) or, if possible, with his KBP,
which often advances to KB4 in support of the KP.

Before examining some variations in detail, we should say a few
words about the "French bishop." The bishop referred to is Black's
QB, which often suffers in this opening from being shut in behind the
pawn at K3. The problem of how best to activate (or exchange) this
piece is never far from the mind of the French Defence player. Although
in general, a bishop is slightly more powerful than a knight, a bad,
passive bishop blocked by its own pawns, is worth far less than a good,
actively posted knight.

CLASSICAL VARIATION

1 P—K4	P—K3
2 P—Q4	P—Q4
3 N—QB3	N—KB3
4 B—KN5	B—K2
5 P—K5	KN—Q2
6 B×B	Q×B
7 P—B4	O—O
8 N—B3	P—QB4
9 B—Q3	P—KB4
10 P×P e.p.	R×P
11 Q—Q2	N—B3
12 P×P	N×P
13 O—O	N×B
14 P×N	

1 P—K4	P—K3
2 P—Q4	

This is obviously the most aggressive and natural reply to 1...P—K3. With this move White strengthens his position in the centre and creates more space for his pieces and more open lines for his development.

2 ...   **P—Q4**

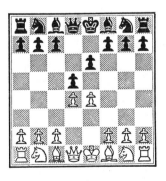

Black wishes to build a "strong point" at his Q4 and to fix White's central pawns. A free, mobile centre is a much more powerful instrument of attack than one which is blocked.

3 N—QB3

Defending the KP with a developing move. This is White's most natural third move, although both 3 N—Q2 and 3 P—K5 are frequently played. These moves are considered in separate variations. Note that 3 P×P is not to be recommended, for after 3...P×P, Black's QB is restored to full freedom of activity.

3 ...   **N—KB3**

Black also develops a piece and continues to apply pressure to the White KP. An important alternative is 3...B—N5 (the Winawer Variation) which we consider later.

(For 3...P×P see p. 109)

4 B—KN5

Another natural move which develops a piece and pins the Black knight, thus relieving the attack on the KP. Now White threatens 5 P—K5.

(For 4 P—K5 see p. 109)

4 ...   **B—K2**

The best way to unpin the Black KN.

(For 4...B—N5 see p. 110)

5 P—K5

There is no good way to maintain the KP on K4; e.g., after 5 B—Q3 Black could play 5...N×P; 6 N×N, P×N; 7 B×P, when he has exchanged a pair of knights, thereby freeing his game. As a general rule the side which has a cramped position should strive to swap off pieces, leaving more room for his remaining forces to manoeuvre.

After the text, White's pawns are fixed, and thus become easier objects to attack. In compensation, however, White does enjoy superiority in space.

5 ...   **KN—Q2**

The attacked knight retreats and chooses a square where it can both support the advance ...P—QB4, and also cover the White KP should this pawn become weak later in the game.

6 B×B

Does this exchange favour White or Black? The reader might suppose from our previous comments that the exchange of pieces will only help liberate Black's position. In contrast, we have also stressed that the usefulness of a bishop is seriously reduced by the presence of a chain of pawns fixed on squares of the same colour as the bishop – so here White is getting rid of his "bad" bishop for Black's "good" one. In any case, retreating the bishop involves loss of tempo which Black could use to play ...P—QB4.

(For 6 P—KR4 see p. 110)

6 ...   Q×B
7 P—B4

White's most energetic continuation. In positions where the centre is blocked, speed of development is less important than correct placement of pawns and pieces; so White can afford to delay activating his KN until he has first advanced his KBP. The pawn on KB4 adds to White's control of K5 and this is very important as we shall see later.

7 ...   O—O

Black hastens his king to safety, which move also brings a rook to the useful KB file. Black will soon advance his own KBP in order to counteract White's growing pressure.

8 N—B3

A natural developing move. KB3 is the best square on which to put the knight, since from there it guards the key points Q4 and K5.

8 ...   P—QB4

Black strikes back in the centre and attacks one of the base pawns in White's chain.

9 B—Q3

Developing the bishop and introducing a terrible threat – the sacrifice of the bishop on KR7. Although the study of tactical motifs belongs more to a book on middle game play than to one on opening strategy, the reader would be well advised to acquaint himself with this combination, since it occurs frequently in actual play. The main idea is 10 B×P ch, K×B; 11 N—KN5 ch, K—N1; 12 Q—R5, and Black cannot avoid mate; e.g., 12...R—Q1 (vacating KB1 for the king); 13 Q—R7 ch, K—B1; 14 Q—R8 mate. Black cannot escape his fate by bringing his king out into the open: 11...K—N3; 12 Q—Q3 ch, P—KB4 (if 12...K—R3 or ...K—R4, then 13 Q—R3 ch, K—N3; 14 Q—R7 mate); 13 Q—R3, and Black must give up several pieces to stop 14 Q—R7 mate.

9 ...   P—KB4

White's last move forces an immediate reaction on the K side. With this move Black threatens to block the pawn position still further, thus making progress more difficult for White.

10 P×P e.p.

White, with his superior development, wishes to open up the game. After the text, Black's KP, which can now be attacked from the front, will eventually become weak.

10 ...   R×P

(For 10...Q×P see p. 111)

11 Q—Q2

White must protect his attacked KBP. The text is better than 11 P—KN3, since it enables White to bring his QR into play more easily.

11 ...   N—B3

Attending to his backward development. Opening up the game still further by an immediate 11...P×P would not be to Black's advantage, but after the text move he does threaten 12...P×P.

12 P×P   N×P

The move 12...Q×P prevents White from playing 13 O—O, but 12...N×P is to be preferred because it not only threatens to exchange off White's active KB but clears the square Q2 for Black's QB, thus speeding up his Q-side development.

13 O—O   N×B
14 P×N

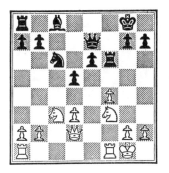

The removal of White's KB has lessened the chances of a successful direct attack on Black's king. Put positionally, Black's game is far from happy. His KP is "backward", (see p. 25). This, coupled with the fact that Black's QB is still inactive (a typical "French bishop" in fact), gives White the advantage.

3...P×P

3...P×P. This move introduces **Rubinstein's Variation**, which is not highly regarded by theorists because it seems to give White too free a hand in the centre. For instance, after 4 N×P, N—KB3 (usually a good developing move, but here not the most accurate); 5 N×N ch, Black is faced with the difficult choice of whether to recapture with the KNP, weakening his K side, or with the queen, which will cost him tempi, since the queen can then be attacked with developing moves (e.g., 6 N—KB3 followed by 7 B—KN5). A better plan for Black (after 4 N×P) is to play **4...N—Q2;**

but White should still be able to keep the upper hand.

One interesting idea that sometimes occurs in this line is the fianchetto of Black's QB. In the game TARRASCH–MIESES, Match 1916, play went:
4...N—Q2; 5 N—KB3, KN—B3; 6 N×N ch, N×N; 7 B—Q3, P—QN3!?; 8 Q—K2.
Aiming to control the weakened light squares on the Q side, and freeing Q1 for a rook. White's subsequent plan is designed to make it difficult for Black to play the freeing move ...P—QB4, which liquidates the centre. The attempt to win a pawn by 8 N—K5?! does not work, since after 8...B—N2; 9 B—N5 ch, P—B3; 10 B×P ch, B×B; 11 N×B, Black has 11...Q—Q4, hitting both N and KNP.
8...B—N2; 9 B—KN5, B—K2; 10 O—O, O—O; 11 QR—Q1.
White still has the better game. The move 11...P—QB4? would be a blunder, losing to 12 P×P, for Black cannot recapture because of 13 B×P ch, discovering an attack on the queen.

---

4 P—K5

4 P—K5. This move was much favoured by the first world champion Steinitz. After 4...KN—Q2, one idea for White is to play 5 QN—K2 in order to be able to support his QP with P—QB3. This leads to positions similar to those encountered in the Advance Variation (p. 119), but Black should find it easier to equalize here than in the main line of the Advance. After all, the move 5 QN—K2 does represent a vast loss of time – not only is the same piece moved twice, but also on K2 the knight shuts in the KB. The reader is recommended to read the section on the Advance Variation and then compare it with the following continuation: **5 QN—K2, P—QB4; 6 P—QB3, N—QB3; 7 P—KB4, P—KB3; 8 N—B3, Q—N3,** and now Black has equalised.

4...B—N5

4...B—N5. The MacCutcheon Variation. Black revives his attack on the KP by pinning the White QN, but the move 4...B—N5 suffers from the defect that it leaves Black's KNP undefended. White can usually profit from this by forcing Black to compromise his K-side position. White's strongest reply is the obvious **5 P—K5,** and now the only way for Black to save his pinned, attacked knight is by **5...P—KR3.** Now 6 P × N, P × B; 7 P × P, R—N1 is probably satisfactory for Black. Better is **6 B—Q2,** when White should keep an edge. Play might continue:

6...B × N.

6...N—Q2 is very passive, so Black exchanges pieces in order to advance his knight to the more active square K5. Note that the immediate 6...N—K5?? loses a piece after 7 N × N.

7 P × B, N—K5; 8 Q—N4.

Now Black's KNP is attacked. He cannot defend it by 8...O—O, because of the reply 9 B × P, so he must play either 8...P—N3, weakening his K-side pawn formation, or 8...K—B1, after which his K and KR are awkwardly placed.

6 P—KR4

6 P—KR4. This interesting gambit idea is called the **Alekhine/Chatard Attack.** Accepting the offered pawn with 6...B × B; 7 P × B, Q × P is dangerous, for White gets a raging attack along the open KR file and an extra tempo by attacking the Black queen with a developing move. If Black's defence is even slightly inaccurate he often gets smashed from the board in short order.

As a sample of White's attacking power, consider the following miniature game, KERES–WADE, USSR *v* England 1954:

6...B × B; 7 P × B, Q × P; 8 N—R3.
Better in this position than N—B3, because the knight can go immediately to KB4, where it is very actively placed.

8...Q—K2; 9 N—B4, P—QR3.
To stop White pieces invading via QN5.

10 Q—N4, K—B1.
Better is 10...P—KN3.

11 Q—B3!.
Threatening 12 N—N6 ch.

11...K—N1; 12 B—Q3, P—QB4.
Better is 12...P—R3, to stop White's next move.

13 B × P ch, R × B; 14 R × R, K × R; 15 O—O—O.
Bringing his other rook into play.

15...P—B4.
Hoping in vain to use KB2 as an escape square for his king.

16 R—R1 ch, K—N1; 17 R—R8 ch.
Black resigns in view of 17...K—B2; 18 Q—R5 ch, P—N3; 19 Q—R7 mate; or 17...K × R; 18 N—N6 ch, followed by 19 N × Q and 20 N × B, winning vast amounts of material.

The soundest reply to 6 P—KR4 is probably the immediate counter-thrust

6...P—QB4, when White's best plan is to embark on a very sharp line of play which forces a draw (so don't play 6...P—QB4 as Black, if you have to win at all costs).

The drawing line runs:

7 N—N5.

Threatening 8 N—Q6 ch.

7...P--B3!; 8 B—Q3, P—QR3!.

Attacking a second piece – after 8...P×B the reply 9 Q—R5 ch favours White.

9 Q—R5 ch, K—B1.

Not 9...P—N3?; 10 B×P ch.

10 R—R3, P×N; 11 B—R6, Q—R4 ch.

11...P×B; 12 Q×P ch, K—K1; 13 Q—R5 ch is a draw by perpetual check.

12 B—Q2, Q—B2; 13 R—N3.

After 13 B—R6??, P×B Black wins because his king can now hide on Q1.

13...P×QP; 14 N—B3, N×P.

Black has nothing better in view of White's numerous threats.

15 R×P!, P—R3.

Not 15...K×R, because of 16 B—R6 ch, K—N1; 17 Q—K8 mate; nor 15...N×N ch, when White will reply 16 K—Q1, after which Black has no more checks and will soon be mated. The text move sets the cunning trap 16 B×RP?, R×B; 17 Q×R, B—N5 ch, followed by 18...Q×R.

16 B—R7, K×R; 17 Q×P ch, K—B2; 18 Q—R5 ch, K—N2.

A draw by perpetual check. ROSETTO-STAHLBERG, Vina del Mar 1947.

10...Q×P

10...Q×P. This is a good alternative to the move in the text, but White should have an advantage after **11 N—KN5**, e.g., **11...Q×BP; 12 B×P ch, K—R1; 13 Q—Q2** (13 Q—R5, Q—B7 ch; 14 K—Q1, N—KB3 is good for Black), **13...Q×QP; 14 Q×Q, P×Q; 15 N—N5, N—R3** (stopping 16 N—B7); **16 N×QP, N—B3; 17 B—Q3,** and White stands much better in the ending. RAVINSKY–ORLOV, Moscow 1964.

WINAWER VARIATION

1 P—K4	P—K3
2 P—Q4	P—Q4
3 N—QB3	B—N5
4 P—K5	P—QB4
5 P—QR3	B×N ch
6 P×B	N—K2
7 Q—N4	P×P
8 Q×NP	R—N1
9 Q×RP	Q—B2
10 K—Q1	QN—B3
11 N—B3	P×P
12 N—N5	N×P

13 P—B4	R×N
14 P×R	N(K4)—N3

1 P—K4	P—K3
2 P—Q4	P—Q4
3 N—QB3	B—N5

This move inaugurates the Winawer Variation, which is currently Black's most popular system in the French Defence complex. Black's strategy is to launch a vigorous attack on the queen's wing; White's play will be mostly on the

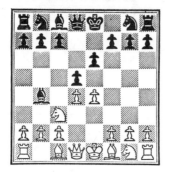

K side, where he may attempt to profit from the absence of Black's KB by attacking Black's unguarded KNP. The play can become much more complicated than in most other variations of the French Defence – both kings often get stuck in the centre of the board.

The text, by pinning White's QN, renews the attack on White's KP.

4 P—K5

(For 4 P—QR3 see p. 113)

4 ...   **P—QB4**

White advances in the centre, and Black reacts promptly by attacking the base of the newly-formed pawn chain.

(For 4...N—K2 see p. 113)

5 P—QR3

The pin has become very annoying and White decides he must end it, even at the cost of playing a non-developing move.

Another way of breaking the pin is 5 B—Q2, but this modest move should cause Black no problems. After 5 B—Q2, Black's best is 5...N—K2, rapidly developing his K side. The reply 5...P × P is bad because of 6 N—N5, when the Black bishop has no good retreat square (6...B—K2 blocks the KN, while 6...B—B4 is met by 7 P—QN4); and, if Black exchanges bishops, his Q3 square becomes weak.

(For 5 Q—N4 see p. 113)

5 ...   **B × N ch**

Black cannot maintain the pin with 5...B—R4, because of 6 P—QN4!; e.g., 6...P × NP; 7 N—N5, P × P dis ch;

8 P—QB3, B—B2 (preventing 9 N—Q6 ch); 9 B × P, and White is well ahead in development and has a strong attack for the sacrificed pawn.

6 P × B   **N—K2**

Black develops his K side before the White queen arrives, making life difficult.

(For 6...Q—B2 see p. 114)

7 Q—N4

This is White's sharpest continuation. 7 N—B3 would allow Black to develop normally and consolidate his position, after which the weaknesses in White's Q-side pawn structure should ensure Black of adequate counter-play.

(For 7 P—QR4 see p. 114)

7 ...   **P × P**

After 7...O—O, simple developing moves would give White a strong attack; e.g., 8 N—B3, QN—B3; 9 B—Q3 (threatening the sacrifice on KR7), 9...P—B4; 10 P × P e.p., R × P; 11 B—KN5.

The text move fits in more logically with Black's plan of immediate counter-attack.

8 Q × NP   **R—N1**
9 Q × RP

Now White has completed the demolition of Black's K wing, but the position on the other side of the board is far from clear since White is now behind in development.

9 ...   **Q—B2**

Black now has the powerful threats of...Q × BP ch and...Q × KP ch.

(For 9...Q—R4 see p. 115)

10 K—Q1

An interesting defensive resource. Now both 10...Q × KP; 11 N—KB3, and 10...Q × BP; 11 R—N1 are bad, because they aid White's development.

(For 10 N—K2 see p. 115)

10 ...   **QN—B3**

Bringing another piece into action with further threats against White's KP.

11 N—B3

White rushes another piece into the attack, planning 12 N—N5, with threats against KB7.

| 11 . . . | P×P |

Regaining the sacrificed pawn.

| 12 N—N5 | N×P |
| 13 P—B4 | |

Driving away the defending knight. Black's next move is virtually forced.

| 13 . . . | R×N |
| 14 P×R | N(K4)—N3 |

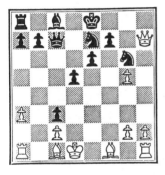

Shutting in White's queen and preventing 15 Q—R8 ch. We have been following analysis by Keres and have reached a very interesting position. Black has considerable compensation for the sacrificed exchange. He has an extra pawn and an impressive, mobile central pawn mass. Both kings are somewhat exposed, but White's more so than Black's (Black is threatening to bring his king to relative safety by playing . . .B—Q2, followed by . . .O—O). In addition, White's queen is out of play. All in all Black has the better prospects.

4 P—QR3

4 P—QR3. This is sometimes seen as an alternative to 4 P—K5, but it is probably not good enough to yield White any advantage. After **4. . .B×N ch; 5 P×B,**

P×P; 6 Q—N4, Black can develop his KN to a more active square than in the main line: **6. . .N—KB3; 7 Q×NP, R—N1; 8 Q—R6,** and then lash out at White's centre with **8. . .P—B4.** White also has some difficulty in completing his development.

4. . .N—K2

4. . .N—K2. This move usually transposes back into the main line after **5 P—QR3, B×N ch; 6 P×B, P—QB4.** If White tries to vary with 5 Q—N4, Black can play 5. . .N—B4, and if White continues 6 B—Q3 (threatening 7 B×N, followed by 8 Q×NP) Black can reply 6. . .P—KR4 (6. . .Q—R5??; 7 B×N loses a piece); 7 Q—B4, Q—R5, with easy equality since the exchange of queens is forced.

5 Q—N4

5 Q—N4. This is less accurate than 5 P—QR3, although after 5 Q—N4, N—K2, White can still play 6 P—QR3, transposing. Other sixth moves are not

so good; e.g., 6 Q×NP? loses to 6...R—N1; 7 Q×RP, P×P; 8 P—QR3, Q—R4!, while, after 6 P×P, Black can play 6...B×N ch; 7 P×B, N—Q2, and White's many weak pawns give Black plenty of chances.

he can start building up an attacking formation on the K side with N—N5 (to force the weakening ...P—KR3), followed by N—R3—B4 and B—R3.

Another try for Black is 8...QN—B3; e.g., 9 Q—Q2 (covering the K1—QR5 diagonal in preparation for moving B—R3); 9...P—B3 (attacking the centre immediately makes it hard for White to keep an advantage); 10 KP×P, NP×P; 11 B—K2, P—B5 (closing the Q side, since Black plans to shift his pieces to the KN file and play ...O—O—O); 12 Q—R6, N—N3; 13 N—R4, R—KN1; 14 B—R5, Q—N2, with equal chances (SMYSLOV–BONDAREVSKY, Parnu 1947).

The next note deals with similar continuations.

6...Q—B2

6...Q—B2. This is a common alternative to the text move. After 7 Q—N4, N—K2 (7...P—KB4 and 7...P—KB3 are also possible); 8 Q×NP, R—N1; 9 Q×RP, P×P, we are back in the main line. Another quieter line for White which holds more promise is **7 N—KB3, N—K2; 8 P—QR4.**

This move holds back the Black Q-side pawns, which might otherwise advance with uncomfortable rapidity. It also frees the square QR3 for later occupation by a Bishop.

Black's best defensive plan is not precisely clear. If **8...P—QN3** (intending ...B—R3 activating or exchanging Black's QB), an important continuation is **9 B—N5 ch, B—Q2; 10 O—O, B×B; 11 P×B** (STEIN–R. BYRNE, Sousse 1967). White is now getting much the better game, for his QNP is preventing Black's knights from reaching active posts and

7 P—QR4

7 P—QR4. The motivation behind this move has already been discussed in the previous note so we shall confine ourselves here to giving other plausible continuations.

(1) **7...QN—B3; 8 N—B3, B—Q2; 9 B—K2, Q—B2; 10 O—O, P—B3.** Attacking White's centre in this way gives Black an equal game. If **11 KP×P,** Black will recapture 11...NP×P and then continue with ...O—O—O, when he has a good game. White can also try **11 R—K1** (seeking to maintain a pawn on K5), but, after 11...P×KP; 12 P×KP, O—O, the game is level. Note that 12...N×P??; 13 N×N, Q×N; 14 B—R5 ch, loses the queen.

(2) **7...Q—R4; 8 B—Q2, QN—B3; 9 N—B3, B—Q2; 10 B—K2, P—B5.** Closing the QB file in this way, leaves Black with very little counter-play.

Black's strategy in this variation is based almost entirely on his Q-side play. **11 O—O, P—B3; 12 P×P, P×P; 13 N—R4** (preventing 13...N—B4, and threatening 14 B—R5 ch). White is left with a slight advantage.

9...Q—R4

9...Q—R4. This leads to variations similar to the main line, but the positions reached are more favourable to White. One example is:

10 R—N1, Q×BP ch; 11 B—Q2, Q—B2.

11...Q×RP gives White the chance to play 12 B—N4, attacking the queen while also threatening 13 B×N, followed by 14 Q×R.

12 P—KB4.

Protecting the KP.

12...QN—B3; 13 N—B3, B—Q2; 14 N—N5.

Attacking KB7, which cannot be easily defended; e.g., 14...N—Q1; 15 B—N4, when Black is in bad shape.

14...R×N; 15 P×R, Q×P ch; 16 K—Q1.

White has much the better game.

10 N—K2

10 N—K2. An interesting alternative, but probably no better than the text. White's KB is now shut in and he can no longer execute the attacking manoeuvre N—N5. The reply 10...Q×KP will only help White to develop faster (11 B—B4), but if Black simply brings out his pieces with **10...QN—B3; 11 P—KB4, B—Q2,** he should keep the game balanced. White is too under-developed to be able to retain his extra material.

TARRASCH VARIATION

1 P—K4	P—K3	9 N—N3	B—Q3
2 P—Q4	P—Q4	10 QN—Q4	O—O
3 N—Q2		11 B—K3	B—KN5
3 ...	P—QB4		
4 KP×P	KP×P		
5 KN—B3	N—QB3		
6 B—N5	B—Q3	1 P—K4	P—K3
7 O—O	N—K2	2 P—Q4	P—Q4
8 P×P	B×P	3 N—Q2	

At first sight this move looks strange, for Q2 is certainly a less active post for a knight than QB3 and, furthermore, the knight on Q2 blocks lines of action for both White's QB and his queen. On the other hand, 3 N—Q2 avoids the Winawer (3...B—BN5? would be answered by 4 P—QB3) and, in some lines, allows White to support his QP by playing P—QB3, as in the Advance Variation.

3 ...   P—QB4

This move and 3...N—KB3 are seen with about equal frequency in tournament play (3...N—QB3 is also quite common). 3...N—KB3 invites White to play 4 P—K5, and set up the usual French Defence pawn chain, which Black will then proceed to attack. The text move prevents the advance P—K5 by applying immediate pressure to White's QP; so White must try to secure an advantage in other ways.

(For 3...N—KB3 see p. 117)

4 KP×P

White decides on an immediate exchange in the centre, hoping to land Black with an isolated pawn. (The owner of an isolated pawn faces two disadvantages. First, his pawn can no longer be protected by another pawn, so that when it is attacked he must use pieces to defend it. Secondly, the square in front of an isolated pawn sometimes becomes very weak and may serve as a useful outpost for his opponent's pieces, for a piece placed directly in front of an isolated pawn cannot be dislodged by a pawn advance, because the pawns on adjacent files are no longer on the board).

4 ...   KP×P

Black accepts the possibility that his QP will, in the future, become isolated and expects to obtain compensation for this weakness through active development and piece play. In particular, the development of Black's QB is no longer a serious problem.

(For 4...Q×P see p. 117)

5 KN—B3

Isolating Black's QP immediately with 5 P×P would be wrong, since Black would reply with a developing move (5...B×P), and gain a tempo. White should delay the move P×P until after Black has already moved his KB, if he can. In the meantime, rapid development of his K side is White's most sensible policy.

(For 5 B—N5 ch see p. 118)

5 ...   N—QB3

Black also wishes to get his pieces quickly into action. This move is more precise than 5...N—KB3, since if White puts his KB on QN5, the Black KN might be better placed on K2.

6 B—N5

A good developing move which pins the Black QN, taking the pressure off the P at Q4.

6 ...   B—Q3

Black has no time to break the pin by (say) 6...P—QR3, because after the forced reply 7 B×N ch (not 7 B—R4??, P—QN4; 8 B—N3, P—B5, when White loses a piece), White will play 8 O—O, followed by 9 R—K1, and the new pin on the K file will be much more troublesome than the old one. For similar reasons both 6...N—KB3 and 6...B—K2 are inferior; e.g., after 6...N—KB3 there would follow 7 O—O (threatening 8 R—K1 ch), 7...B—K2; 8 P×P, and then Black cannot recapture 8...B×P, because of 9 R—K1 ch, B—K2; 10 Q—K2, and Black cannot castle without losing a piece.

7 O—O

Completing the development of the K side, and threatening 8 R—K1 ch.

7 . . .   N—K2

Virtually forced. Any other continuation leaves Black at a considerable disadvantage.

8 P×P

At last White returns to the basic positional theme of isolating Black's QP.

8 . . .   B×BP
9 N—N3

This knight is, of course, headed for the fine outpost Q4. Along the way it attacks Black's bishop.

9 . . .   B—Q3

The bishop is best placed on the QN1—KR7 diagonal.

(For 9. . .B—N3 see p. 118)

10 QN—Q4   O—O
11 B—K3

This bishop is logically posted here to help control the squares Q4 and QB5.

11 . . .   B—KN5

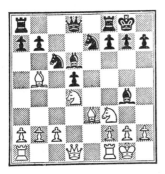

Despite his isolated QP, Black has emerged from the opening with an equal game, for his pieces are actively placed and he has no other weaknesses. PACHMANN–PORTISCH, Bled 1961, continued from this position:

12 P—KR3, B—R4; 13 Q—Q2, R—B1; 14 B—K2, B—N1.

In conjunction with Black's next move, this produces a configuration of pieces, which exerts great pressure both along the open QB file and against White's king. White must now play defensively.

15 P—QB3, Q—B2.

Threatening 16. . .N×N, followed by 17. . .B×N and 18. . .Q—R7 mate.

16 P—KN3, Q—Q2.

Attacking the KRP.

17 K—N2.

Neither side seemed to be making progress.

---

3. . .N—KB3

3. . .N—KB3. With this move Black wishes to provoke White into closing the centre. The most common continuation is: **4 P—K5, KN—Q2; 5 B—Q3, P—QB4; 6 P—QB3.** Black's best equalizing method is then to adopt a strategy similar to that employed in the Advance Variation: **6. . .N—QB3; 7 N—K2** (White develops his KN to K2 so that his QN can use the square KB3), **7. . . Q—N3; 8 N—B3, P×P; 9 P×P,** and now **9. . .P—B3!** attacks the pawn chain from the other end and gives Black full equality.

---

4. . .Q×P

4...Q×P. Avoiding being landed with an isolated QP. But the move suffers from the usual defect that arises from moving the queen early in the game – White can gain a tempo by attacking the queen with a developing move (B—B4). A frequent continuation is: **5 KN—B3, P×P; 6 B—B4, Q—Q3; 7 O—O, N—QB3; 8 N—N3, N—B3.**

Black is now too far behind in development to consider trying to hold on to his extra pawn with 8...P—K4, for not only does this move fail to activate a piece, but it also weakens Black's KB2 by exposing it to attack from the White QB; e.g., 9 N—N5, N—R3; 10 P—KB4, and White has a great advantage. **9 N(N3)×P, N×N; 10 N×N.** White's pieces are now well placed and he has the freer game.

---

5 B—N5 ch

5 B—N5 ch. This will transpose back into the main line after **5...N—QB3; 6 KN—B3.** If White plays 6 Q—K2 ch (hoping for the ending after 6...Q—K2; 7 P×P, Q×Q ch; 8 N×Q, B×P; 9 N—QN3, B—N3, in which White has some advantage, since Black's QP is the only weakness on the board), Black should probably continue 6...B—K2; e.g., 7 P×P, N—KB3; 8 N—N3, O—O; 9 N—B3, R—K1; 10 B—K3, N—K5; 11 O—O, N×QBP, and Black will regain his pawn with good play.

Another common reply to 5 B—N5 ch is **5...B—Q2.** In the ending which arises after 6 Q—K2 ch, Q—K2; 7 B×B ch (Black was threatening...B×B himself, so this exchange is more or less forced), 7...N×B; 8 P×P, N×P; 9 N—N3, Q×Q ch; 10 N×Q, N×N; 11 RP×N, B—B4, White's advantage is minimal.

9...B—N3

9...B—N3. This is the other possible retreat for Black's bishop. White's best reply is probably Botvinnik's suggestion **10 B—K3,** with the positional idea that White's control of the squares Q4 and QB5 will be enhanced after the dark-squared bishops are exchanged; but after **10...B×B; 11 B×N ch, P×B** (11...N×B; 12 R—K1 is doubtful for Black); **12 P×B, B—N5,** Black has equalized here as well.

ADVANCE VARIATION

1 P—K4	P—K3
2 P—Q4	P—Q4
3 P—K5	
3 . . .	P—QB4
4 P—QB3	N—QB3
5 N—KB3	Q—N3
6 B—K2	P×P
7 P×P	KN—K2
8 N—R3	N—B4
9 N—B2	B—N5 ch
10 K—B1	B—K2
11 P—KN3	B—Q2
12 K—N2	

1 P—K4	P—K3
2 P—Q4	P—Q4
3 P—K5	

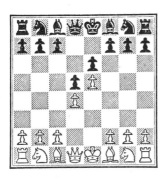

This unforced second push of the White KP gives the "advance" variation its name. Already on the third move White's general strategy is becoming clear. He has chosen to convert his temporal advantage into a spatial one which he hopes will be more enduring. While this plan is in itself logical, the loss of tempo involved hands the initiative over to Black for some considerable time: so this line, while considered sound, is not highly regarded by modern masters, who prefer a more dynamic approach to opening play.

3 . . .   P—QB4

The natural (and best) reply. Black gains space on the Q side and strikes immediately at the base of White's pawn chain.

4 P—QB3

Since Black will sooner or later try to undermine White's centre with ...P×P, White takes steps to ensure that he can meet this move with a pawn recapture, and thereby maintain his advanced chain of pawns.

(For 4 N—KB3 see p. 120)

4 . . .   N—QB3

Black's counter-strategy is to attack the White QP with all the force at his disposal. Although he does not really expect to win this pawn, he hopes to tie down most of the White pieces to its defence.

(For 4...Q—N3 see p. 121)

5 N—B3

Developing a piece and adding another guardian to the pawn at Q4.

5 . . .   Q—N3

An important exception to the rule that the queen should not move early in the game. The Black queen is immune from attack on QN3 and also beautifully placed, for not only does she add another attacker to White's QP but she also restricts the scope of the White QB, which cannot move without exposing the QNP to capture.

6 B—K2

The choice of whether to put this bishop on K2 or Q3 is one of the most important decisions White must make in this opening. Nimzowitsch, who first developed the theory of this variation, held that B—K2 "protects" the PQ4 more thoroughly than B—Q3 – by which he meant that B—K2 does not deprive the QP of the defensive services of the White queen.

(For 6 B—Q3 see p. 121)

6 . . .   P×P

This exchange is a natural part of Black's plan. If Black delays it any longer White might himself try P×P (cf. note on 6 B—Q3, B—Q2, p. 121).

7 P×P   KN—K2

Black intends to increase the pressure on White's QP by manoeuvring his KN to KB4.

8 N—R3

White replies by rushing another defender to his poor besieged pawn – this knight is heading for QB2.

(For 8 N—B3 see p. 122)

8 . . .   N—B4
9 N—B2   B—N5 ch

An interesting idea. White's pieces are overloaded by the necessity to guard Q4 and QN2, and as a result White must now move his king and therefore lose the right to castle.

10 K—B1

White can no longer defend his weak pawns after either 10 N×B, or 10 B—Q2. Thus, the king must take a walk. After the text however, White too has some threats. If permitted he will play P—QR3 and P—QN4, increasing his spatial advantage while getting rid of one of his pawn weaknesses.

10 . . .   B—K2

Removing his bishop so that he can meet 11 P—QR3 with 11...P—QR4.

11 P—KN3

White makes some space for his king so that his KR is not left out of play in the corner.

11 . . .   B—Q2

Black has still not solved the problem of how to activate his QB – always a worry in the French Defence. For the moment he puts it on Q2 so as to free the square QB1 for a rook, which will be well placed on the open file.

12 K—N2

This position has been reached several times in master practice. It is possibly a

little better for White, who has maintained his advantage in space in spite of all Black's efforts. Black, however, should not be discouraged. Apart from a mild case of cramp his position is free from weaknesses. He has forced White's pieces into somewhat defensive positions and should in the future be able to continue his thematic assault on White's pawn centre by preparing the advance ...P—KB3.

4 N—KB3

4 N—KB3. This move inaugurates a slightly different strategy from that of the main variation. Instead of setting up a full cramping pawn chain, White is satisfied with maintaining his pawn at K5 as a "strong point." After 4...P×P, White should temporarily sacrifice the pawn by playing 5 B—Q3, since 5 N×P, N—QB3; 6 N—KB3, B—B4 gives Black easy equality.

One famous game in this variation is ALEKHINE–EUWE, Nottingham 1936, which went: 5 B—Q3, N—QB3; 6 O—O,

P—KB3; **7 B—QN5!** (Paradoxical but brilliant – White wastes a tempo and gives up the two bishops, all in order to retain control of his K5 square), **7...B—Q2; 8 B×N, P×B; 9 Q×P, P×P?!; 10 Q×KP, N—B3; 11 B—B4,** and White stood better. White's central pawns have gone, but pieces have come to take their place, and these effectively blockade the Black position.

Of course, after **4 N—KB3,** Black need not play **4...P×P,** but can instead continue simply with **4...N—QB3** or **4...Q—N3,** which will usually transpose back into the main line.

4...Q—N3

4...Q—N3. In the main line Black's moves ...N—QB3 and ...Q—N3, can be played in either order, but if ...Q—N3 is played first, a new defensive possibility arises. Since the passive QB is usually Black's main problem in the French Defence, Black's first task should be to exchange this piece for White's more active KB. Black can accomplish this by delaying the move ...N—QB3, and playing instead ...Q—N3, ...B—Q2, and ...B—N4. Since the centre is closed the tempi lost by moving the QB are not of great importance. This idea often works quite well. For instance, after **4...Q—N3; 5 N—B3, B—Q2; 6 B—K2, B—N4; 7 O—O, B×B; 8 Q×B, Q—R3** (offering the exchange of queens), the game usually peters out into a dull sort of equality. However, prospective players of this line should be warned that there is a complicated tactical variation beginning **7 P—QB4,** which we do not analyse here.

---

6 B—Q3

6 B—Q3. This is a very important alternative to the text. Nowadays, it is usually played with the intention of offering the QP as a gambit pawn. Note that the QP cannot immediately be captured, for after 6 B—Q3, P×P; 7 P×P, N×P??; 8 N×N, Q×N??; 9 B—QN5 ch, Black loses his queen. Black must first guard against this terrible check by playing...B—Q2.

However, 6...B—Q2 is inaccurate, since White can surprisingly gain an advantage by 7 P×P. It would seem as though this capture should weaken White's hold on the centre, but closer study reveals that this is not the case. White's advantage lies in the fact that Black's game is cramped. This cramp is caused by White's pawn chain, not directly, but because it is preventing Black's own pawns from advancing. Removing the pawns is, in itself, not enough – Black must struggle to gain control of the squares they occupy and then he will be able to push his own pawns forwards.

Thus, in the game NIMZOWITCH–SALWE, Carlsbad 1911, play continued: 6...B—Q2; 7 P×P, B×P; 8 O—O, P—KB3; 9 P—QN4, B—K2; 10 B—KB4, P×P; 11 N×P, N×N; 12 B×N, and Black found that although the White pawns have disappeared, White still controlled the vital squares Q4 and K5, and White's spatial advantage was enhanced rather than diminished. (This would not be the case if Black could challenge the White QB by playing 12...B—KB3; but this move has a tactical refutation: 12...B—KB3; 13 Q—R5 ch, P—N3; 14 B×P ch, P×B;

15 Q×P ch, K—K2; 16 B×B ch, N×B; 17 Q—N7 ch, and White wins.)

We conclude that after 6 B—Q3 Black should play **6...P×P**, and only after **7 P×P**, should he continue with **7...B—Q2.** Now White's QP is genuinely threatened and White must either retreat 8 B—K2, or else sacrifice the pawn boldly with **8 N—QB3.** This sacrifice is called the **Milner-Barry Gambit.** After **8...N×QP; 9 N×N, Q×N; 10 O—O,** White clearly has some compensation for the pawn. He has more pieces developed, the Black king is still dangerously placed in the centre, and White has the powerful threat of 11 N—N5. A thorough analysis of the possibilities is beyond the scope of this book, so we confine ourselves to listing a couple of plausible continuations:

(1) **10...Q×KP?!, 11 R—K1,** Q—Q5 (if 11...Q—N1, then 12 N×P is strong); **12 N—N5,** Q—N3; **13 Q—B3,** B—Q3; **14 N×B ch,** Q×B; **15 B—KB4,** and White stands well.

(2) **10...P—QR3** (probably best); **11 Q—K2,** N—K2; **12 R—Q1,** N—B3; **13 B—QN5** (13 B×QRP, Q×KP; 14 Q×Q, N×Q; 15 B×P, R—R2 favours Black), **13...Q—N3; 14 B—R4,** with

an unclear position in which it is doubtful whether White really has sufficient compensation for the pawn.

---

8 N—B3

8 N—B3. Played with the idea of continuing 9 N—QR4 and driving the Black queen from its attacking position. After **8...N—B4; 9 N—QR4, Q—R4 ch; 10 B—Q2, B—N5,** the game is equal. In a match game between NIMZOWITCH and STAHLBERG played in 1934, play went **11 B—B3** (to protect the QP), **11...B×B; 12 N×B** (12 P×B fails to 12...P—QN4), **12...Q—N3** (attacking the QP yet again); **13 B—N5,** with level chances

9

CARO-KANN DEFENCE

1 P—K4, P—QB3

The strategical idea behind the Caro-Kann Defence is somewhat similar to that which motivates the French Defence (1 P—K4, P—K3). In both these openings White is allowed to build a full pawn centre with 2 P—Q4, and Black attempts to counteract its influence by establishing a pawn on Q4 himself. Several leading players, including the ex-World Champions Botvinnik and Petrosian, have alternated between playing these two openings several times during their careers.

The question of which opening is "sounder" is difficult to answer. Advocates of the French Defence point out that in the main line of the Caro-Kann, after 1 P—K4, P—QB3; 2 P—Q4, P—Q4; 3 N—QB3, Black has no good way of maintaining his QP on Q4 and must give up the centre by playing 3...P×P. Supporters of the Caro-Kann might reply that the French Defence opening move 1...P—K3 unnecessarily shuts in the QB and dooms this piece to a passive role.

The principal advantage of the Caro-Kann pawn structure is that one of White's central pawns is immediately exchanged so that he cannot exert any lasting central bind as he does in the French Defence. Also, Black's pieces have no difficulty in getting developed, but the posts that they take up are more often defensive than active. The most noticeable defect of this defence is that Black is usually committed to a passive role in which his chances of victory are more dependent on White's mistakes, than on the success of any active plan of his own.

Historically, the Caro-Kann is a much more recent development than the French. The two masters after which the opening is named, H. Caro and M. Kann, were both active in the 1890's, but most of the important theory of the opening dates from Botvinnik's reign as World Champion in the 1950's.

CLASSICAL SYSTEM WITH 4. . .B—B4

1 P—K4	P—QB3
2 P—Q4	P—Q4
3 N—QB3	
3 . . .	P×P
4 N×P	B—B4
5 N—N3	B—N3
6 P—KR4	P—KR3
7 N—B3	N—Q2
8 P—R5	B—R2
9 B—Q3	B×B
10 Q×B	Q—B2
11 B—Q2	P—K3
12 Q—K2	KN—B3
13 O—O—O	O—O—O
14 N—K5	N×N
15 P×N	N—Q2
16 P—KB4	

---

1 P—K4	P—QB3
2 P—Q4	

(For 2 N—QB3!? see p. 126)

2 . . .	P—Q4
3 N—QB3	

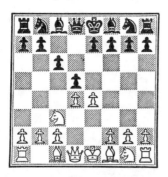

The most obvious continuation, developing a piece and protecting the KP.

3 . . .   P×P

Black has no good alternative to this capture. Protecting the centre still further with 3. . .P—K3 would simply lead to a sort of French Defence in which White

has an extra move, for Black would almost certainly have to spend a tempo later in advancing . . .P—QB4. Simple development with 3. . .N—KB3 is also unappealing, for White could reply with 4 P—K5, driving away the knight without loss of time, and after 4. . .KN—Q2 White can play the enterprising pawn sacrifice 5 P—K6!, P×P; 6 N—B3, establishing a lasting bind on Black's position. (Black will find it difficult to develop his pieces.)

4 N×P   B—B4

Although Black has had to surrender the centre with 3. . .P×P, he now hopes to profit from the exposed position of White's QN by attacking it with a developing move. If White now retreats the knight to QB3 Black has gained a clear tempo, but if White moves the knight to KN3 Black will not gain time, for he must then in turn retreat his bishop. An alternative . . .N—B3 is considered in a separate section.

5 N—N3

This is White's best move.

5 . . .   B—N3

No other retreat should be considered for long – 5. . .B—K3 blocks the KP and thus makes it difficult for Black to develop his KB; 5. . .B—Q2 hinders the QN and will leave the bishop incarcerated after Black subsequently plays . . .P—K3; and after 5. . .P—K3, 6 N×B; Q—R4 ch, and 7. . .Q×N, Black has surrendered the bishop pair.

6 P—KR4

Threatening to win the bishop with 7 P—R5. Normally such moves should be played with great caution, for they may create weaknesses in front of White's king. However, in this position White plans to castle on the Q side, so no such weaknesses will occur.

(For 6 N—B3 see p. 126)

6 . . .   P—KR3

The alternative 6. . .P—KR4?! is very doubtful, since White could continue with the manoeuvre N—R3—B4, which forces either the exchange of Black's QB for a knight or the win of the KRP.

7 N—B3

Developing a piece and threatening N—K5.

(For 7 KN—K2!? see p. 126)

7 . . .	N—Q2
8 P—R5	

Inaugurating a plan to immobilize completely Black's K side.

8 . . .	B—R2
9 B—Q3	

From White's point of view, Black's QB has served its function by acting as a target for the White KRP. The next logical step is to exchange it off, for it is still quite well posted and restricts the freedom of action of White's knight on KN3.

9 . . .	B×B
10 Q×B	Q—B2

This is more accurate than 10. . .P—K3 or 10. . .KN—B3, after which White's QB could seize the more active post KB4.

11 B—Q2	P—K3
12 Q—K2	

The next stage in White's plan is to prepare the move N—K5.

12 . . .	KN—B3
13 O—O—O	O—O—O

The attempt to cover the K4 square by 13. . .B—Q3 fails to 14 N—B5!. If Black then continues 14. . .B—B5, the sacrifice, 15 N×NP ch!, K—B1; 16 N×P ch, P×N; 17 Q×P, gives White three pawns and a raging attack for his piece.

14 N—K5

Assuming a powerful post in the centre of the board and attacking KB7.

14 . . .	N×N

The knight was really too strong to be allowed to live. Other methods of defending the KBP don't have much to recommend them; e.g., 14. . .N—N3 would be met by 15 B—R5.

15 P×N	N—Q2

15. . .N—Q4 may be an improvement, but the knight will eventually be driven away by P—QB4.

16 P—KB4

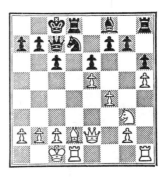

Supporting the KP, White now has a substantial bind on the K side, and Black will have to play carefully to avoid being strangled slowly to death! The game we are following is SPASSKY-PETROSIAN, Thirteenth Game, World Championship Match 1966, which continued:

16. . .B—K2; 17 N—K4, N—B4.
Hoping to relieve his position by exchanges.
18 N—B3, P—B3!?.
This involves a weakening of the KP, but the alternative 18. . .KR—K1; 19 P—KN4 (to be followed by 20 P—N5) leaves Black very cramped.
19 P×P, B×P; 20 Q—B4.
The attempt to win a pawn by dislodging the knight with 20 P—QN4? does not work: 20. . .B×N; 21 B×B, Q×P ch.
20. . .Q—N3; 21 P—QN4.
Not 21 B—K3?, N—N6 ch.
21. . .N—R3; 22 N—K4.
Black's KP still cannot be captured; e.g., 22 Q×P ch, K—N1; 23 P—R3, R×B!; 24 R×R, B×N; or 24 K×R, Q—Q5 ch.
22. . .N—B2.
Defending the KP.
23 KR—K1, R—Q5?!.

A possible improvement is the line 23...B—K2; 24 P—R3, N—Q4.

24 Q—N3, Q—N4; 25 P—B3.

Now, because of the threat of 26 N—B5 followed by 27 N×KP or 27 P—R4, Black was compelled to sacrifice the exchange with 25...R×N; 26 R×R, Q×RP. For brevity we shall not give the rest of this game, since after this exchange sacrifice Petrosian defended tenaciously, and it was not until move ninety-one(!) that Spassky finally managed to force his resignation.

2 N—QB3!?

2 N—QB3!?. Naturally White is not forced to play 2 P—Q4 merely because his opponent has invited him to do so! One popular method of meeting the Caro-Kann is to omit this move in favour of quick development of the knights. After **2...P—Q4; 3 N—B3,** Black has his choice of three continuations (3...B—N5, 3...P×P, and 3...N—KB3), of which the best and most common is **3...B—N5.** White usually tries to break the force of this pin at once with **4 P—KR3,** and now Black has the further choice between the retreat 4...B—R4 and the exchange 4...B×N.

The retreat 4...B—R4 leads to very sharp play if White chooses the continuation 5 P×P, P×P; 6 B—N5 ch, N—QB3; 7 P—KN4, B—N3; 8 N—K5, when he has good attacking chances. However, Black can avoid most of the complications by playing 4...B×N. After the usual 5 Q×B, N—KB3; 6 P—Q3, P—K3, White has the bishop pair, but Black's position is very solid and it

is difficult for White to open the game up enough to make his two bishops an important factor. This system was elaborated in several games of the 1958 Smyslov-Botvinnik, World Championship Match, but theory currently believes that White's practical winning prospects are not very high.

6 N—B3

6 N—B3. Continuations which don't involve the advance of the KRP seem to be insufficiently challenging to Black, and usually only lead to drawish positions; e.g., 6 N—B3, N—B3; 7 B—B4, P—K3; 8 O—O, QN—Q2; 9 R—K1, B—K2, and Black's defensive formation is very difficult to penetrate.

7 KN—K2!?

7 KN—K2!?. The alternative development of the KN, played with the idea of continuing 8 N—B4. (White cannot get his KN to B4 via KR3 because of the tactical possibility 7 N—R3, P—K4; 8 P×P, Q—R4 ch; 9 B—Q2, Q×P ch.

After 7 KN—K2, this line is not good for Black; e.g., 7 KN—K2, P—K4; 8 P×P, Q—R4 ch; 9 B—Q2, Q×KP; 10 B—B3, with obvious advantage to White.) After 7...P—K3; 8 N—B4, B—R2; 9 B—B4, N—B3; 10 O—O, B—Q3, Black's game is positionally quite healthy, and if White plays quietly

Black may even get the better of things. However, White has at his disposal the speculative piece sacrifice **11 N×P!?**, P×N; **12 B×KP**. White obtains two pawns for his piece and disrupts Black's position, leaving the Black king exposed. A definite conclusion as to the merit of this sacrifice has yet to be reached.

CLASSICAL SYSTEM WITH 4...N—B3

1 P—K4	P—QB3
2 P—Q4	P—Q4
3 N—QB3	P×P
4 N×P	N—B3
5 N×N ch	NP×N!?
6 P—QB3	B—B4
7 N—K2	P—KR4
8 P—KR4	N—Q2
9 N—N3	B—KN5
10 B—K2	B×B
11 Q×B	Q—R4
12 O—O	O—O—O
13 P—QB4	P—K3

1 P—K4	P—QB3
2 P—Q4	P—Q4
3 N—QB3	P×P
4 N×P	N—B3

(For 4...N—Q2 see p. 128)

The main alternative to 4...B—B4, but this line is double-edged and the complications can often favour White.

5 N×N ch

This capture is best because it does not waste time and it poses Black immediate problems about how he should recapture. After 5 N—N3 Black can liquidate the centre immediately with 5...P—B4!

5 ...   NP×N!?

The other possibility 5...KP×N is less risky, but it leaves White with a lasting advantage due to his superior pawn structure (for a discussion of why the pawn structure after 5...QP×N favours White, the reader should consult the section on the Exchange Variation of the Ruy Lopez, p. 84).

After the text, the position becomes sharp. Black has seriously compromised his K side, and his king can certainly not find refuge there. His future plan must be to develop his Q side quickly, play ...O—O—O, and seek attacking chances along the open KN file.

6 P—QB3

It is not easy to determine White's best continuation; the text is the most common. It protects the QP, strengthens the centre, and in some lines prevents tactical possibilities based on the rapid transfer of Black's queen to the K side via the intermediate move ...Q—R4 ch.

| 6 . . . | B—B4 |
| 7 N—K2 | |

Heading for KN3 to harass Black's bishop and protect the K side. An instructive error is 7 Q—N3?!, Q—B2; 8 B—KB4?, when White sacrifices a bishop in order to win Black's QR. However, after 8...Q×B; 9 Q×NP, B—R3 (threatening mate by 10...Q—Q7); 10 N—B3, O—O; 11 Q×R, Q—B2, White's queen is trapped. It cannot be saved by 12 P—Q5, because of 12...Q—N3; 13 B—B4 (there is no better move), 13... B—B1 (threatening...B—N2); 14 P×P, N×P, and now ...B—N2 cannot be stopped.

| 7 . . . | P—KR4 |

With the idea of either depriving the knight of the KN3 square or facilitating the exchange of light-squared bishops. After a developing move such as 7... N—Q2, Black's bishop would be driven to a bad position; e.g., 8 N—N3, B—N3; 9 P—KR4, P—KR3; 10 P—R5, B—R2; 11 B—B4, and White has the initiative.

8 P—KR4

Ensuring that White's knight can be permanently maintained on KN3. Less accurate is 8 N—N3, B—N5; 9 B—K2, B×B; 10 Q×B, Q—Q4!; 11 O—O, P—R5; 12 N—K4, N—Q2; 13 B—B4, O—O—O; 14 P—KR3, R—N1, when Black has counter-play on the KN file.

8 . . .	N—Q2
9 N—N3	B—KN5
10 B—K2	

10 P—B3 weakens White's K side.

10 . . .	B×B
11 Q×B	Q—R4
12 O—O	O—O—O

Black has completed the first part of his plan, but too slowly, for White's attack is ready to begin.

| 13 P—QB4 | P—K3 |

This position arose in AVERBACH-SOKOLSKY, 18th USSR Championship. In that game White tried 14 P—R3, intending a pawn storm on the Q wing, but this move gave Black time to get his KB into play with 14...B—Q3!. Instead,

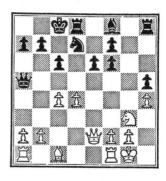

Boleslavsky recommends 14 B—B4, after which White has excellent attacking chances, since his pieces are better coordinated; e.g., 14...B—R3?; 15 B×B, R×B; 16 P—Q5!, BP×P; 17 P×P, Q×P; 18 Q—K3, with a simultaneous attack on the KR and QRP.

4...N—Q2

4...N—Q2. Played with the idea of bringing the knights into play quickly, without risking the doubled pawns which occur in the main line. This system used to be considered a little passive but ultra-solid (it was a favourite of Petrosian), but it has fallen slightly out of fashion because of **5 N—QB4, KN—B3; 6 N—N5,** attacking KB7. This forces Black to play **6...P—K3,** shutting in the QB and leaving himself somewhat cramped. Play might now continue: **7 Q—K2** (threatening 8 N×BP!), **7...N—N3; 8 B—Q3, P—KR3; 9 N(5)—B3, P—B4; 10 P×P, N(N3)—Q2** (if 10 ...B×P; 11 N—K5, and White keeps a slight plus); **11 N—K5, N×N; 12 Q×N,**

Q—R4 ch; 13 B—Q2, Q×BP; 14 N—B3, | N—K5; 17 N—Q3, B—Q3; 18 B—K3
Q×Q; 15 N×Q, B—B4; 16 B—K2, | with a slight advantage to White.

PANOV ATTACK

1 P—K4	P—QB3
2 P—Q4	P—Q4
3 P×P	P×P
4 P—QB4	
4 . . .	N—KB3
5 N—QB3	P—K3
6 N—B3	B—K2
7 P—B5!?	O—O
8 B—Q3	P—QN3!
9 P—QN4	P—QR4
10 N—QR4	QN—Q2
11 P—QR3	RP×P
12 RP×P	NP×P
13 NP×P	P—K4
14 N×P	B×P!
15 O—O	N×N
16 P×N	N—K5

---

1 P—K4	P—QB3
2 P—Q4	P—Q4
3 P×P	P×P

After 3...Q×P? White would gain a tempo by 4 N—QB3, attacking the queen with a developing move.

4 P—QB4

With this move White inaugurates the Panov attack. In the 1930's this system was believed to refute the Caro-Kann, but since then sufficient defensive improvements have been found to restore the theoretical equilibrium. If Black now plays 4...P×P, White will be left with an isolated QP, but he has no need to be afraid; e.g., 5 B×P, P—K3; 6 N—KB3, and now the opening has effectively transposed into a Queen's Gambit Accepted. In such positions the

isolated pawn is known to be a strength rather than a weakness because of the attacking potential which it generates.

4 . . .   N—KB3

Defending the QP with a developing move. 4...N—QB3?! is less accurate, for, after 5 P×P, Q×P, Black's queen has again reached a rather exposed position, and White will be able to play a subsequent N—QB3 with gain of time (after defending his QP).

5 N—QB3   P—K3

The most solid defence, ensuring that Black can maintain a pawn on Q4.
(For 5...N—QB3 and 5...P—KN3 see p. 131)

6 N—B3   B—K2
7 P—B5!?

7 B—N5 would be answered by 7...O—O or 7...N—K5, both of which should lead to equality. So White tries for an advantage through the quick advance of his Q-side pawns.

7 . . .   O—O
8 B—Q3

Keeping Black's knight away from K4. After the immediate 8 P—QN4, there would follow 8...N—K5!; 9 Q—B2 (9 N×N, P×N; 10 N—K5, P—B3; 11 N—B4, N—B3 would cost White a pawn), 9...N—B3; 10 P—QR3, P—K4!, with advantage to Black; e.g., 11 P×P, N×N; 12 Q×N, B—N5, with a strong attack looming, since White has not yet brought his king into safety.

8 ... P—QN3!

Launching a counter-attack against White's advanced QB pawn so that White does not have time to consolidate his forces.

9 P—QN4 P—QR4
10 N—QR4

Attacking the QN pawn. The immediate 10 P—QR3? would not help preserve White's pawn chain, because, after 10...RP×P, the QRP is pinned on the rook.

10 ... QN—Q2

After 10...NP×P?; 11 NP×P, White's protected passed QB pawn will cause Black trouble. The text is a slight improvement over 10...KN—Q2, to which White can reply 11 P—N5 (threatening 12 P—B6), 11...P×P; 12 P×P, P—K4! (not 12...N×P?; 13 N×N, B×N; 14 B×RP ch, etc.); 13 P—B6, P—K5; 14 P×N, N×P; 15 O—O, and White still has a small advantage.

11 P—QR3

White's chain of pawns still looks quite imposing, but in fact Black has at his disposal a simple equalizing combination. This provides a good illustration of the maxim that a pawn chain becomes weaker as the base of the chain moves up the board.

11 ... RP×P
12 RP×P NP×P
13 NP×P

After 13 QP×P, P—K4, Black's central pawns are better than White's on the Q side.

13 ... P—K4!
14 N×P

Other possibilities are worse; e.g., 14 P×P, N×BP!; 15 P×N (15 N×N allows 15...R×R), 15...N×B ch; 16 Q×N, B×P; 17 N—Q4, Q—K1 ch; 18 B—K3, R×N; or 14 P—B6, P—K5; 15 P×N, B×P.

14 ... B×P!
15 O—O

15 N×N, B—N5 ch; 16 B—Q2, B×B ch; 17 Q×B, B×N, wins for Black, since White cannot save the knight on QR4.

15 ... N×N

15...B×P would be answered by 16 B×P ch.

16 P×N

16 P×B? would be a mistake, as 16...N×B; 17 Q×N, B—R3 wins the exchange.

16 ... N—K5

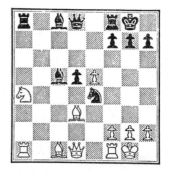

Also possible is the speculative 16...N—N5!?; e.g., 17 B—KB4 (developing a piece and protecting the KP), 17...B×P ch; 18 R×B, N×R; 19 K×N, Q—R5 ch; 20 B—N3 (or 20 P—N3, Q×RP ch), 20...Q—Q5 ch; 21 K—B1, K—R1 (to prevent 22 B×RP ch, winning the queen), and Black has some winning chances, because of the bad knight on QR4 and the exposed position of White's king.

After the text move the position is completely equal. Best play for White is 17 B×N, P×B; 18 Q×Q (18 N×B?

still allows 18...R×R), **18...R×Q; 19 B—N5, R—Q4** (to protect the bishop, since White's knight is now unpinned); **20 N×B,** (20 KR—B1? would be met by 20...B—Q5), **20...R×R; 21 R×R, R×N,** with a quick draw to follow.

5...N—QB3

5...N—QB3. This looks like a natural developing move but is probably not so strong as 5...P—K3, for the knight on QB3 makes it more difficult for Black to counter efficiently the advance of White's QB pawn. A common continuation is **6 B—N5** (after 6 N—B3 Black can hold his own with 6...B—N5), **6...P—K3** (necessary to protect the QP); **7 P—B5, B—K2; 8 B—N5, O—O,** and now White can keep a modest but lasting advantage with **9 B×QN!, P×B; 10 N—B3;** e.g., **10...N—K5; 11 B×B, Q×B; 12 O—O, N×N; 13 P×N.** In this position White's knight is better than Black's bishop which is hampered by its own pawns.

Another incorrect defence is:

5...P—KN3

5...P—KN3. With the idea of fianchettoing the KB. However, after the aggressive **6 Q—N3!,** Black is obliged to sacrifice his QP with **6...B—N2,** since he has no good way of keeping the pawn. (6...P×P; 7 B×P, P—K3; 8 P—Q5 gives White a strong attack as Black is behind in development.)
7 P×P, O—O; 8 B—K2.
Intending to put the KB on KB3 to support the extra pawn.
8...QN—Q2; 9 B—B3, N—N3; 10 B—N5!, B—N5!.
The only way to regain the pawn.
11 B×N, B×KB; 12 N×B, P×B!.
Keeping White's knight away from K5.
13 O—O.
Black can now recapture his sacrificed pawn by the manoeuvre 13...Q—Q2, followed by 14...QR—Q1 and 15...N×P; but the position still favours White, because of his passed QP and the possibility of his rooks invading Black's seventh rank.

ADVANCE VARIATION

1 P—K4	P—QB3
2 P—Q4	P—Q4
3 P—K5	

3 . . .	B—B4
4 P—QB4!?	P×P
5 B×P	P—K3
6 N—QB3	N—Q2
7 KN—K2	N—K2
8 O—O	N—QN3
9 B—N3	Q—Q2
10 P—QR4!	P—QR4
11 N—N3	B—N3
12 B—B2!	B×B
13 Q×B	N(K2)—Q4
14 N(B3)—K4	N—N5
15 Q—K2	N(N3)—Q4

1 P—K4	P—QB3
2 P—Q4	P—Q4
3 P—K5	

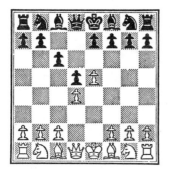

The reader should compare this position with that position reached in the Advance Variation of the French Defence (1 P—K4, P—K3; 2 P—Q4, P—Q4; 3 P—K5), which is treated on pages 119–122.

There are two significant differences:

(i) In the French Defence, Black normally pushes his QBP to QB4 in order to attack the base of White's pawn chain. This advance effectively costs Black a tempo in the Caro-Kann, because he has already played this pawn to QB3.

(ii) In the French Defence, Black's QB is shut in behind the pawn on K3 and, because of the closed nature of the position, it usually remains inactive for some considerable time. In contrast, after 3 P—K5 in the Caro-Kann, Black is at liberty to develop this piece to the aggressive post KB4.

Chess theory holds that, from White's point of view, the advantage (i) is outweighed by the disadvantage (ii), and so this line is not very highly regarded.

3 . . .	B—B4

It is best to develop this bishop immediately, since Black will soon want to play . . .P—K3, fixing White's pawns and strengthening his centre.

4 P—QB4!?

An interesting and instructive continuation which gives this variation a character of its own. It looks at first sight as though Black can exploit this move by the capture 4. . .P×P, followed by . . .P—K3, leaving White saddled with a weak backward QP for which he will have no clear compensation. However, this is not the full story; White's advanced KP will continue to give him some spatial superiority and, even more important, if the Black pawn disappears from Q5, White will regain the use of his K4 square, which can serve as a valuable outpost for his knights.

(For 4 P—KR4!? see p. 134)

4 . . .	P×P

Accepting the challenge.
(For 4. . .P—K3 see p. 135)

5 B×P	P—K3

Fixing White's QP by permanently preventing the advance P—Q5.

6 N—QB3	N—Q2
7 KN—K2!	

This is much more logical than 7 N—

KB3, because in this variation White's KN really belongs on KN3, where it can keep a watchful eye on K4 and perhaps later assist the advance of the KB pawn (one of White's long-term positional threats is the manoeuvre P—B4—B5).

7 ...   N—K2

There is not much point in developing the KB with 7...B—QN5, for Black is never seriously threatening to exchange this bishop for a white knight. If Black does play ...KB×N and White replies P×B, the net effect is to strengthen White's weak QP and to create a hole, Black's Q3 square, for White's remaining knight to occupy. Thus, after 7...B—QN5, White could simply drive away the bishop with pawn moves while gaining extra space on the Q side.

8 O—O   N—QN3

While White's pieces are struggling to gain control of K4, one of Black's knights is aiming to occupy his Q4 square.

9 B—N3   Q—Q2

Preparing for Q-side castling, which will increase the pressure on the Q file against White's backward pawn.

10 P—QR4!

Playing to discourage 10...O—O—O; e.g., 11 P—R5, N(N3)—Q4; 12 N—R4, with Q-side pressure.

10 ...   P—QR4

Stopping the troublesome advance of White's QRP. Of course, it is now quite risky to play ...O—O—O, because Black's Q-side pawns are compromised, but, in compensation, Black has gained QN5 as another outpost square for his knights.

11 N—N3   B—N3

Black would not like to concede the advantage of the two bishops. Also after this retreat, he threatens 12...N—B4, increasing the pressure on the QP.

12 B—B2!

Preventing ...N—B4 and forcing the exchange of light-squared bishops, after which White has undisputed control of K4. Of course, this move involves a potential pawn sacrifice, which we will discuss further in our next note.

12 ...   B×B
13 Q×B   N(K2)—Q4

Accepting the sacrifice with 13...Q×P?! is very dangerous; e.g., 14 B—K3, Q—QN5 (or 14...Q—Q1; 15 Q—N3); 15 R—R3 (threatening to win the knight after 16 R—N3), 15...N(K2)—Q4; 16 R—N3, N×B; 17 P×N, Q—B4; 18 Q—B2, and Black cannot defend both his knight and his weak KB2 square.

14 N(B3)—K4   N—N5
15 Q—K2   N(N3)—Q4

15...Q×P?! is still doubtful, as White could play 16 B—K3, Q—Q1; 17 Q—N4, threatening 18 N—R5. After the text, however, Black has good play for his knights and should not be at much of a disadvantage. We are following the game TAL–GOLOMBEK, Munich Olympiad 1958. Golombek himself has always maintained that he got a good game out of the opening and was only outplayed later on. The game concluded:

16 P—B4, P—KN3.

Weakening the dark squares on the K side, but probably necessary to prevent P—B5.

17 R—R3, B—K2; 18 B—Q2, N—B7?!.

The prophylactic 18...P—QN3, keeping White's pieces away from QB4, is preferable here. Black's position then seems very solid.

19 R—Q3, N(Q4)—N5; 20 B×N,

N×B; 21 R(Q3)—Q1, R—Q1; 22 K—R1.

A useful waiting move which removes the king from possible checks on the diagonal.

22...P—R4?.

A mistake, which weakens the dark squares still further. Probably Black had over-estimated the strength of his position.

23 N—B6 ch.

The start of a typically brilliant Tal attack.

23...B×N; 24 P×B, K—B1.

Something had to be done to prevent 25 P—B5, so Black moves his king to unpin the KP; 25...O—O? would have been met by 26 N×P, P×N; 27 Q×P, with an unstoppable mate on KN7.

25 N—K4, P—R5?!.

25...N—Q4 was better, but Black is probably lost now anyway.

26 N—B5, Q—B1; 27 P—B5!, NP×P; 28 Q—K3, P—N3; 29 Q—N5.

White does not waste time moving the knight; his attack on the KN file is overwhelming.

29...R—R2.

Or 29...P×N; 30 Q—N7 ch, K—K1; 31 Q×R ch, etc.

30 R—B4!, P×N.

There is nothing better.

31 R×RP, R×R; 32 Q—N7 ch!.

There is no need even to capture the rook – White is out for bigger game.

32...K—K1; 33 Q—N8 ch, K—Q2; 34 Q×P ch, K—Q3; 35 Q—K7 ch.

Black resigned. It is mate in two, after 35...K—Q4 by 36 Q×BP ch, K—K5; 37 Q—K5 mate.

---

4 P—KR4!?

---

4 P—KR4!?. A continuation which had a short vogue after Tal employed it in his 1961 World Championship Match with Botvinnik, but which has since sunk back into obscurity. The idea is to gain space on the K side and force Black's QB back to Q2, where it will be shut in after Black's KP advances to K3. A

dreadful blunder now would be: 4...P—K3??, for after 5 P—KN4, B—N3; 6 P—R5, B—K5; 7 P—KB3, the bishop is lost. The best reply is believed to be **4...P—KR3** (4...P—KR4!? is also possible), threatening to maintain the bishop on its good diagonal by retreating it to R2 (after consolidation with 5...P—K3). The only way for White to prevent this is by **5 P—KN4!?** immediately, which forces **5...B—Q2** (since 5...B—R2? gives White the advantage after 6 P—K6!, P×P; 7 B—Q3, B×B; 8 Q×B, when Black's K1—KR4 diagonal has become very weak).

In the game TAL–PACHMANN, Bled 1961, Tal carried this plan to its logical extreme when he continued (after 4...P—KR3; 5 P—KN4, B—Q2) with the moves:

6 P—R5, P—QB4; 7 P—QB3, P—K3; 8 P—KB4.

This is an amazing position, for White has played eight pawn moves without developing a single piece! However, Tal's way is not to be recommended to lesser mortals (or perhaps even to Tal), for White's somewhat unwarranted pawn avalanche must surely carry with it the seeds of its own destruction if Black plays carefully.

The game continued:

8...Q—N3; 9 N—B3, N—QB3; 10 N—R3.

10 B—R3, hoping to force P—B5 later, may be better – but probably only good enough to equalize.

10...P×P; 11 P×P, O—O—O; 12 N—B2, K—N1.

Removing the king from the open QB file, which can then be used by a rook.

13 B—Q3, KN—K2.

Black should have the better prospects.

4...P—K3

4...P—K3. Black can, of course, refuse to play ...P×P, and simply continue with his development instead. This is less ambitious but should also lead to equality.

5 N—QB3, N—Q2; 6 P×P.

The cramping advance 6 P—B5? fails to 6...P—QN3!; 7 P—QN4, P—QR4, when White's centre starts to collapse. After **6...BP×P**, White has no way to keep a real advantage. One continuation is:

7 KN—K2, N—K2; 8 N—N3, B—N3; 9 B—Q3, N—B3; 10 O—O, Q—R5 (STOLTZ–GOLOMBEK, Dubrovnik Olympiad 1950).

The chances are level.

QUEEN'S PAWN AND FLANK OPENINGS

INTRODUCTION

By playing P—K4 on his first move White not only stakes a claim in the centre, which is normally an advantageous principle to follow, but also prepares swift development by opening diagonals for his queen and KB. After 1 P—K4, White is often able to launch an attack based on his rapid development potential. If Black stonewalls in reply with 1...P—K4, White can exploit the fact that the Black KP lacks protection to mobilize his forces quickly – with constant threats to the KP, as in the Ruy Lopez.

1 P—Q4, although optically similar to 1 P—K4, leads to an entirely different concept of opening play. Admittedly, White still stakes his claim in the centre, but 1 P—Q4 does not allow White to develop his pieces so rapidly as does 1 P—K4. Furthermore, if Black replies with 1...P—Q4, the QP is lent automatic protection by the Black queen; so the simple developing move 2 N—QB3 achieves nothing but the obstruction of White's QBP. This is a bad thing, since the QBP is normally required as a central lever to attack the opponent's QP in Q-side openings.

After 1 P—Q4 White's main aim is not rapid development of pieces, but the attempt to form a massive central pawn structure, under cover of which he can prepare an assault on the Black position.

We will examine three types of Black response to this White strategy:
1. Black fights the formation of a White pawn centre by occupying the centre himself with pawns (Queen's Gambit).
2. Black fights the formation of a White pawn centre by controlling key central squares with his pieces (Nimzo-Indian Defence).
3. The most contemporary treatment – Black positively encourages the formation of a White pawn centre, hoping to prove that such structures are over-extended and prone to contain weaknesses (King's Indian Defence and one line of the Modern Defence).

Before moving on to an analysis of specific variations, let us first take a look at a game, opening 1 P—Q4, in which White carries out his ideal strategy. The game can be divided into the following stages:
1. White forms a powerful pawn centre.
2. White masses his pieces in preparation for the attack, shielded by his pawns.
3. White throws forward his pawns to clear lines of attack for his massed piece army.

4. White's emancipated pieces converge on Black's king and deliver mate.

Note how central control in this game allows White to choose his object of attack. Black's pieces are strewn round the edge of the board and cannot offer effective resistance.

The game was played in 1962 in a match between two famous Soviet Grandmasters, KERES playing the White pieces, GELLER the Black.

Stage 1: 1 P—Q4, N—KB3; 2 P—QB4, P—K3; 3 N—KB3, P—Q4; 4 N—B3, P—B4; 5 BP × P, N × P; 6 P—K3, N—QB3; 7 B—B4, N × N?. Not to be recommended. This strengthens White's centre, by allowing him to capture with a wing pawn towards the centre (NP × N), without granting Black any means of counter-attacking or undermining it. 8 P × N, B—K2; 9 O—O, O—O; 10 P—K4.

Stage 2: 10...P—QN3; 11 B—N2, B—N2; 12 Q—K2, N—R4; 13 B—Q3, R—B1; 14 QR—Q1.

Stage 3: 14...P × P; 15 P × P, B—N5; 16 P—Q5!.

Suddenly all of White's pieces are pointing at Black's unhappy king. **16...P × P; 17 P × P, Q—K2** (17...Q × P?; 18 B × RP ch wins the queen, while 17...B × NP; 18 Q—K5, P—B3; 19 Q—R5, is also disastrous for Black, who cannot parry the threats to his king's position, e.g., 19...P—N3; 20 B × P, P × B; 21 Q × P ch, K—R1; 22 N—N5, Q—Q2; 23 R × B!); **18 N—K5, P—B3; 19 Q—R5.**

Stage 4: 19...P—N3; 20 N × P. A very common type of sacrifice to demolish the pawn barrier protecting a king. We have already seen something similar to this in the note to move 17. **20...P × N; 21 B × NP, Q—N2.**

Keres himself wrote of this position: "Black's defence is exceedingly difficult. White has already two pawns for the sacrificed piece and in addition practically all his pieces stand ready to attack the weakened enemy king. Even on general grounds it seems that Black can scarcely hope to emerge from his hopeless position safe and sound."

22 R—Q3, B—Q3; 23 P—B4, Q—R1; 24 Q—N4, B—B4 ch; 25 K—R1, R—QB2; 26 B—R7 dble ch, K—B2 (26...K × B; 27 R—KR3 mate); **27 Q—K6 ch, K—N2; 28 R—N3 ch,** and mate next move, after **28...K × B; 29 Q—R3.**

After this impressive example of central control leading to a crushing attack, we direct our attention to concrete analysis of the Queen's Gambit.

10

QUEEN'S GAMBIT

1 P—Q4, P—Q4; 2 P—QB4

Until the last quarter of the 19th century it was normal to play P—K4 on move 1 in international tournaments. (Of course, other moves were not unknown.) However, at this stage in the development of chess, 1 P—Q4, also became popular, and Black invariably responded with ...P—Q4, leading to the Queen's Gambit. The Gambit accepted has cropped up sporadically over the last 100 years, but it has never been taken up with general enthusiasm. The defences to prove most popular initially, were the Orthodox (Black resorts to trench warfare), and Tarrasch (activity at the cost of pawn weaknesses). Although they both suffered a decline with the onset of the Hypermodern ideas (e.g., Nimzo-Indian) in the 1920's, they still retain many devotees to the present day. While Tarrasch was elaborating his defence to the Queen's Gambit at the close of the 19th century, the great Russian Master Mikhail Tchigorin was pioneering his own highly individualistic approach. Although the Russian's idea never found general acceptance, it still offers fascinating and unexplored paths in the defence of the Queen's Gambit.

After 1 P—Q4, the copycat reply 1...P—Q4 is the most obvious way of preventing White from increasing the scope of his pawn-centre with 2 P—K4. We have seen that 1 P—Q4, P—Q4; 2 N—QB3 is pointless, because Black's QP is automatically protected by his queen, therefore White will normally offer a gambit at this stage with 2 P—QB4, hoping to lure away the Black QP so that White can build up his centre in peace.

We now examine three modes of Black response to the Queen's Gambit:

(1) The Queen's Gambit Accepted – Black takes the pawn and relies for his counterplay on the fact that White must waste time in regaining his material. This is a very risky course for Black, since White normally gains control of the centre – although he may have to accept an isolated queen's pawn in order to achieve this.

(2) Black launches a rapid counter-attack against White's QP – either with pieces (The Tchigorin Defence), or with pawns (The Tarrasch Defence).

(3) Black staunchly defends his QP at Q4 against all of White's assaults (The Orthodox Defence).

QUEEN'S GAMBIT ACCEPTED

1 P—Q4	P—Q4
2 P—QB4	P×P
3 N—KB3	N—KB3
4 P—K3	P—K3
5 B×P	P—B4
6 O—O	P—QR3
7 P—QR4!	N—B3
8 Q—K2	P×P
9 R—Q1	B—K2
10 P×P	O—O
11 N—B3	N—Q4
12 B—Q3!	

---

1 P—Q4	P—Q4
2 P—QB4	P×P

(For 2...P—K4 see p. 140)

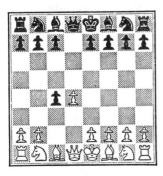

Ostensibly this falls in with all of White's plans. Black gives up his foothold in the centre and cedes White a central pawn majority. Furthermore, White can easily regain his pawn by attacking it with his KB, and, if necessary, QN and queen. However, White cannot realize his objective immediately with 3 P—K4, in view of ...P—K4! (see p. 140); so he must expend a tempo with:

3 N—KB3

...in order to prevent Black's thrust. But now Black is given some time in which to organize counterplay. Nevertheless, the Queen's Gambit Accepted

remains a very risky defence for Black. 3 Q—R4 ch is another way of regaining the pawn, but it is better to develop the KB, rather than the queen at QB4 so early in the game.

(For 3 P—K4 see p. 140)

3 ...	N—KB3

Development is essential for Black. 3...N—KB3 also prevents 4 P—K4. Attempts to cling to the pawn are examined in the notes.

(For 3...P—QN4 see p. 141)

4 P—K3

Preparing to regain the pawn, simultaneously developing the KB on a very useful square.

4 ...	P—K3

Black wants to play ...P—QB4 to attack White's QP. The text move allows Black's KB to cover the QB4 square.

(For 4...B—N5 see p.141)

5 B×P	P—B4
6 O—O	

6 P×P, allowing the exchange of queens and dissolving White's central pawn majority, is clearly futile. But it is often chosen when White only wants a draw.

6 ...	P—QR3

This looks like an irrelevant pawn move, but Black now threatens ...P—QN4 and ...B—N2, developing his QB on a fine diagonal with gain of time. Of course, White stops this.

7 P—QR4!

Now White is getting ready to mass his pieces for the attack behind his central pawns, which act as a kind of shield.

7 ...	N—B3
8 Q—K2	P×P
9 R—Q1	B—K2

Not 9...P—K4?; 10 P×P, and the

KP is pinned. 9...B—B4 looks good, developing and protecting the pawn, but, after 10 P×P, N×P; 11 N×N, B×N; 12 B—K3, the pin is too powerful.

10 P×P   O—O
11 N—B3

White is fully developed and ready for the disruptive advance P—Q5; therefore Black blockades the isolated QP in the approved fashion:

11 . . .   N—Q4
12 B—Q3!

Pointing aggressively at Black's king.

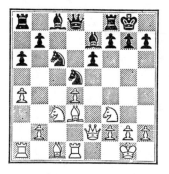

We have reached a typical position arising from the Queen's Gambit Accepted. Positions similar to this have occurred on many thousands of occasions in tournament play.

This is a case where the isolated QP is a positive advantage for White, since it gives him a firm grip on the centre, while Black is insufficiently well developed, and his pieces are not efficiently placed to exploit the pawn's weakness. Compare the section on the Tarrasch Defence (p. 144) where White, by virtue of moving first, can co-ordinate his pieces ideally to exploit Black's isolated QP.

GLIGORIC–PORTISCH, from Board 1 of a Yugoslavia-Hungary match in 1971 continued:

12...N(3)—N5; 13 B—N1.

It is worth boxing in the rook to maintain the bishop on its wonderful diagonal.

13...P—QN3; 14 P—R5!, B—Q2; 15 N—K5.

Moving forwards to occupy one of the squares controlled by the isolated QP.

15...P×P; 16 R—R3.

Threatening a typical mate by means of 17 N×N, followed by 18 B×KRP ch, K×B; 19 R—R3 ch, and 20 Q—R5. Black must weaken the pawn cover around his king to ward off this menace, so we can see the worth of 13 B—N1.

16...P—B4; 17 N×N, N×N; 18 N×B, Q×N.

18...B×R??; 19 Q×P ch, R—B2; 20 N—K5.

19 R×P.

White has a very good position, with his two bishops and open lines against Black's QRP and KB. White also has a fine square on K5 for a piece, while Black has no pressure to speak of against the isolated QP.

2...P—K4

2...P—K4 (Albin's Counter Gambit). This is a rather silly gambit continuation which, however, does deserve a brief mention. As one might expect, the position after 3 QP×P, P—Q5, favours White, who has won a centre pawn free of charge. A good line for White now is 4 N—KB3, N—QB3; 5 P—KN3, B—K3; 6 QN—Q2, Q—Q2; 6 B—N2, O—O—O; 7 O—O, followed by P—QR3 and P—QN4.

---

3 P—K4

3. P—K4 This looks ideal for White, who has a pawn centre ready-made and will

soon develop his KB on the useful square QB4, capturing a pawn in the process. However, after **3...P—K4!**, Black can exploit his temporary extra pawn to complete his development. Unpalatable for White now are:

(a) 4 P—Q5, which obstructs the paths for his KB by putting too many pawns on light squares. Black replies 4...B—QB4, followed by ...N—K2 and...P—KB4 with an active game.

(b) 4 P×P, Q×Q ch; 5 K×Q, N—QB3; 6 P—B4, P—B3; 7 P×P, N×P; 8 P—K5, N—KN5, followed by...B—K3 and...O—O—O. Black has a big lead in development, and White's king is prone to harrassment.

So White must enter an unclear gambit line with **4 N—KB3, P×P; 5 B×P**, but now Black can hold his QP with ...B—N5 ch and ...N—QB3, so we cannot honestly recommend this line for White. N.B. Black should avoid the trap 5...P—QB4?; 6 N—K5!, B—K3; 7 B×B, P×B; 8 Q—R5 ch, P—N3; 9 N×P.

3...P—QN4

3...P—QN4. Clinging to the pawn involves expenditure of too many pawn moves at the cost of development. White easily regains his pawn while maintaining a superior position:

4 P—QR4, P—QB3; 5 P—K3.
Threat: 6 P—QN3, hacking a path through Black's forest of pawns to the vulnerable one on QN5.

5...Q—N3; 6 P×P, P×P; 7 N—K5.
Threat: Q—B3, attacking QR8 and KB7. Already, Black's neglect of development has permitted White a powerful attack.

7...B—N2; 8 P—QN3, P×P; 9 Q×P.
Simultaneously attacking QN5 and KB7. It is difficult to see a defence for Black in view of his chronic lack of development.

4...B—N5

4...B—N5. A modern idea in the Queen's Gambit Accepted. After **5 B×P** there is a threat of 6 B×P ch, K×B; 7 N—K5 ch, so Black must play 5...P—K3. Now White can win a pawn at the cost of development by means of 6 Q—N3, B×N; 7 P×B, QN—Q2; 8 Q×P, P—B4, but it is not worth the danger involved. White does better to develop normally: **6 P—KR3, B—R4; 7 N—B3, QN—Q2; 8 O—O, B—K2; 9 P—K4, O—O; 10 B—K3**, with a solid, well centralized position and some White advantage.

TCHIGORIN DEFENCE

1 P—Q4	P—Q4
2 P—QB4	N—QB3
3 N—QB3	P×P
4 N—B3	B—N5
5 P—Q5!	B×N
6 KP×B	N—K4
7 B—B4!	N—Q2
8 KB×P	P—QR3
9 O—O	KN—B3
10 R—K1	

---

1 P—Q4	P—Q4
2 P—QB4	N—QB3

This defence was pioneered by the great 19th century Russian Master, Tchigorin. Black plans a quick counter-attack against White's centre by means of piece activity. However, 2...N—QB3 flouts an important principle – that the QBP should not be blocked by a knight in the QP openings. This error could be compared to blocking the QP by B—Q3 in a KP opening – although it is by no means so heinous. The Tchigorin Defence is almost playable, but here we offer analysis that suggests that Black cannot equalize if White plays correctly.

3 N—QB3!

Increasing the pressure against Black's QP is the correct procedure. Black must now surrender his grip on the centre

since he is unable to support his QP with his QBP.

(For 3 N—KB3 see p. 143)

3 ...   P×P

Black could maintain his QP by means of 3...P—K3, but that would lock in his QB in sad fashion, and with his knight already on QB3, Black would have great difficulty in freeing his cramped position by means of ...P—QB4.

(For 3...N—B3 see p. 143)

4 N—B3

This developing move towards the centre is best. White need be in no hurry to regain his sacrificed pawn. Incidentally, this developing move also reinforces White's own QP, which was indirectly threatened by Black's second move.

(For 4 P—Q5 see p. 144)

4 ...   B—N5

Black pursues his theme of attacking White's QP with pieces. After 4...N—B3; 5 P—Q5, N—QR4; 6 Q—R4 ch, P—B3; 7 P×P, N×P; 8 P—K4, followed by B×P, White's superior development guarantees him the advantage.

5 P—Q5!

Only now does White displace Black's poor QN. Thus we see a further defect of 2...N—QB3.

5 ...   B×N

Consistent but useless. Black removes White's KN in order that his own QN may take up a post in the centre.

6 KP×B

Usually it is recommended to capture with a wing pawn towards the centre, but here KP×B is correct, since it opens the path of White's KB so that it can join in a dangerous attack against Black's still uncastled king.

6 ...   N—K4

7 B—B4!

Still harrassing the wretched knight. Now if 7...N—N3, then 8 KB×P!, N×B; 9 B—N5 ch, P—B3; 10 P×P, and White has a winning attack.

    7 . . .   **N—Q2**
    8 KB×P

Threatening N—N5, which Black prevents.

    8 . . .   **P—QR3**
    9 O—O

White completes his mobilization.

    9 . . .   **KN—B3**
    10 R—K1

Automatically occupying the open file leading to Black's king. White now has a clear advantage, since he has the bishop pair in an open position, and a vast lead in development, while Black's king is horribly exposed to attack. Here is a possible continuation: **10... N—R4; 11 B—K3, P—KN3; 12 P—Q6!** (clearing lines for attack). **12...BP×P; 13 Q—N3, P—K3; 14 B—Q4, B—N2; 15 B×KP!, P×B** (15...B×B; 16 B×N dbl ch, K×B; 17 Q×NP ch, Q—B2; 18 R—K7 ch, etc.); **16 Q×KP ch, K—B1; 17 Q×P ch, K—B2; 18 Q—K6 ch, K—B1; 19 QR—Q1,** and wins.

Conclusion: The doubt we have cast on Tchigorin's Defence to the Queen's Gambit reveals an important principle: The requirements of long-term strategy can be far more important than speedy development in the Q-side openings.

---

3 N—KB3

3 N—KB3. This has been a popular continuation in the past, but it is too passive, Black can obtain a fine position with the following manoeuvre:

    3...B—N5; 4 P×P, B×N.

4...Q×P?; 5 N—B3, and Black loses time with his queen, which he has prematurely developed.

    5 P×N.

If 5 NP×B, then Q×P; 6 P—K3, P—K4; 7 N—B3, B—N5, and Black can maintain his queen on its powerful central square.

    5...B×BP; 6 N—B3.

"Threatening" P—K4.

    6...P—K3; 7 P—K4, B—N5; 8 P—B3 (forced), **Q—R5 ch.**

To weaken the pawn structure around White's king.

    9 P—N3, Q—B3.

Continuing with ...O—O—O, Black has great piece pressure against White's unwieldy centre.

3...N—B3

3...N—B3. This has been recommended

by the Russian Masters Panov and Estrin, as a method of keeping a grip on the centre, but it fails to **4 N—B3**. Now White threatens 5 P×P, KN×P; 6 P—K4, and 4...P×P; 5 P—Q5 transposes into the note to Black's fourth move in the text. Perhaps Black should play the unattractive ...P—K3. Panov and Estrin give **4...B—N5**, but overlook that **5 N—K5!** gives White a tremendous position:

(*a*) **5...N×N;** 6 P×N, winning a pawn.

(*b*) **5...P×P;** N×B, N×N; 7 P—K3, N—B3; 8 B×P, with the bishop pair in an open position. Also White has a central pawn majority and leads in development.

(*c*) **5...B—B4;** 6 N×N, P×N; 7 P—K3, and Black has an appalling set of doubled pawns, which White can fix as permanent weaknesses with an imminent P—B5.

---

4 P—Q5

---

4 P—Q5. This thrust is premature. Black has two playable possibilities:

(*a*) **4...N—K4; 5 B—B4, N—N3.** Now White must lose a move with his bishop – compare the note to White's seventh move in the main text. **6 B—N3, P—K4; 7 P×P e.p., B×P.** Black has a fully satisfactory position with free development and (temporarily at least) an extra

pawn – GLIGORIC–SMYSLOV, Amsterdam 1971.

(*b*) **4...N—QR4,** offering a fascinating piece sacrifice, which White must accept; if White does not take up the challenge he will never retrieve his lost pawn. **5 Q—R4 ch, P—B3; 6 P—QN4.** Note that 6 P×P, N×P; 7 Q×BP, B—K3, is not encouraging for White, who will have to lose a lot of time with his queen, which has been brought into the game much too soon. **6...P—QN4!.** A necessary piece sacrifice. 6...P×P e.p.; 7 RP×P, P—N3; 8 P×P, is clearly disastrous for Black. **7 Q×N, Q×Q; 8 P×Q, P—N5; 9 N—Q1, P×P; 10 P—K4, P—K3.**

An examination of this position reveals that Black has for the exchange of a knight two very strong pawns which form part of a powerful central pawn majority. In addition Black can develop his pieces easily. Finally White's pawns are not particularly healthy. We must conclude that Black has good compensation for his piece and does not stand worse.

TARRASCH DEFENCE

1 P—Q4	P—Q4	8 O—O	O—O
2 P—QB4	P—K3	9 B—K3	
3 N—QB3	P—QB4		
4 BP×P	KP×P		
5 N—B3	N—QB3	1 P—Q4	P—Q4
6 P—KN3!	N—B3	2 P—QB4	P—K3
7 B—N2	B—K2	3 N—QB3	

The best developing move, since it puts pressure on Black's QP.

3 ...   P—QB4

The key move of the Tarrasch. Black seeks at all costs to gain active play in the centre for his pieces. At the beginning of this century, under the influence of the great German Master, Dr Siegbert Tarrasch, this was considered to be the "only correct" defence to the Queen's Gambit; but, as chess theory developed, the Tarrasch fell into disrepute. Black nearly always finds himself saddled with an isolated QP in the Tarrasch (the price he has to pay for his early activity), and since the 1920's, Masters have regarded this weakness in Black's position as too much of a liability. In recent games, however, it has become slightly more respectable, after it was used to good effect in the 1969 World Championship Match.

4 BP×P

The attack against Black's QP is the theme of the whole opening, so this is, once again, best. Simple development by 4 N—B3 is insufficiently to the point here, while the other capture, 4 QP×P?, would allow Black to make an important advance in the centre: 4...P—Q5, displacing White's newly developed knight. After 5 N—R4, Black can easily regain his pawn with the small trick 5...B×P; 6 N×B, Q—R4 ch; 7 B—Q2, Q×B, and Black's control of the centre (the advanced QP) gives him reasonable chances. His queen has come out rather early, we must admit, but

White is insufficiently well developed to exploit this. In fact, Black's queen on QB4 attacks White's QBP, and White must expend a tempo to protect it.

4 ...   KP×P

(For 4...BP×P see p. 146)

5 N—B3

Once again the surrender of the Q4 central square, with 5 P×P, P—Q5; 6 N—R4, is not to be recommended. If White wishes to attack Black's QP where it stands, he must keep a very firm grip on his own Q4 square to prevent the QP from advancing.

White's plan is to play QP×P at a moment when Black cannot play P—Q5 at once in reply. White will then blockade the QP (usually by planting a knight on his own Q4) and will proceed to mass his pieces to attack the Black QP.

A useful rule coined by Nimzowitsch for situations where you want to attack a weak pawn is: first restrain the pawn weakness, then blockade it (so that it cannot advance into safety), and then destroy it.

5 ...   N—QB3

5...P×P?; 6 KN×P would help White by bringing his KN to Q4, free of charge.

6 P—KN3!

A highly effective development for White's KB. From KN2 it can direct its fire in the most efficient manner possible at Black's QP.

6 ...   N—B3

Black's opening play in the Tarrasch consists almost entirely of mobilizing his pieces sensibly and quickly on their most attractive central squares – i.e.: a "classical" development as opposed to White's "modern" development of a bishop on the flank square KN2.

(For 6...P×P see p. 147)

7 B—N2	B—K2
8 O—O	O—O
9 B—K3	

(For 9 B—N5 see p. 147)

At move nine White has several possibilities. 9 P×P is still premature. After 9...P—Q5!; 10 N—QR4, Black's QP escapes from the blockade and, once again, White's QN is chased to the edge of the board. Although White then has some chances to retain his extra QBP, most Master players would avoid this line for White in view of the active play Black gains for his pieces, and the strength of the QP, which increases in power the nearer it comes to the White position. Continuing with 10...B—B4 intending ...P—Q6, Black maintains a dangerous initiative.

9 B—N5 was Petrosian's choice in his 1969 World Championship match with Spassky.

The text (B—K3) was played by Spassky in a game from board one of the USSR v Canada match in the 1970 World Team Championships. Black was Yanofsky.

With 9 B—K3, White attacks Black's QBP with a second piece, while also increasing his control of his own Q4 square. The further course of the game revealed in startling fashion the potential weakness of an isolated QP.

9...P×P; 10 KN×P.
This is very important because the blockading knight reaches the key Q4 square. Half the battle is won now for White.

10...P—KR3.
Black fears B—N5, attacking his KN, which is propping up the isolated QP.

11 R—B1, N—QR4; 12 P—N3!.
Black's control over his QB5 and K5 squares is one of his main forms of compensation for an isolated QP. With 12 P—N3!, White takes away the use of

one of these squares which Black threatened to occupy.

12...N—B3; 13 Q—Q3.
Intending to build up behind the knight with KR—Q1.

13...N—K4; 14 Q—B2.
Now concentrating on the open file.

14...Q—R4; 15 N(B3)—N5, B—Q2; 16 Q—B7!.
Occupying the seventh rank with queen or rook is nearly always advantageous.

16...Q×Q; 17 N×Q, QR—Q1; 18 N×P, N×N; 19 B×N, B—KR6; 20 B—N2.
White has won Black's isolated QP where it stood. Black has zero compensation (20...B×B; 21 K×B, N—N5; 22 N—B5!, N×B ch; 23 N×N, R—Q7; 24 R—B2!), and lost after 42 moves.

Black should meet 9 B—K3 with ...N—KN5!, threatening ...N×B. After 10 B—B4, White has to lift some of the pressure from Black's QBP, but Black's KN is slightly offside. White has a small advantage.

4...BP×P

4...BP×P. Also playable, but it leads to the loss of a pawn: 5 Q×P, N—QB3; 6 Q—Q1, P×P; 7 Q×P, B—Q2. (Black should not exchange queens a pawn to the bad.) In this position Black has many open lines for his pieces and can gain time by attacking White's queen, but White has an extra pawn.

You could play this gambit to great effect against someone you know to be timid, but it could backfire horribly against a good defender. Here is one example: (POLUGAIEVSKY–I. ZAITSEV, Alma Ata 1969):

8 N—B3, N—B3; 9 Q—Q1, B—QB4; 10 P—K3, Q—K2.

Preparing to castle on the opposite wing from White, and then launch a pawn-storm against White's king.

11 B—K2, O—O—O; 12 O—O, P—KN4.

Of course, it would be time-wasting and dangerous for White to take this pawn sacrifice – he prefers to centralize.

13 N—Q4!, P—N5; 14 P—N4!?.

Giving back the pawn in the interests of opening a file towards Black's king – Petrosian recommends 14 B—N5, and considers that White is on top.

14...B×P; 15 B—N2, P—KR4.

15...N×N is an improvement.

16 N(3)—N5, K—N1; 17 Q—R4, P—R3; 18 N×N ch, B×N; 19 B×N, Q×B; 20 Q×B, P×N; 21 B×QNP, Q—Q3; 22 QR—N1.

White still has an extra pawn and also Black's king is the more exposed. White naturally won.

6...P×P

6...P×P. Quite anti-thematic, since it brings White's KN to the vital square Q4, in front of Black's QP. But in 1963 a German player, Dr W. Alles, published an analysis which claimed to demonstrate that Black could safely defy established positional principles in this fashion in view of certain tactical tricks available to him:

7 KN×P, Q—N3.

Bringing the queen out early as well! Black hopes for 8 N×N, which fails to 8...B—QB4!, gaining a tempo on White's KBP. White's knight has no time to escape; e.g., 9 N—K5, B×P ch; 10 K—Q2, Q—K6 ch.

8 N—N3.

Discovering an attack on the QP, which can now advance, but White gains time by chasing Black's queen.

8...P—Q5; 9 N—Q5, Q—Q1; 10 B—N2, B—K3; 11 P—K4.

To support the knight.

11...KN—K2; 12 B—N5, P—KR3.

Here Alles ended his analysis, concluding that White must exchange on K7, when Black has a fine game with his strong, advanced, passed QP. But he overlooked that White can refute Black's whole play with **13 B—B6!!**, attacking Black's QP from the rear. 13...P×B? allows 14 N×BP mate. So, a "tactical trick" comes to White's aid to justify his positionally correct play – but this is only what we should expect. Tactics should flow naturally from good positional play. KEENE–MORRIS, Dulwich 1963, concluded:

13...B×N; 14 P×B, N—N5.

14...P×B; 15 P×N, N×P; 16 B×N ch, P×B; 17 Q×P. Black's pawn structure is appalling.

15 B×QP, N(2)×P; 16 O—O.

White's bishops and superb development must win for him.

16...R—B1; 17 P—QR3, N—B7; 18 R—B1, N×B; 19 Q×N, N—B2; 20 KR—K1 ch, N—K3; 21 Q—R4 ch, K—K2.

21...Q—Q2; 22 R×R ch.

22 Q—N4 ch, K—K1; 23 Q—N5 ch, K—K2; 24 Q×P ch.

White has won a whole rook.

---

9 B—N5

9 B—N5. This looks good because it increases the pressure against the isolated QP. However, it is probably too blunt to win the QP.

Black can keep afloat as follows:

9...B—K3; 10 P×P, B×P; 11 B×N, Q×B! (11...P×B? destroys his own pawn structure and is clearly out of the question); **12 N×P, Q×P,** and Black has maintained material equality.

ORTHODOX DEFENCE

1 P—Q4	P—Q4
2 P—QB4	P—K3
3 N—QB3	N—KB3
4 B—N5	B—K2
5 N—B3	O—O
6 P—K3	QN—Q2
7 R—B1	P—B3
8 B—Q3	P×P!
9 B×P	N—Q4!
10 B×B	Q×B
11 O—O	N×N
12 R×N	P—K4
13 Q—B2	P×P
14 P×P	

1 P—Q4	P—Q4
2 P—QB4	P—K3

(For 2...P—QB3 see p. 149)

Sturdily defending the QP. The "defence" by 2...N—KB3 is illusory. After 3 P×P, N×P; 4 P—K4, White's pawn centre has become a dangerous, mobile majority.

3 N—QB3	N—KB3
4 B—N5	

Developing with threats and continuing the assault on the QP by pinning Black's KN. Now 4...P—KR3 would be disastrous for Black: 5 B×N!, P×B (5...Q×B; 6 P×P, wins a pawn for nothing); 6 P×P, P×P, and Black has been hamstrung by one of the most loathsome of all weaknesses – an isolated doubled pawn. Note that the square KB5 (from White's side) could thus become an ideal outpost for White's pieces from which to threaten Black's position (e.g., B—Q3/N—K2—N3) and that Black's lack of pawns on the K and KN files, would mean a White piece established on KB5 could never be driven away.

(For 4 P×P see p. 150)

4 ...	B—K2

Breaking the pin.

5 N—B3	O—O
6 P—K3	

It is best to develop White's KB on Q3 in this line. The fianchetto development with 6 P—KN3 and B—N2 would be out of place here, since Black's QP is heavily protected. At Q3 the KB stares aggressively at Black's king.

6 ...	QN—Q2

Reinforcing his KN. The more natural move 6...N—B3 is a mistake, since it obstructs the Black QBP. Once again, we must stress that this obstruction should be avoided in the queen's pawn openings.

(For 6...P—KR3 see p. 150)

7 R—B1

Occupying a file which can later be opened by means of BP×P. Later on we will see just how useful this can be.

7 ...   P—B3

Lending the QP extra protection. Black prepares slowly, but surely, to free his game by exchanging pieces.

8 B—Q3   P×P!

Surrendering the centre now forces White to move his KB a second time. This gives Black the opportunity to set in motion an exchanging manoeuvre devised by the great Cuban World Champion, Capablanca. Black follows the principle: in a cramped position try to exchange pieces to free yourself.

9 B×P   N—Q4!

Now White's QB has no retreat, so ...

10 B×B   Q×B
11 O—O

Completing development.

11 ...   N×N
12 R×N

12 P×N would strengthen the centre, but would also box in the rook.

12 ...   P—K4

The final link in the freeing manoeuvre. The position has occurred many times in master play. After 13 P×P, N×P; 14 N×N, Q×N; 15 P—B4, Q—K5; 16 B—N3 (planning B—B2), 16...B—B4, Black has equal chances. In order to retain the initiative White must play:

13 Q—B2

Now White's bishop points at the traditionally vulnerable Black KB2 square, and his queen points at Black's KR2 square. White has the makings of a powerful assault on Black's king.

13 ...   P×P

(For 13...P—K5 see p. 151)

14 P×P

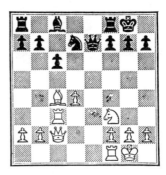

Producing a clear case of a situation where one should voluntarily accept an isolated queen's pawn in order to retain control of key central squares and open lines for the pieces. White has a small advantage here, especially in view of his control of the K file.

One possible continuation which includes a brilliant combination of the type that can actually be learnt by the student is:

14...N—B3; 15 R—K1, Q—Q3; 16 N—N5, B—N5.

16...Q×QP; 17 R—B3, threatening both 18 R×N and 19 Q×RP mate, and 18 N×BP, R×N; 19 R—K7.

17 R—KN3, B—R4; 18 R—KR3, B—N3?. 18...Q—N5! is necessary, and Black can still fight successfully.

19 Q×B!!, P×Q; 20 B×P ch, R×B; 21 R—R8 ch, K×R; 22 N×R ch, K—N1; 23 N×Q, R—Q1; 24 R—K6.

After this brilliant piece of pyrotechnics White has a winning ending.

2...P—QB3

2...P—QB3. The Slav Defence. Black plans to accept the gambit pawn on his own terms and therefore prepares ...P—QN4. However, White can now bring about a symmetrical position in which his extra move gives him the advantage:

3 P×P, P×P; 4 N—QB3, N—QB3;

5 N—B3, N—B3; 6 B—B4, B—B4.

6...P—K3 locks in the QB, but may be a slight improvement.

7 P—K3, P—K3; 8 N—K5!.

Threatening 9 B—QN5, and 9 P—KN4, B—N3; 10 P—KR4, P—R3; 11 N×B, P×N; 12 B—Q3, and Black's position is a wreck.

8...N×N; 9 B×N, B—K2; 10 B—N5 ch.

Black now has problems completing his development.

---

4 P×P

4 P×P. The Exchange Variation. White plans to give Black a majority of pawns on the queen side (Black pawns on QR/QN/QB files against White's QR and QN pawns), and then to rush his own minority (QR and QN pawns) up the board to attack Black's pawn constellation.

Typical play from now on would be:

4...P×P.

As usual 4...N×P; 5 P—K4 is horrible for Black.

5 B—N5, B—K2; 6 P—K3, P—B3; 7 B—Q3, O—O; 8 N—B3, QN—Q2; 9 O—O, R—K1; 10 Q—B2, N—B1.

Black brings his pieces over to the K wing to counter-attack in that sector, while White prosecutes his Q-side advance.

11 QR—N1, N—K5; 12 B×B, Q×B; 13 P—QN4, P—QR3.

Holding up P—N5.

14 P—QR4, N—N3; 15 P—N5, RP× P; 16 P×P, B—N5.

Black has play in the centre and on the K side to compensate for White's Q-side initiative.

An entirely different, but quite playable idea for White in the Exchange Variation is to play 8 KN—K2, and then follow up with Q—B2/O—O/QR—K1/P—KB3/P—K4, attempting to make use of his majority of pawns in the centre.

6...P—KR3

6...P—KR3. This move introduces an idea which was very popular with the former Soviet World Champion, Boris Spassky. Black wants to free his game with ...P—QB4 without allowing himself to be given an isolated QP. This is a more active plan than Capablanca's freeing manoeuvre, but Black still runs the risk of obtaining some weak points in his pawn structure:

7 B—R4, P—QN3.

Oddly, this move does not mean that Black intends to develop his QB on QN2 – it is just played to back up ...P—QB4.

8 P×P, N×P.

Again, Black frees his position by exchanges – it is now possible to capture with the knight at Q4, since White cannot advance his centre pawns quickly (as he could after: 1 P—Q4,

P—Q4; 2 P—QB4, P—K3; 3 N—QB3, N—KB3; 4 P×P, N×P?; 5 P—K4!); e.g., 9 B×B, Q×B; 10 P—K4?, N×N; 11 P×N, B—N2; 12 B—Q3, P—QB4, followed by ...N—B3 and KR—Q1, with a lot of pressure against White's QP.

9 B×B, Q×B; 10 N×N, P×N; 11 R—B1, B—K3; 12 Q—R4, P—QB4; 13 Q—R3.
Pinning Black's QBP.
13...R—B1; 14 B—N5.
Intending to exchange the bishop for Black's knight when it is developed and thus expose Black's QBP to severe pressure from White's pieces.
14...P—QR3; 15 P×P, P×P; 16 O—O.
The advantage is with White, since Black has "hanging pawns" (i.e., an isolated duo of pawns), which White can attack with all his pieces.

This position arose in the sixth game of the 1972 FISCHER–SPASSKY World Championship Match. Fischer, as White, went on to win the game most convincingly.

13...P—K5

13...P—K5. Hoping to block off the action of White's queen towards Black's king. However, after 14 N—Q2, N—B3; 15 R—B1, B—B4; 16 P—QR3, QR—Q1; 17 P—QN4, P—QR3; 18 B—N3, KR—K1; 19 R—B5. White has the advantage, in spite of Black's very well centralized and developed position. In effect, Black has made all the progress he can in this position, while White can push his Q-side pawns forward in a "minority attack" which will be even more deadly if he can support his pawn advance by manoeuvring his knight to K5 (e.g., N(Q2)—B4—K5).

11

NIMZO-INDIAN DEFENCE

1 P—Q4, N—KB3; 2 P—QB4, P—K3; 3 N—QB3, B—N5

One of White's main ambitions in this opening is to establish a powerful pawn-centre behind which he may mass his pieces in tranquillity for attack. After 1 P—Q4, White threatens 2 P—K4, partially achieving his goal; in the previous section we saw Black parrying this threat with the copycat or stonewalling 1...P—Q4. Here 1...N—KB3 achieves the same end, but with piece development instead of pawn movement. After 2 P—QB4, P—K3; 3 N—QB3, White once again threatens the powerful P—K4 and – once more – Black prevents this, with the pin ...B—N5, rather than with the pawn-blockade...P—Q4.

Play against White's K4 square forms one of the leitmotifs of Black's strategy in the Nimzo-Indian Defence, and Black will often reinforce this theme by developing his QB on QN2, pressing against the vital point.

In the long run Black may not be able to prevent White from advancing P—K4, but in compensation he will be able to inflict doubled pawns on his opponent by playing...B×QN. The originator of the Nimzo-Indian Defence, Grandmaster Aron Nimzowitsch, who was a challenger for the World Championship in the late 1920's and early 1930's, was a great expert in handling situations in which he had inflicted a doubled pawn complex on his opponent.

We comment on pages 30–34 on the relative strengths and weaknesses of doubled pawn complexes. Since they arise so frequently in the Nimzo-Indian Defence, three of our four sections will examine situations in which Black creates doubled pawns in White's camp. By studying these, the reader will be able to discern which types of doubled pawn structures favour White and which Black. In the final section (page 162), we look at lines in which White avoids doubled pawns, by protecting his QN with a piece on move four.

Any defence in which Black voluntarily renounces the bishop pair, thereby also creating an unbalanced pawn structure, tends to sharp and dynamic situations in which draws are unlikely. The Nimzo-Indian Defence therefore appeals to positional players who are ambitious to win games as Black against 1 P—Q4.

SÄMISCH VARIATION

1 P—Q4	N—KB3
2 P—QB4	P—K3
3 N—QB3	B—N5
4 P—QR3	

4 . . .	B×N ch
5 P×B	O—O
6 P—K3	P—B4
7 B—Q3	N—B3
8 N—K2	P—QN3
9 P—K4	N—K1!
10 O—O	

---

1 P—Q4	N—KB3
2 P—QB4	P—K3
3 N—QB3	

(For 3 N—KB3 see p. 155)

3 . . .	B—N5
4 P—QR3	

For 4 B—N5 see p. 155)

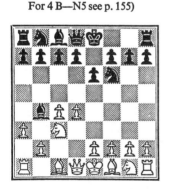

Bringing about the doubled pawn complex in its most extreme form. White forces Black to exchange bishop for knight, reasoning that the doubled pawns will lend his own centre increased resilience.

4 . . .	B×N ch
5 P×B	O—O

Black removes his king from the centre before concentrating his attack on the doubled pawns. This is a sensible precaution in view of the fact that White's central pawns may soon rush forward. Black's king is safer out of the path of their advance.

6 P—K3

Essentially White wants to establish a vast roller of pawns stretching from QB4 to KB4. There are two methods of achieving this desired formation: (*a*) P—K3/B—Q3/P—K4, and then P—KB4, and (*b*) P—KB3/P—K4/B—Q3 and P—B4. Both methods entail the loss of one tempo, either with the KP or KBP. Method (*b*) will be examined in the notes.

(For 6 P—B3 see p. 155)

6 . . .	P—B4

Most important! Black blockades the front QBP in preparation for his assault, which will involve the following moves: . . .N—QB3—QR4/. . .B—QR3/. . .R—QB1 (threatening QBP×QP, discovering an attack on White's QBP) . . .Q—Q2—QR5, or (if Black omits . . .P—Q3), . . .N—K1—Q3. Black's sixth move fixes his target (front White QBP) very firmly in place.

7 B—Q3

7 P×P? is suicidal. The gain of a pawn is temporary. After 7. . .N—R3 and . . .Q—R4, the front tripled pawn falls quickly and White will be left with one of the weaknesses to be avoided at all costs: an isolated doubled pawn on an open file.

7 . . .	N—B3
8 N—K2	

Here, rather than KB3, since White does not want to block the path of his KBP.

8 . . .	P—QN3

Preparing . . .B—R3.

9 P—K4

Threatening B—N5 and P—K5, so Black prevents the pin before it comes.

9 ...   N—K1!

A brilliant move originated by Capablanca. Another method of preventing the aforementioned pin is 9...P—KR3, but that would weaken the pawns in front of Black's king and is therefore best avoided.

There is a further idea behind this retreat of the knight: Black's play is animated by the desire to blockade the position in order to minimize the scope of White's bishops, and halt the advance of White's central pawn avalanche. Thus the way is made clear for the Black KBP to advance to B4, blocking the action of White's KB and obstructing the path of White's KBP. Black will support his blockading pawn on KB4 by means of ...P—KN3 and ...N(K1)—KN2.

In such a closely blockaded situation Black's knights would be fully the equal of White's bishops.

10 O—O

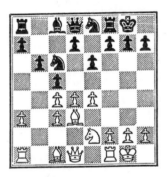

In a sense this represents an ideal position, where both sides have carried out their respective strategies in the most efficient manner possible.

Both Black and White have scored brilliant triumphs from this position, and we give one sample of each in the main text to illustrate the respective strengths and weaknesses of the doubled pawns.

First we have a game where Black is bowled over by the advance of White's KBP, which he carelessly fails to hinder. The second case is a magnificent example of restraint. At no time does Black allow his opponent the ghost of an attacking chance, and White eventually succumbs

in the ending as a result of his pawn weaknesses:

(a) BRONSTEIN–NAJDORF, Budapest 1950:

10...P—Q3; 11 P—B4, B—R3?.

11...P—B4 was essential.

12 P—B5!, P—K4.

Hoping to block the entire position after 13 P—Q5, N—R4; 14 Q—R4, P—B3.

13 P—B6!!.

Brilliant. 13...P×BP; 14 B—R6, N—N2; 15 N—N3, is horrible for Black, while 13...N×BP; 14 B—N5, followed by B×N is equally unpleasant. However, Black cannot long avoid this variation.

13...K—R1.

Ignoring the pawn in the hope that it will go away – but it doesn't.

14 P—Q5, N—R4.

The attack on White's QBP is no longer relevant.

15 N—N3, P×P.

15...N×KBP; 16 B—N5, and N—R5 is even worse.

16 N—B5.

An ideal blockading square for a knight in front of Black's doubled pawns, which have become considerably more of a liability than White's.

16...B—B1; 17 Q—R5, B×N; 18 P×B, R—KN1; 19 R—B3.

Threat: 20 Q×P ch, K×Q; 21 R—R3 ch, K—N2; 22 B—R6 ch, K—R2; 23 B—B8 mate.

19...R—N2; 20 B—R6, R—KN1; 21 R—R3, Resigns.

(b) BOTVINNIK–RESHEVSKY, World Championship Tournament, 1948:

10...B—R3; 11 B—K3, P—Q3; 12 N—N3, N—R4; 13 Q—K2, Q—Q2?!.

Threatening...Q—R5 in some lines and also supporting ...P—B4 by lending extra protection to his own KB4 square.

14 P—B4.

14 P—K5 is stronger, opening a line for his KB.

14...P—B4!; 15 QR—K1, P—N3; 16 R—Q1, Q—KB2.

16...Q—R5; 17 P—Q5 is too risky. Black concentrates on a K-side blockade.

17 P—K5, R—B1.

Incidentally attacking White's QB4.

18 KR—K1, QP×P; 19 QP×P, N—KN2; 20 N—B1, KR—Q1.

If all the major pieces are exchanged, Black will automatically win White's forward QBP.

21 B—KB2, N—R4; 22 B—N3, Q—K1; 23 N—K3, Q—R5 (at last!); 24 Q—R2, N×B; 25 P×N, P—R4.

Paralysing White's second set of doubled pawns.

26 B—K2, K—B2; 27 K—B2, Q—N6; 28 Q×Q, N×Q; 29 B—Q3, K—K2; 30 K—K2, N—R4; 31 R—Q2, R—B2; 32 P—N4, R(B)—Q2.

Black can even ignore White's sacrifice, so strong is his position.

33 P×BP, NP×P; 34 R(K1)—Q1, P—R5; 35 K—K1, N—N6.

What follows is pure desperation by White.

36 N—Q5 ch, P×N; 37 B×P, N×R; 38 R×N, P×P; 39 B×R, R×B; 40 R—KB2, K—K3; 41 R—B3, R—Q6; 42 K—K2, and White resigned.

---

3 N—KB3

3 N—KB3. In this fashion White can avoid the Nimzo-Indian, but Black need not be diverted from his theme of controlling White's K4 square with pieces. To this end he should adopt the **Queen's Indian Defence** 3...P—QN3, bringing his QB to bear on the vital square with the utmost speed. Here is a typical sequence:

3 N—KB3, P—QN3; 4 P—KN3.

To challenge control of the long White diagonal. With 4 N—B3, B—N5, we would be back in a Nimzo-Indian.

4...B—N2; 5 B—N2, B—K2; 6 O—O, O—O; 7 N—B3, N—K5!; 8 Q—B2, N×N; 9 Q×N.

Now Black can choose between 9...P—KB4, followed by...P—Q3, and...N—Q2—KB3, continuing the struggle for White's K4 square, and 9...P—QB4, intending...B—KB3 and...N—QB3, putting pressure on White's pawn centre. Both courses promise Black good chances for an equal game.

---

4 B—N5

4 B—N5. The **Leningrad Variation,** popularized by the Soviet ex-World Champion Boris Spassky. Black's best course is 4...P—KR3; 5 B—R4, P—B4!; 6 P—Q5, B×N ch; 7 P×B, P—Q3, followed by...P—K4, inflicting doubled pawns on White, and blocking the centre quickly to muffle White's bishops.

Black can also play an unclear pawn sacrifice to gain a dangerous central pawn majority: 6...P—QN4; 7 P×KP, BP×P; 8 P×P, P—Q4, but such exciting adventures are not to everyone's taste.

---

6 P—B3

6 P—B3. The alternative method of erecting a huge centre, but it should not prove unduly troublesome to Black:

6...N—K1; 7 P—K4, P—QN3; 8 B—Q3, B—R3.

In this line Black hits hard at White's QB4 with his pieces. Only then does he fix the weakness by means of ...P—QB4.

9 N—K2, N—QB3; 10 N—N3, N—R4.

This procedure should be familiar to the reader by now.

11 Q—K2, N—N6; 12 R—QN1, N×B; 13 R×N, P—QB4.

Black has a fine position. White still is saddled with his doubled pawns, and yet he has shed the bishop pair.

BLACK FIANCHETTOES HIS QB

1 P—Q4	N—KB3
2 P—QB4	P—K3
3 N—QB3	B—N5
4 P—K3	
4 ...	P—QN3
5 B—Q3	B—N2
6 N—B3	N—K5
7 O—O	B×N
8 P×B	P—KB4
9 P—Q5!	N—B4
10 B—R3	QN—R3
11 B—B2	

---

1 P—Q4	N—KB3
2 P—QB4	P—K3
3 N—QB3	B—N5
4 P—K3	

This is the fourth move choice in about

75 per cent of modern Master games with the Nimzo-Indian. White firmly refuses to waste a move (P—QR3) in forcing Black to exchange his KB for knight. 4 P—K3 also prepares normal, classical development with B—Q3, N—B3, O—O. On top of this, White introduces the option of KN—K2, enabling a recapture on QB3 with a piece, thus eschewing any possible disadvantages that might arise from a doubled pawn complex.

4 ...   P—QN3

Black logically continues the fight for White's K4 by developing his QB on QN2.

(For 4...O—O see p. 157)

5 B—Q3

(For 5 KN—K2 see p. 158)

5 ...   B—N2
6 N—B3

6 P—B3 would muffle the range of Black's QB, but would also deprive White's KN of a useful square.

6 ...   N—K5

Taking hold of White's K4, Black hopes with tempo, since this attacks White's QN a second time, and before White can play Q—B2, which would permanently conquer K4 and simultaneously negate the pawn doubling threat to the QN. A playable alternative is 6...O—O; e.g., 7 O—O, P—Q4; or

7 O—O, P—B4; 8 N—QR4, but then Black would have to renounce the strategy of inflicting doubled pawns on White in the QB file.

7 O—O!

A very promising sacrifice of a pawn; acceptance is analysed in the notes, as is the natural protective move 7 Q—B2.

(For 7 Q—B2 see p. 158)

7 ...   B×N

The doubled pawn complex comes into being.

(For 7...N×N see p. 159)

8 P×B   P—KB4

This weakens Black's K wing and deprives the KP of protection, but it does increase control of White's K4 and also supports the knight on that square. Now 9 Q—B2 would transpose into the note on 7 Q—B2, and the only way for White to exploit the dynamic potential of his doubled pawns is to advance them boldly as sacrifices, to open paths for his bishops.

(For 8...N×QBP see p. 159)

9 P—Q5!

If now 9...P×P, then 10 P×P, B×P; 11 P—B4, B—N2; 12 N—Q4, or 12 B—N2, and White's bishops radiate power. Black's best course is to attempt to blockade (hem-in) the dangerous bishops with ...

9 ...   N—B4

but after ...

10 B—R3   QN—R3

Protecting its colleague. If 10...N×B, then 11 Q×N, and Black cannot castle.

11 B—B2

Black's knights are tied in knots and out of play, stranded on the edge of the board. The main trouble with Black's position is that his pieces are directed towards control of White's K4, and not to the restraint of White's doubled pawns, which have become a powerful force in controlling the centre. This suggests that the plan connected with 6...N—K5 and 7...B×N is faulty.

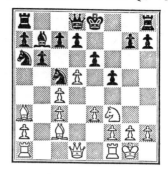

After 11 B—B2, White has exploited to the full the dynamic potential of the doubled pawns and has a considerable advantage in terms of space and open lines for his better placed pieces.

From this position GLIGORIC–CAFFERTY, Teeside 1972, continued:

11...O—O; 12 N—Q4!.

An important centralization, with indirect threats to Black's KBP.

12...R—B3.

Gligoric: "This attack is unsound and merely makes the position more difficult for Black."

13 P—B3, R—R3; 14 Q—K2, Q—B3; 15 QR—K1.

Massed pieces behind the pawn-centre; all according to rule!

15...R—K1; 16 B—B1.

The bishop aims a blow at Black's wandering rook.

16...P—KN4; 17 P—N4.

Smashing open the position for the bishops – a useful principle to follow, if you have the bishop pair!

17...KP×P; 18 N×P, R—N3; 19 P×P, B×P; 20 P—QB4, B—B2; 21 N—Q4, N—N5; 22 B—N1, R—N2; 23 B—N2.

Look at these bishops. It's not worth giving up one of them for a mere rook!

23...Q—Q1; 24 Q—Q2, P—QR4; 25 N—B5, R—N3; 26 Q—Q4, Resigns.

4...O—O

4...O—O. This move is commonly met in tournament play, with the almost invariable continuation: **5 B—Q3, P—**

B4; 6 N—B3, P—Q4; 7 O—O. Although Black has good chances of equality in this line, and interesting positions may occur from the position after move seven, we believe that this treatment for Black shies away from the main issues of the Nimzo-Indian with which we are here concerned, namely, the question of the doubled pawn complex.

The clash of centre pawns after 7 O—O suggests that the tension may soon be cleared completely by exchanges, and dull, level games do frequently result from this sequence. Here is one example (SPASSKY–FISCHER, First game World Championship 1972).

7...N—B3; 8 P—QR3, B—R4; 9 N—K2, QP×P; 10 B×BP, B—N3; 11 P×P, Q×Q; 12 R×Q, B×P; 13 P—QN4, B—K2; 14 B—N2, B—Q2. Equality, since 15 B×N, B×B; 16 R×B fails to 16...B×R.

5 KN—K2

5 KN—K2. A very interesting move. White plans: 6 P—QR3, B×N ch; 7 N×B!. Black can only seek to cross White's strategy by counter-attacking against his QBP with 5...B—R3; e.g., 6 P—QR3, B×N ch; 7 N×B, P—Q4; 8

P—QN3 (8 P×P allows the exchange of one bishop, and White's only advantage here is his bishop pair), 8...O—O 9 B—K2, N—B3!. A purely temporary obstruction of the QBP. Black intends an instant...N—QR4, with active play and unpleasant pressure against White's QBP.

6 N—N3! is a more exciting try, intending B—Q2, followed by P—K4. Black can then win a pawn, but it is very dangerous. 6...B×N ch (now or never); 7 P×B, P—Q4 (challenging White's projected P—K4. Black is not really liquidating White's doubled pawns, since 8 P×P?, B×B; 9 K×B, P×P, would also deprive White of a valuable bishop); 8 B—R3!. The gambit: White has a powerful pawn centre and two bishops as compensation. Furthermore, Black has problems with the position of his king. In the game PORTISCH–FISCHER, World Team Championship 1970, these compensating advantages brought White close to victory after: 8...P×P; 9 P—K4, Q—Q2; 10 B—K2, and White eventually pushed forward his central majority with P—Q5.

7 Q—B2

7 Q—B2. Not good. White wastes a move to cover his knight, and with the extra tempo Black has sufficient time to deal with the doubled pawns.

In the following game Black drums up an attack on the K side which forces the exchange of queens, and then he turns all his attention to the doubled pawns:

7...P—KB4; 8 O—O, B×N; 9 P×B, O—O; 10 N—K1.
Also possible is 10 N—Q2, Q—R5; 11

P—B3; but not 11 R—N1?, N×N; 12 B×N, B×P!!; 13 K×B, Q—N5 ch; 14 K—R1, Q—B6 ch; 15 K—N1, R—B3; 16 KR—B1, R—N3 ch; 17 K—B1, R—N7; 18 B—K1, R×RP, and wins – this is another combination of the type that can be learnt, since the required positional contours for its execution often arise.

10...Q—R5; 11 P—B3, N—KB3; 12 Q—B2, Q×Q ch; 13 R×Q, P—B4.

Black's play from now on is a model exploitation of the doubled pawn complex.

14 R—N2, B—R3; 15 N—B2, N—B3; 16 N—R3, KR—B1; 17 B—B1, N—QR4; 18 R—QB2, N—K1; 19 B—N2, R—B2.

Intending to double rooks on the QB file and then play...P×P.

20 R—Q1, N—Q3; 21 P×P, N(3)×P; 22 R—Q4, N×N; 23 B×N, B×B; 24 P×P, P×P; 25 B—Q6, R—B3; 26 Resigns (POLLAK–KEENE, Student Match, Erlangen 1968).

7...N×N

7...N×N. Accepting the pawn sacrifice here, or on the subsequent move, is extremely hazardous. In general, master players tend not to accept pawn-sacrifices that grant the opponent a prolonged initiative, as in this case: 8 P×N, B×P; 9 R—N1; now...O—O; 10 Q—B2 is worrying, and meanwhile White threatens B—R3. The only safe square for Black's KB is QR4, but there it is woefully out of play. We must conclude that the increased activity of White's

pieces represents ample compensation for the pawn.

8...N×QBP

8...N×QBP. This was once thought to be good enough for a draw, but a game between Keres and Spassky played in 1965 in a World Championship eliminating match changed that opinion. Keres demonstrated convincingly that White's two bishops, mobile pawns, and open lines for the rooks, are more than sufficient compensation for the loss of even two pawns:

9 Q—B2, B×N.

Otherwise the knight is lost.

10 P×B, Q—N4 ch; 11 K—R1, Q—R4.

Hoping for...Q×BP ch, with a draw.

12 R—KN1!, Q×BP ch; 13 R—N2, P—KB4.

To rescue the knight. 14 Q×N?, Q—Q8 ch is still a draw.

14 B—R3, N—K5; 15 R—KB1, R—N1; 16 B—K2, Q—R6; 17 P—B3, N—KB3; 18 P—Q5!.

Opening lines at all costs for the bishops. Bishops hate closed and blocked positions. They feel flattered if their own pawns lay down their lives for the benefit of their superior clergy.

18...K—B2; 19 P—K4, P—B4; 20 B—N2, P—B5; 21 P—K5, N—R4; 22 K—N1, P—N3; 23 R—N4, R—Q1; 24 B—Q3, R—N1.

B×P ch is threatened.

25 R—B2, Resigns.

The White KB is about to show his gratitude by trapping Black's queen (26 B—KB1).

HÜBNER'S VARIATION

1 P—Q4	N—KB3
2 P—QB4	P—K3
3 N—QB3	B—N5
4 P—K3	P—B4
5 B—Q3	N—B3
6 N—B3	B×N ch
7 P×B	P—Q3
8 P—K4	P—K4
9 P—Q5	N—K2
10 N—R4	P—KR3
11 P—B4!	N—N3
12 N×N	P×N

---

1 P—Q4	N—KB3
2 P—QB4	P—K3
3 N—QB3	B—N5
4 P—K3	P—B4

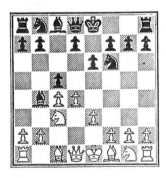

Angling for White to play P—QR3, when Black could revert to a Sämisch with White's QB pawns already blockaded. But what if White refuses to oblige?

5 B—Q3

(For 5 KN—K2 see p. 161)

5 . . .	N—B3
6 N—B3	B×N ch

The alternative is 6...O—O and ...P—Q4, which we mentioned in the section dealing with 4...P—QN3 (p. 156). With the text, Black surrenders a tempo to inflict White with doubled pawns, but in view of the missing tempo (White has not expended a move with P—QR3 to force ...B×N ch as in the Sämisch), it is here too risky for Black to attack White's QBP with ...N—QR4. Therefore Black chooses a different plan, involving the transfer of his QN to the K side. This plan is a great favourite with the young West German Grandmaster, Hübner.

7 P×B   P—Q3

Black prepares to block the centre with 8...P—K4 to minimize the scope of White's bishop pair. You must keep the position closed if your opponent has two bishops against two knights or bishop and knight. Conversely, if you possess the bishop pair, you must seek to open the position even at the cost of a pawn sacrifice.

8 P—K4

(For 8 O—O see p. 161)

8 . . .   P—K4
9 P—Q5

Of course, it would be a major positional crime to play 9 P×BP or 9 P×KP. White's isolated, doubled QB pawns would be hopelessly exposed, and White could never manoeuvre a knight to Q5 to shield their weakness; e.g., 9 P×BP, P×P; 10 Q—B2, B—K3!; 11 N—Q2, N—QR4, and White has not enough time to play N—B1—K3—Q5 (analysis by Gligoric).

9 . . .   N—K2

Now Black threatens to implement a dangerous K-side attack with ...P—KR3, ...P—KN4, and ...N—N3, so White must take measures to prevent this.

10 N—R4!   P—KR3

Preparing for ...P—KN4. Not 10

...N—N3, because 11 N—B5 is good for White.

11 P—B4

Hoping that Black will fall for the very plausible attempt to win material by 11...P×P; 12 B×P, P—KN4; but then comes 13 P—K5! with a powerful attack. (For 11 P—B3 see p. 162)

11 ...   N—N3!

A brilliant riposte, which wipes out White's play on the KB file. Furthermore, it eliminates White's most aggressively placed piece, since 12 N—B5 fails to 12...B×N; 13 P×B, N×BP.

12 N×N   P×N

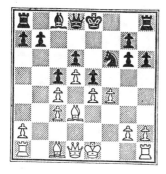

Black has at least an equal game. White's bishops are not very impressive and his doubled pawns are more vulnerable than Black's. The Yugoslav Grandmaster Gligoric made the following assessment of the position after twelve moves: "The position is blocked and White simply has nothing. Black can easily defend his weak spots, while White's are not less in number."

SPASSKY–FISCHER, World Championship 1972, saw Black exploiting White's pawn weaknesses in most efficient fashion:

13 P×P, P×P; 14 B—K3, P—N3; 15 O—O, O—O; 16 P—QR4, P—QR4; 17 R—N1, B—Q2; 18 R—N2, R—N1; 19 R(2)—KB2, Q—K2; 20 B—B2, P—KN4; 21 B—Q2, Q—K1; 22 B—K1, Q—N3; 23 Q—Q3, N—R4; 24 R×

R ch, R×R; 25 R×R ch, K×R; 26 B—Q1, N—B5; 27 Q—B2?, B×P!; 28 Resigns (28 Q×B, Q×P is fatal).

5 KN—K2

5 KN—K2. White thus avoids doubled pawns, but this move locks in the KB. With 5...P×P; 6 P×P, P—Q4, Black assures himself of a foothold in the centre and an easy development.

Equally, 5...P×P; 6 P×P, O—O is not bad, and Black has no problems in completing mobilization, while White still cannot develop his KB.

8 O—O

8 O—O. If White avoids P—K4 and P—Q5, it is hard to see a plan for him; e.g., 8 O—O, P—K4; 9 Q—B2, O—O, and White has advanced very little. Meanwhile Black threatens to push forward in the centre with ...R—K1 and ...P—K5.

11 P—B3

11 P—B3. If White plays 11 P—B3, there follows **11...P—KN4!; 12 N—B5, B×N; 13 P×B, Q—R4,** and Black has succeeded in making the position a very closed one, in which White's bishops no longer constitute any danger to Black. The chances are approximately equal.

WHITE AVOIDS DOUBLED PAWNS

1	P—Q4	N—KB3
2	P—QB4	P—K3
3	N—QB3	B—N5
4	Q—B2	

4	...	O—O
5	P—QR3	B×N ch
6	Q×B	P—QN3
7	B—N5	B—N2
8	P—K3	P—Q3
9	P—B3	QN—Q2
10	B—Q3	P—B4
11	N—K2	R—B1

1	P—Q4	N—KB3
2	P—QB4	P—K3
3	N—QB3	B—N5
4	Q—B2	

The only method of avoiding doubled pawns that is current in Master play. (Other moves to prevent the doubling of the QB pawns are very insipid – see pp. 163–4 for 4 B—Q2, 4 Q—Q3 and 4 Q—N3.) Theoretically White's idea (to obtain the bishop pair without allowing his QB pawns to be doubled) is very sound, but the time consumed by White's queen in travelling from Q1 to QB3 in the opening gives Black plenty of counterplay. Fourth move alternatives

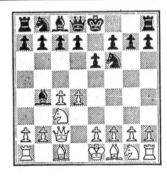

with similar objectives are examined in the notes.

4 ...   O—O

A sensible reaction, since castling on the Q side is not likely to come into consideration.

(For 4...P—B4, 4...P—Q4, 4...N—B3 see p. 164)

5 P—QR3

White could try to rush forward into the centre with 5 P—K4, but this would fail to a typical combination: 5...P—B4!; 6 P—Q5 (6 P—K5?, P×P); 6...P×P; 7 BP×P, N×KP!; 8 Q×N, R—K1, and Black wins. 7 KP×P, R—K1 ch is also good for Black.

5 ...   B×N ch

If 5...B—K2, White would indeed

play 6 P—K4, and Black would be crushed by White's centre.

6 Q×B   P—QN3

As so often in this defence, Black piles up on White's K4 square to prevent the formation of a massive White pawn centre.

7 B—N5

Pinning the KN to reduce Black's piece influence on K4.

7 . . .   B—N2
8 P—K3

A normal move to complete development.

8 . . .   P—Q3
9 P—B3

White is prepared to sacrifice the development of his KN on its best square in order to assert his control over K4, but this cedes Black more time to complete his own mobilization.

9 . . .   QN—Q2

Supporting his KN so that the queen can move. Black certainly does not want to allow his own KB pawns to be doubled.

10 B—Q3   P—B4

While White is still bringing out his pieces, Black is already in a position to attack White's pawn centre. The plan associated with 4 Q—B2 is too artificial and insufficiently sharp to be of any real concern to Black.

11 N—K2   R—B1

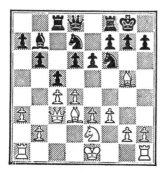

Black concentrates his fire on White's QBP. He has easy development and a ready-made plan to compensate for White's bishops. A game between two leading English players from the 1971 British Championship continued:

12 O—O, P—KR3; 13 B—R4, B—R3.
One more piece on the QBP. White must do something about this.

14 P—Q5, N—K4; 15 P—K4, N×B; 16 Q×N, P—K4.
Complete equality. The position is blocked and White no longer has the two bishops. A draw was soon agreed. (WHITELY–CAFFERTY, Blackpool 1971)

---

4 B—Q2

4 B—Q2. Black now obtains good chances with 4...P—QN3, reaching a position from Variation 2 (Q-side fianchetto by Black), in which White has the useless move B—Q2 – useless, because after; e.g., 4 B—Q2, P—QN3; 5 P—QR3, B×N; 6 B×B, Black could even play 6...N—K5, and White doesn't keep his bishops after all.

---

4 Q—Q3

4 Q—Q3. Contravenes the principle concerning early development of the queen. Well, so does 4 Q—B2, but on Q3 the queen also robs the White KB of its best square. After 4...P—Q4 White's position is already beginning to look rather silly. Black will certainly gain more development time by attacking White's queen (e.g.,...P—QN3,...B—R3).

4 Q—N3

4 Q—N3. Not as bad as the two previously examined alternatives. But on N3 the queen is very exposed to attack from Black's minor pieces. Here is one example:

4...P—B4; 5 P×P, N—B3; 6 N—B3, N—K5; 7 B—Q2, N×QBP; 8 Q—B2. One tempo lost, and Black's knight on QB4 is well placed.

8...P—B4; 9 P—K3, O—O; 10 B—K2, P—QN3; 11 O—O—O, P—QR4!.

Black has a good attack, with all his minor pieces clustered near White's king. (BOGOLYUBOV–NIMZOWITSCH, San Remo 1930.)

4...P—B4, 4...P—Q4, 4...N—B3

On move four, Black has a very large choice of playable alternatives; e.g., 4...P—B4 or 4...P—Q4 (meeting 5 Q—R4 ch with ...N—B3, and White has wasted time with his queen), or even 4...N—B3 blocking the QBP and planning ...P—Q3 and ...P—K4. It is sufficient for the reader to note that theory considers all of these moves to be fully adequate for Black, which suggests that 4 Q—B2 is really not very terrifying. However, we regard the move 4...O—O, given in the main text, to be best of all for Black at move four.

12

KING'S INDIAN DEFENCE

1 P—Q4, N—KB3; 2 P—QB4, P—KN3; 3 N—QB3, B—N2;

This defence goes one step further even than the Nimzo-Indian Defence and allows White to form his cherished pawn centre virtually unchallenged, in the belief that this centre is not really so terrible for Black after all.

In the late 19th and early 20th century, a Master player would consider that he had virtually a winning game if he could establish pawns unchallenged on QB4, Q4, and K4 in the opening stages. But in the 1920's and 30's such views were overturned by the so-called "Hypermodern" masters (Nimzowitsch, Réti, Breyer), who demonstrated that a massive pawn centre can also contain the germs of defeat, since it is exposed to counter thrusts by the opponent's pawns which have been deliberately held back. The King's Indian Defence belongs to this category and was finally elaborated in the 1940's and 1950's by Soviet Grandmasters, notably Boleslavsky and Bronstein. Since then it has occupied a respectable position in the repertoire of every leading Grandmaster.

The King's Indian Defence is a sharp opening, with many tactical chances and surprise blows available to both sides. It is considerably more risky than the Queen's Gambit Declined or Nimzo-Indian and its appeal is to players who prefer tactically sharp positions, with good possibilities of attacks on the kings of both players, and who don't object to their fair share of interesting wins and losses.

Black's strategy is based on a delayed attack on the White centre, by ...P—QB4, inviting P—Q5, when Black will undermine White's centre by means of the thrusts ...P—K3 and ...P—QN4. Alternatively Black may play ...P—K4 (instead of ...P—QB4) and, if White gains space with P—Q5, Black can move his KN to K1 or KR4 and commence a K-side advance with ...P—KB4. Such an attack, with ...P—KB4 – KB5 and ...P—KN4, can often turn out to be an automatic winner for Black if White has castled K side.

In our first section we take a look at the misfortunes that can befall White if he occupies the centre on megalomaniac proportions with pawns stretching from QB4 via Q4 and K4 to KB4. In subsequent sections we analyze systems for White that concentrate on cementing his already existing central territorial conquests.

CLASSICAL VARIATION

1 P—Q4	N—KB3
2 P—QB4	P—KN3
3 N—QB3	B—N2
4 P—K4	P—Q3
5 B—K2	
5 . . .	O—O
6 N—B3	P—K4
7 O—O	QN—Q2
8 P—Q5	N—B4
9 Q—B2	P—QR4

1 P—Q4	N—KB3
2 P—QB4	P—KN3

(For 2. . .P—QB4 see p. 167).

In this section devoted to the King's Indian Defence we feel that we should also give a brief mention to the two important sub-divisions of the King's Indian Defence, which in modern tournament practice have blossomed into fully fledged opening systems in their own right. We refer to the Benoni (see p. 167) and the Grünfeld (see p. 168). Although we have not elected to use these openings as illustrations of the strategic principles of opening play, the reader should know of them. In each one we will restrict our treatment to the suggestion of one reliable line for White.

3 N—QB3	B—N2

(For 3. . .P—Q4 see p. 168)

4 P—K4	P—Q3
5 B—K2	

The hallmark of the Classical system. White develops his pieces rapidly on good central squares. With 5 B—K2 White intends O—O as quickly as possible, followed by an advance of his Q-side pawns. 5 B—Q3 is less good. There is no chance of a K-side attack involving the KB, and on Q3 it would be exposed to attack if Black's QN reached . . .QB4.

5 . . .	O—O
6 N—B3	P—K4

Almost universally chosen here. Black hopes for White to play P—Q5, stabilizing the centre, when Black will move his KN and advance his KBP, setting in motion the well-known K-side pawn avalanche. Development by 6. . .N—B3 is out of place. After 7 P—Q5 the QN has no useful escape square. However, 6. . .P—B4 is reasonable; e.g., 7 P—Q5, P—K3, reaching a type of Benoni position.

7 O—O

Acceptance of Black's pawn offer achieves nothing. This is analysed in the note. 7 B—K3 is possible here, and this natural developing move is a favourite of the American Grandmaster Reshevsky. Normally such a move would be inferior in view of 7. . .N—N5, but here White could move his bishop, with tempo, on Black's queen: 8 B—N5, P—KB3; 9 B—R4, with equal chances.

(For 7 P × P see p. 168)

7 . . .	QN—Q2

Supporting the KP and also preparing 8. . .P × P; 9 N × P, N—B4, and . . .R—K1, pressurizing White's KP. Therefore White disarms this threat.

(For 7. . .N—B3 see p. 168)

8 P—Q5	N—B4

The knight comes to a good central

square with gain of tempo. White must now protect his KP with . . .

(For 8. . .N—R4 see p. 169)

9 Q—B2

. . . which gives Black time to safeguard the position of his QN:

9 . . .   **P—QR4**

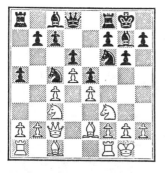

If Black did not play this, White would play P—QN4, chasing away Black's knight, and gaining space on the Q side. It would then be easy for White to arrange to play P—QB5; e.g., by placing his QB on QR3 and a rook on QB1. White would then be all set to invade Black's Q side with P(QB5)×QP, followed by N—QN5 and Q—B7. Black's undefended QP would be a target for White's pieces.

In this position Black is all ready to move his KN and play . . .P—KB4, which would be unpleasant for White. White has no choice but to go in for the following manoeuvre, which has occurred many times in Master play:

10 B—N5.

Pinning the KN.

10. . .P—KR3 .

Black has to break the pin.

11 B—K3, N—N5.

De-obstructing the KBP with gain of tempo on White's QB.

12 B×N!.

Normally it is very bad to give bishop for knight like this in the King's Indian Defence, since White needs his QB to protect the dark squares, but here there are some exceptional tactical points.

12. . .P×B; 13 P—KR3!, N—B3.

Where else? Black deprived his KN of

a possible retreat to KR3 when he broke the pin on move ten.

14 N×P, N×QP.

Discovering an attack on White's knight. This is the only way to regain the pawn.

15 BP×N!.

Capturing towards the centre.

15. . .B×N; 16 P—B4, B—Q5 ch; 17 K—R2.

As compensation for Black's bishop pair White has a very powerful centre, which can be supported by B—B4 and QR—K1. We slightly prefer White's chances, but a powerful argument for the other side is that Fischer has played such a position with success for Black.

---

2. . .P—QB4

2. . .P—QB4. The **Benoni.** White gains space in the centre with **3 P—Q5** and Black challenges White's QP with **3. . .P—K3.** After **4 N—QB3, P×P; 5 P×P, P—Q3; 6 P—K4, P—KN3,** a very sharp position has arisen, which was a favourite (as Black) with the brilliant Latvian, Tal. White has a central pawn majority and free development, but Black can attack White's KP with a rook on the open K file and he can also use his fianchettoed KB to support a dangerous advance of his own Q-side pawns. Here we recommend for White a solid, but aggressive system: **7 B—Q3, B—N2; 8 KN—K2, O—O; 9 O—O,** and White will follow up with P—KB4, Q—B3, B—Q2, QR—K1, etc., aiming for P—K5. In fact, this was the system used by Penrose of England, when he defeated Tal in the 1960 World Team Championships.

3...P—Q4

3...P—Q4. Grünfeld's Defence, to which we alluded in our introduction. There we pointed out that the natural line 4 P×P, N×P; 5 P—K4, N×N; 6 P×N, is not as strong as it looks, since White's centre is exposed to a powerful counter-attack from Black's pieces. A rather uncommon but good alternative for White is **4 B—N5!**, putting immediate pressure on Black's QP. After 4...P×P; 5 P—K4, White has a fine position, while 4...B—N2?; 5 B×N!, followed by 6 P×P, wins Black's QP for nothing. Another way of losing at once is 4...P—B3?; 5 B×N!, P×B; 6 P×P, P×P; 7 Q—N3, and White wins a pawn for no compensation. Best is 4...N—K5!.

Here is a typical continuation from Master play: **5 B—R4, N×N; 6 P×N, P—QB4; 7 P—K3, B—N2; 8 P×QP, Q×P; 9 N—B3, P×P; 10 KP×P, N—B3; 11 B—K2, O—O; 12 O—O.** (GLIGORIC–DUEBALL, Berlin 1971). White has hanging pawns, but they are mobile, and can advance to attack Black's pieces. Also White has pressure on Black's KP plus good files for his rooks (QN and K). We conclude that White has a small advantage.

7 P×P

7 P×P. This gets White nowhere: 7...P×P; 8 Q×Q, R×Q; 9 N×P, N×P!, discovering an attack on White's knight and bringing Black's KB to vigorous life.

After 7 P×P, P×P, White can hardly

avoid this continuation, since he has a hole on his Q4 square (which Black could try to occupy with the manoeuvre: ...Q—K2 ...R—Q1 ...QN—Q2—QB4—K3—Q5), while Black can protect *his* Q4 by means of...P—QB3.

7...N—B3

7...N—B3. A popular alternative to 7...QN—Q2. We give one example of it here as an illustration of the vital importance of a major King's Indian theme: the K-side pawn avalanche, which can be an automatic winner if it is successfully set in motion. We follow the game SZABO–SPASSKY, from the international tournament at Bucharest in 1953.

8 P—Q5, N—K2; 9 N—K1.
9 N—Q2!; 9 B—Q2!; 9 P—QN4! are very good alternatives; they all intend a Q-side advance with P—QN4 and P—QB5, which is the basis of White's strategy in this line.

9...N—Q2.
Freeing the KBP for its advance.
10 B—K3?.
Now when Black plays...P—KB5, as he surely will, it gains a tempo by attacking the QB. 10 N—Q3 was best.

10...P—KB4; 11 P—B3, P—B5!.
Very important. The pawn on KB5 acts like a brick wall preventing White from bringing over defensive pieces to the aid of his king. Black will then rush his KNP and KRP up the board to open lines for his pieces on to White's unfortunate monarch.

12 B—B2, P—KN4.
The avalanche begins to slide.

13 P—QN4, R—B3; 14 N—Q3, R—N3; 15 P—B5, N—KB3, 16 Q—N3, K—R1.
It is normally good to move your king off the same diagonal as your opponent's queen.

17 KR—B1, P—N5; 18 KBP×P, B×P; 19 B—B1, B—B6; 20 Q—B4, B×NP!; 21 B×B, P—B6; 22 N—K1, P×B; 23 N×P, B—R3; 24 R—B2, Q—KN1.
White's king no longer has any shelter.

25 B—N3, R×B!.
Winning a piece, since 26 P×R, Q×NP leaves White helpless against the threat of ...N—N5. White resigned after another four moves.

26 P×P, P×P; 27 Q—B7, R—N2; 28 Q×QP, N—N5; 29 K—R1, R—Q1.

8...N—R4

234

8...N—R4. Threatening ...N—B5 and ...P—KB4, but this is too crude an implementation of Black's strategic idea. After 9 P—KN3 (preventing ...N—B5); **9...P—KB4; 10 P×P!, R×P; 11 N—K4,** White has gained control of the ideal blockading square K4 with a piece, which can never be challenged by Black pawns. This blockade of Black's KP shuts Black's KB out of play for ever. It is a "bad bishop" in an extreme sense.

10...P×P is positionally superior, since it controls White's K4 and stifles any blockade possibility; but after 11 N—KN5!, threatening B×N and N—K6, Black loses material.

Black must always be alert to such light square accidents in the King's Indian Defence.

FOUR PAWNS ATTACK

1 P—Q4	N—KB3
2 P—QB4	P—KN3
3 N—QB3	B—N2
4 P—K4	P—Q3
5 P—B4	
5 ...	O—O
6 B—K2	P—B4!
7 P—Q5	P—K3

8 N—B3	P×P
9 BP×P	
1 P—Q4	N—KB3
2 P—QB4	P—KN3
3 N—QB3	B—N2
4 P—K4	P—Q3
5 P—B4	

White takes the opportunity, granted by Black's opening moves, to occupy the centre with pawns in the most extreme fashion possible. In the early days of the King's Indian Defence such a territorial conquest by White would have been considered nearly decisive, but now we recognize that White's broad pawn centre contains weaknesses. In particular the move P—KB4 weakens the squares around White's king. Black can assault White's distended centre with ...P—QB4, luring forward White's QP, and then commence undermining operations with ...P—K3 and ...P—QN4.

The Four Pawns Attack is no longer very popular in Master play, but we analyse it here to show that such a broad pawn centre can be rendered innocuous by accurate defensive play on Black's part.

5 ...　　　　　O—O
6 B—K2

White prefers to develop his KB before his KN, since after 6 N—B3 Black could play ...B—N5 followed by ...N—QB3 putting pressure from his pieces on White's Q4 square. This motif will be examined in greater depth in our treatment of the Austrian Attack in the chapter on the Modern Defence.

6 ...　　　　　P—B4!

This strikes at White's QP in the approved fashion. If White now plays 7 P×P, there comes ...Q—R4 with the threat of ...N×KP and Black's excellent development gives him an excellent position. White's safest course is to claim some territory in the centre with ...

7 P—Q5

(For 7 N—B3 see p. 171)

7 ...　　　　　P—K3

The undermining operations commence. If White now plays 8 P×P, hoping to inflict a weak backward QP on his opponent, Black replies ...B×P, followed by ...N—QB3, with rapid development and the possibility of attacking White's KP on the half-open K file. It is better for White to attempt to keep the position closed while he lags in development.

8 N—B3

Sensibly attempting to complete his development.

8 ...　　　　　P×P
9 BP×P

(For 9 KP×P see p. 171)

With this move White attempts to maintain a mobile majority of pawns in the centre. The alternative recapture 9 KP×P is examined in the note. In this position Black has available a very useful tactical device, which is typical of play in such positions against an extended White pawn centre.

Black plays 9...P—QN4, threatening ...P—N5, attacking White's QN and thus allowing Black to capture White's KP free of charge. 9...P—QN4 looks absurd because the pawn is twice en prise, but it is hardly feasible for White to capture. After 10 N×P, Black simply captures White's KP; after 10 B×P, there follows the neat combination 10...N×KP; 11 N×N, Q—R4 ch; 12

K—B2 (if 12 N—B3, then B×N ch; 13 P×B, Q×B, and White's position is a wreck); 12...Q×B; 13 N×QP, Q—R3; 14 N×B, R×N, and Black has sufficient counterplay for his pawn in view of White's ragged position and the exposure of his king.

White does better on move ten to decline the pawn sacrifice, and push forward in the centre with his pawn majority; so he should play 10 P—K5, P×P; 11 P×P; but after 11...N—N5, Black's counter-attack against White's KP would prove more than sufficient to hold the balance for him.

This is a complicated position on which much analysis has been lavished, and it would require a book of specific analysis, rather than a treatise on general principles, to unravel all its secrets. The complicated lines commence after 12 B—N5, Q—N3, but Black also has available – and this is the move we recommend – 12...P—B3; 13 P×P, B×P; 14 B×B, Q×B, with a sound position and some play on the dark squares; in particular White's K3 square is very weak. This line is positionally correct and there is no necessity for the reader at this stage to trouble himself with the complex "theoretical line."

---

7 N—B3

7 N—B3. This move is not uncommon. White hopes for 7...P×P; 8 N×P, transposing into a sort of anti-Sicilian "bind position." But now Black has available a powerful move which underlines the exposed nature of White's centre in the Four Pawns Attack:

8...B—N5!.
If now 9 B×B, then N×B; 10 Q×N, B×N, and Black's bishop, entrenched on White's Q4, is most unpleasant for White. The bishop can be supported by ...N—B3, and meanwhile Black threatens to double White's QB pawns. On top of this, the bishop prevents White from castling.

If 9 B×B, N×B; 10 P—KR3, Black can counter-attack with ...Q—N3; e.g., 11 N—Q5, Q×N; 12 N×P ch, K—R1; 13 Q×Q, B×Q; 14 P×N, R—K1; 15 N—Q5, R×P ch, and White's pawns are rather weak.

Finally, 9 B—K3, Q—B1!; 10 O—O, B×B; 11 Q×B, N—N5 (catching White's QB), is quite good for Black.

---

9 KP×P

9 KP×P. This renounces White's ambition of surging forwards with his centre pawns. Black exploits the vacuum that has been created in the centre with 9...N—R4!; 10 O—O, B×N; 11 P×B, N—N2, with a position reminiscent of the Nimzo-Indian, where White has doubled QB pawns. If Black's knight reaches KB4 it will blockade White's position and render his bishops virtually useless. White could lift the blockade by playing the immediate 12 P—B5, but the pawn-sacrifice does not look sound.

White can hardly avoid doubled pawns after 9...N—R4; e.g., 10 Q—N3, R—K1; or 10 Q—B2, B—B4; or 10 Q—Q2, R—K1 – in each case White wastes time with his queen, while Black's development proceeds apace. Black's control of the K file is especially valuable.

FIANCHETTO VARIATION

1 P—Q4	N—KB3
2 P—QB4	P—KN3
3 N—KB3	B—N2
4 P—KN3	

4 . . .	O—O
5 B—N2	P—Q3
6 O—O	QN—Q2
7 N—B3	P—K4
8 P—K4	P—B3
9 P—KR3	Q—N3
10 P—Q5	

1 P—Q4	N—KB3
2 P—QB4	P—KN3
3 N—KB3	B—N2
4 P—KN3	

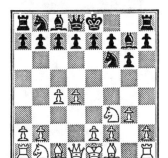

This is a highly positional line that suggests a cautious attitude on White's part. He prepares for O—O with great speed, and forgoes the immediate construction of a pawn centre. Only after White has developed his pieces will he attempt to take control of the central zone with his pawns.

4 . . .	O—O
5 B—N2	P—Q3
6 O—O	QN—Q2

Black prepares to strike out in the centre with P—K4.

(For 6...P—B4 and 6...N—B3 see pp. 173—4)

7 N—B3

Developing a piece, controlling K4, and preparing to advance the KP.

7 . . .   **P—K4**

Black intends a manoeuvre like ...R—K1 followed by ...P—QB3. Black would then be in a position to advance in the centre and claim some valuable territory with ...P—K5. White cannot allow this.

8 P—K4   **P—B3**

Now Black's strategy is to attack White's QP in the hope of forcing P—Q5 stabilizing the centre. After this, Black will as usual move his KN, and then advance his KBP with a traditional Black K-side King's Indian attack operation. Of course Black wishes to avoid if possible ...KP × P, since this would grant White control of the centre with his pieces.

9 P—KR3

White wants to develop his QB on K3, but if he were to play this now Black would reply ...N—N5, a very familiar motif, which in this case is most embarrassing for White.

9 . . .   **Q—N3**

Putting more pressure on White's QP. White now disarms this pressure with:

(For 9...P × P see p. 174)

10 P—Q5

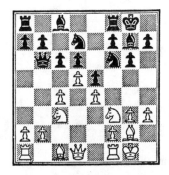

It would be wrong to play 10 P×P, P×P, since White would have a hole on his own Q4 square, while Black's Q4 is guarded by his pawn on QB3.

After 10 P—Q5, Black's best is to blockade the centre with 10...P—B4, after which he can prepare his flanking blow...P—KB4. Meanwhile White will attempt to advance with P—QR3, R—QN1 and P—QN4. The chances in this position are about equal.

Less good is 10...N—B4, since after 11 R—K1 (protecting the KP); 11...B—Q2 comes 12 R—N1. The centre is still fluid and therefore it is difficult for Black to arrange to play ...P—KB4 in safety. Moreover, White has the possibility of playing P—QN4 more or less unimpeded, since Black has a knight rather than a pawn on his QB4 square.

We now follow the game KEENE-PENROSE, English Counties Championship 1970, which illustrates one of the most important positional themes in the King's Indian Defence, to wit, the power of a White knight established on its own K4 square, blocking in Black's KB, which is impeded by its own KP. In Master chess such an advantage would be considered of nearly decisive proportion. The game continued:

12...P×P; 13 BP×P, P—QR4; 14 B—B1, KR—B1; 15 B—K3, Q—Q1; 16 N—Q2, N—K1.

At last Black sets out to play...P—KB4.

17 P—QR4.

A very important move. White plans to play B—QN5, swopping off the light-squared bishops, when he will have complete control of the light squares.

17...P—B4; 18 N—B4, P×P; 19 B×N, R×B; 20 N×P(K4), R—B2; 21 N—N6.

21 N(K4)×QP, N×N; 22 N×N, B×QRP, and White has got nowhere.

21...R—N1; 22 N×B, R×N; 23 B—N5, R—K2; 24 B×N, R×B.

Now White has the strategically winning position we mentioned in the preliminary note to this game. He can open lines for his rooks against Black's pawn weaknesses, and Black's KB is powerless to help. The White knight on K4 dominates the board.

25 P—QN4, P×P; 26 R×P, R—K2; 27 Q—N3, R—Q2; 28 R—N6, Q—

K2; 29 R—N1, R—R1; 30 R×NP, R×R; 31 Q×R, Q×Q; 32 R×Q, R×P; 33 R—N8 ch, B—B1; 34 N—N5, R—R2; 35 N—K6, R—KB2; 36 K—B1, R—B3; 37 K—K2, R—B2; 38 R—Q8, R—B3; 39 K—K3, R—B2; 40 P—B3, R—B3; 41 K—K4, P—R4; 42 P—R4, R—B2; 43 K—K3, Resigns.

White can win any time he pleases with N×B, followed by R×QP. Alternatively, he can play P—B4 and then move his king to QB6. At this point he can liquidate all the pieces on Black's KB1 and play K×QP with a winning king and pawn ending. Note how White's knight moving on the light squares, dominated Black's KB throughout the entire game.

6...P—B4

6...P—B4. This is a common device in the King's Indian Defence. Black strikes at White's QP in the hope of maximizing the range of his KB. After the stock space-gaining response, 7 P—Q5, Black relies for his counterplay on a flanking assault against White's centre with ...P—QN4. 7...N—R3 (developing a knight on the edge, but it is coming to QB2 to support the Q-side thrust); 8 N—B3, N—B2; 9 P—QR4 (clamping down on ...P—QN4), 9...R—N1; 10 B—B4, P—QR3, and White cannot really prevent ...P—QN4 for much longer; but after 11 P—K4 (planning P—K5), White's possibilities of advancing in the centre grant him some edge over Black's demonstration on the Q side.

6. . .N—B3

6. . .N—B3. A popular plan known as the Panno system, after its inventor, the Argentine Grandmaster, Oscar Panno. Black plans . . .P—QR3 and . . .P—QN4. The Black QBP is only temporarily obstructed, since Black's knight aims for QR4 to pressurize White's QBP. However, White maintains a small plus as follows: 7 N—B3, P—QR3; 8 P—Q5!, N—QR4; 9 N—Q2, P—B4; 10 Q—B2, R—N1; 11 P—N3, P—QN4; 12 B—N2, and White's QBP is adequately protected. White can also counter Black's pressure in the QN file with QR—N1.

A major defect of Black's set-up is the off-side position of his QN. White may steamroller through the centre with P—K4—K5 while Black's QN looks on, a forlorn spectator. 11 P—N3 is a vital link in White's scheme. Not only does it lend much needed protection to the QBP, it also prepares to fianchetto White's QB, thus challenging the power of Black's KB. If ever these dark-squared bishops are exchanged, the defences of Black's king will be sorely depleted.

After Black has played . . .P—QN4, White must never go in for QBP×QNP. This would hand Black a compact central pawn majority, and also deprive the White QP of a considerable portion of its support.

9. . .P×P

9. . .P×P. Weak. Black hopes to attack White's KP, but it is well protected by White's fianchettoed KB. Giving up the centre in this fashion is a positional error. After 10 N×P, N—B4; 11 B—B4!, Black's QP, backward and exposed on an open file, is already a serious and accessible weakness, while White's KP can be protected easily enough (Q—B2/R—K1, etc.).

SÄMISCH VARIATION

1 P—Q4	N—KB3	7 P—Q5	N—R4
2 P—QB4	P—KN3	8 Q—Q2	P—KB4
3 N—QB3	B—N2	9 O—O—O	N—Q2
4 P—K4	P—Q3	10 B—Q3	QN—B3
5 P—B3		11 P×P	P×P
		12 N—R3!	
5 . . .	O—O		
6 B—K3	P—K4		

1 P—Q4	N—KB3
2 P—QB4	P—KN3
3 N—QB3	B—N2
4 P—K4	P—Q3
5 P—B3	

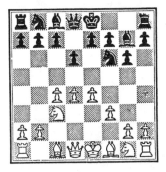

This is the key move of the Sämisch Variation, which was elaborated by the German master, Fritz Sämisch in the 1920's. P—B3 may seem a very strange move, since it does nothing for White's development and also takes away the square KB3 from White's KN. However, 5 P—B3 does have a lot of point and has been favoured by four World Champions – Botvinnik, Petrosian, Tal, and Spassky. This move strengthens White's centre in preparation for moves like B—K3, followed by Q—Q2. White's plan is to castle Q side and then assault Black's king position with an advance of his K-side pawns, supported by the possibility B—KR6. P—B3 not only strengthens White's KP against counter-attack, but also prepares P—KN4, which would support an advance of White's KRP to KR5. If White can succeed in opening the KR file and exchanging Black's KB, he is almost certain to gain a decisive attack against Black's king.

Many examples of this sharp strategy succeeding brilliantly for White will be found in the notes to the main text.

| 5 . . . | O—O |

There is little advantage in delaying this commitment of Black's king to the K wing. It is very difficult for Black to arrange O—O—O.

| 6 B—K3 | |

The best development square for the bishop. White prepares Q—Q2 and O—O—O. Note that the pawn on KB3 prevents Black from playing . . .N—KN5, molesting the QB on K3. Should the QB go to KN5 it could be chased away by P—KR3 by Black, and if it went to KB4 on move six, Black could reply . . .N—B3, threatening a fork trick with . . .N×QP and . . .P—K4.

| 6 . . . | P—K4 |

This is the traditional method of gaining play in the centre for Black in the King's Indian Defence, but possibly here it is too blunt to be an adequate method of countering White's strategic designs. Since White's king is planning to go to the Q side anyway, the planned Black K-side pawn avalanche that follows 6. . .P—K4 will lack its usual force. We suggest some possibly more suitable continuations for Black in the notes, but 6. . .P—K4 is examined in the main text, because it has been the most popular choice for Black at this stage in most Master games.

(For 6. . .N—B3 see p. 177)

| 7 P—Q5 | |

This move not only gains some territory in the centre but also closes the central position and thus minimizes Black's counterplay against White's intended flank attack on the Black king. It is always a good idea to block the centre when planning a wing attack.

| 7 . . . | N—R4 |

Black prepares a typical King's Indian Defence K-side pawn-storm, by means of P—KB4—B5 and P—KN4.

| 8 Q—Q2 | P—KB4 |
| 9 O—O—O | |

White has carried out the first part of his plan.

| 9 . . . | N—Q2 |
| 10 B—Q3 | |

The bishop comes into play on a good central square, where it is also pointing toward Black's king.

| 10 . . . | QN—B3 |

Black's plan is to put pressure on White's KP in the hope that White may abandon the centre with KP×P, thus ceding Black a mobile central pawn majority. However, this is a rather dangerous scheme for Black, since the pawn majority lacks the support of a KNP and could become rather loose, especially on the light squares. Black must always be very careful about light-square invasions by White in the King's Indian Defence. The most cautious method for Black would have been 10...P—B5, attempting to block up the K side, and minimize White's attacking chances there. But with the K side completely blocked White could have attempted an advance on the Q side by moving his king to QN1, and following up with R—QB1 and P—QB5.

11 P×P   P×P

Of course it would be a major strategic error on Black's part to recapture with a piece on his KB4 square. Thus, after 11...B×P?, White would reply 12 KN—K2 and would eventually establish on his own K4 square a piece which would nullify for ever the scope of Black's KB. If White ever establishes on his own K4 a piece which cannot be shifted by Black's KBP and which also blockades Black's KP, which is imprisoning the Black KB, White can normally regard his position as strategically won.

12 N—R3!

Now White has a powerful threat of N—KN5—K6, exploiting the weakness on the light squares in Black's camp

which we have already mentioned. Furthermore White has the possibility of playing a rook to the KN file, following up with P—KN4, opening some lines against Black's king. In view of these possibilities we must conclude that White has a noticeable advantage. The game PORTISCH–GLIGORIC from the World Team Championship at Siegen 1970, continued from this position:

12...P—QB3.

Black could inflict doubled isolated KR pawns on White by means of 12...P—B5; 13 B—KB2, B×N; but after 14 P×B White's KB is completely unopposed by its light-squared Black counterpart, and this would give White complete control of the light squares; e.g., by means of B—KB5—K6 ch. In addition White would have dangerous possibilities on the KN file.

13 KR—N1, P×P; 14 P×P, K—R1; 15 K—N1, B—Q2; 16 N—KN5, Q—K2; 17 B—N5, B—B1.

Of course Black cannot allow the exchange of light-square bishops, since White's knight would have a free passage to K6, and it is well known that an unchallengeable knight established on the sixth rank is virtually a guarantee of victory.

18 B—QB4.

White's KN is coming to K6 anyway. Black will have to exchange his bishop for it, and White will obtain a dangerous passed pawn in its place. White's position is already strategically won.

We continue our treatment of the Sämisch Variation in a manner that differs slightly from the procedure we normally adopt. At this point we give the moves of four complete games which illustrate White's attacking possibilities against Black's king. If the reader plays over these games he will gain a feel for the correct way to carry out these K-side attacks. On page 177 (6...N—B3!) we recommend a playable procedure for Black against the Sämisch.

TAL–TOLUSH, 24th USSR Championship, Moscow 1957.
1 P—QB4, N—KB3; 2 N—QB3, P—KN3; 3 P—K4, P—Q3; 4 P—Q4, B—N2; 5 P—B3, P—K4; 6 KN—K2, QN—Q2; 7 B—N5, P—B3; 8 Q—Q2, O—O;

9 P—Q5, P—B4?; 10 P—KN4, P—QR3; 11 N—N3, R—K1; 12 P—KR4, Q—R4; 13 B—R6, N—B1; 14 P—R5!, Q—B2; 15 B—Q3, P—QN4; 16 O—O—O, P×P; 17 B—N1!, B—R1; 18 QR—N1, R—N1; 19 N—B5!.

This is a very typical sacrifice of a knight on KB5 to break through against Black's king in this variation. 19...N (B3)—Q2; 20 B—N5, B—KN2; 21 N×B, K×N; 22 B—R6 ch, K—N1; 23 P—B4!, P×P; 24 Q×P, Q—Q1; 25 P×P, N×P; 26 Q—R2, N(Q2)—K4; 27 B—B4?, N—B1?; 28 Q—R6, N(K4)—N3; 29 B—N5, P—B3; 30 P—K5!, R×KP; 31 B×N, R—N2; 32 N—K4!, BP×B; 33 R—B1!, R×N; 34 B×R, R—N2; 35 R—B6, B×P; 36 KR—B1, N—Q2; 37 R×P, Q—K2; 38 R×P, K—R1; 39 B×P!, N—N1; 40 B—B5 dis ch, K—N1; 41 B—K6 ch, B×B; 42 R×B, Resigns.

TAL–GLIGORIC, Candidates' Tournament, Bled 1959.
1 P—Q4, N—KB3; 2 P—QB4, P—KN3; 3 N—QB3, B—N2; 4 P—K4, P—Q3; 5 P—B3, O—O; 6 B—K3, P—K4; 7 KN—K2, P—B3; 8 P—Q5, P×P; 9 BP×P, P—QR3; 10 Q—Q2, QN—Q2; 11 P—KN4, P—KR4; 12 P—KR3, N—R2; 13 P—KR4!, P×P; 14 P×P, KN—B3; 15 B—R3, N—N3; 16 B—N5, N—B5; 17 Q—Q3!, Q—B2; 18 P—N3, N—R6; 19 R—QB1!, B×P; 20 B×N!, B×N; 21 K×B!, B×B; 22 N—N1, Q—R4; 23 P—N4, Q×NP; 24 N×N, B×P; 25 N—B4, P—QN4; 26 N—N6, QR—Q1; 27 B—B5!, B—N4; 28 QR—KN1, Q—N7 ch; 29 K—B3, B—B5; 30 R—N2, Q—N5; 31 N—Q7, R—B1; 32 N—B6 ch, K—N2; 33 N—R5 ch, K—N1; 34 B×R, R×B; 35 R—QB2, R×R; 36 Q×R, Q—R6 ch; 37 Q—N3, Q×Q ch; 38 P×Q, P×N; 39 R—R1, P—R5; 40 K—N4, K—K6; 41 R×P, B—B4; 42 K×P, P—B4; 43 P×P, P—K5; 44 P—N4!, B×P; 45 K—N5, K—B2; 46 R—R7 ch, K—K1; 47 P—B6, Resigns.

BOTVINNIK–TAL, 21st game World Championship 1961, Moscow.
1 P—Q4, N—KB3; 2 P—QB4, P—KN3; 3 N—QB3, B—N2; 4 P—K4, P—Q3; 5 P—B3, QN—Q2; 6 B—K3, P—K4; 7 KN—K2, O—O; 8 P—Q5, N—R4; 9 Q—Q2, P—KB4; 10 O—O—O, P—QR3; 11 K—N1, QN—B3; 12 P×P, P×P; 13 N—N3, Q—K1; 14 B—Q3, N×N?!; 15 P×N, P—B4?!; 16 B—R6, Q—N3; 17 P—KN4, P—N4; 18 B×B, K×B; 19 R—R4, P×BP; 20 B—B2, P—R3; 21 QR—R1, Q—N4; 22 Q×Q ch, P×Q; 23 R—R6, P×P; 24 P×P, B×P; 25 R—N6 ch, K—B2; 26 R—KB1, K—K2; 27 R—N7 ch, K—K1; 28 N—K4 (if...N×N, 29 B—R4 ch wins at once), 28...N—Q2; 29 N×P ch, K—Q1; 30 R×R ch, N×R; 31 N×P, B—Q2; 32 R—B7, K—B2; 33 P—Q6 ch, Resigns.

SPASSKY–EVANS, Varna Olympiad 1962.
1 P—Q4, N—KB3; 2 P—QB4, P—KN3; 3 N—QB3, B—N2; 4 P—K4, P—Q3; 5 P—B3, P—B3; 6 B—K3, P—QR3; 7 Q—Q2, P—QN4; 8 O—O—O!, P×P; 9 B×P, O—O; 10 P—KR4!, P—Q4; 11 B—N3, P×P; 12 P—R5!, KP×P; 13 RP×P, RP×P; 14 B—R6!, P×P; 15 R—R4!, N—N5; 16 B×B, K×B; 17 Q×P, N—R3; 18 N—B3, N—B4; 19 R—R2, Q—Q3; 20 N—K5, N—Q2; 21 N—K4, Q—B2; 22 QR—R1, R—KN1; 23 R—R7 ch, K—B1; 24 R×P ch, K—K1; 25 Q×P!, N×N; 26 R—B8 ch, Resigns.

Black's losses in these encounters were due to various causes; for example: blocking the centre when White was preparing an attack on the wing, thus failing to gain sufficient counterplay, or advancing his own K-side pawns, thus creating targets for White's attack.

6...N—B3

6...N—B3. The most accurate move in our opinion. True, it blocks the Black QBP, but Black is relying on the generation of central activity by means of ...P—K4 (backed up by ...P—QN4), to counter White's K-side operations.

White could now play 7 P—Q5, N—K4; 8 P—B4, N(4)—Q2, but in so doing he would render his pawn centre most vulnerable to thrusts, such as ...P—QB3 and ...P—K3. Another line White must avoid is 7 B—Q3, P—K4; 8 KN—K2, N—KN5!, and Black wins after 9 P×N, P×P, regaining the piece and scattering White's centre. This underlines one of the points of 6...N—B3! – quick pressure against White's QP on Q4.

Now let us see what happens if White carries on with his plan of a K-side attack:

7 Q—Q2, R—K1; 8 KN—K2, R—N1. Black puts his rooks on the QN file and K file preparatory to playing ...P—QN4 and ...P—K4. The point is that Black hopes in the future to open both those files, when his rooks will already be well placed.

9 O—O—O.

9 P—Q5?, N—K4; 10 B×P, R—R1, followed by ...N×QBP.

9...P—QR3; 10 B—R6, B×B; 11 Q×B, P—QN4!.

Black's counter-attack is well under way. A better plan for White is the retreat 9 N—B1. White plans to redeploy this piece on QN3 to defend the QP, and then develop his KB on Q3. Black will still obtain adequate counter-play by preparing the advances ...P—QN4 and ...P—K4.

13

DUTCH DEFENCE

1 P—Q4, P—KB4

The Dutch Defence is very popular with aggressive players of the black pieces, whose main aim is to attack the opponent's king. Black's first move already gains some space on the king's wing and Black will normally utilize this space to implement the following manoeuvre: ...P—K3/...N—KB3—K5/...B—K2 or Q3/...O—O, followed by ...R—KB3 and ...Q—K1—KR4. Black can then advance his KNP in an attempt to bludgeon his way through to White's KR2 square. By adopting this plan Black has won many crushing games. However, Black's first move sins against several principles: (i) P—KB4 does not develop any pieces, nor does it aid development; (ii) moving the KBP weakens the position of Black's king. If White plays correctly he should be able to obtain an advantage by advancing P—K4 at the appropriate moment, opening up the centre and exposing all of Black's weaknesses.

White can either go for P—K4 at once, playing a gambit for rapid development, or he can develop his pieces quietly and aim to push P—K4 at a later date. We believe that the latter procedure is more effective. The Dutch Defence weakens Black's position so it is not necessary to sacrifice any pawns to gain an advantage against it.

Many of the lines we have so far examined represent certain historical stages in the development of chess thought. Thus the King's Gambit and Giuoco Piano have vanished almost entirely from modern tournaments, and their place has been taken over by the more sophisticated Ruy Lopez. On the Q side, too, it is evident that the Nimzo-Indian and King's Indian Defences have developed at a later historical stage than the ordinary Queen's Gambit Declined; but the Dutch Defence boasts no such intellectual heritage since it represents no specific stage of chess thought. It has always been a favourite of aggressive players who are not afraid of accepting weaknesses in their own position.

First of all we examine White's gambit line.

STAUNTON GAMBIT

1 P—Q4	P—KB4
2 P—K4	

2 ...	P×P
3 N—QB3	N—KB3
4 P—B3	P×P
5 N×P	P—KN3
6 B—KB4	B—N2
7 Q—Q2	O—O
8 O—O—O	P—Q4
9 N—K5	QN—Q2

---

1 P—Q4	P—KB4
2 P—K4	

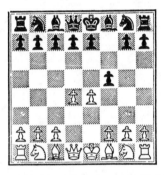

The Staunton Gambit, named after the great English Master Howard Staunton who was active in the mid 19th century. It is the most aggressive answer to the Dutch. Since Black's first move does nothing for his development, White reckons that he can profitably sacrifice a pawn to maximize the efficiency of his own mobilization. However, this gambit does not promise much more than equality. We prefer 2 N—KB3, which is considered under the subsequent three headings.

2 ...	P×P

Black can only test White's gambit by accepting it. (See also note to Black's fourth move.)

3 N—QB3

Both attacking Black's front KP and developing a piece.

3 ...	N—KB3

Likewise, Black defends his extra pawn with a developing move.

4 P—B3

Making a true gambit of the opening. White renounces all hopes of retrieving his pawn and relies on speedy development, followed by a quick attack against Black's king.

(For 4 B—KN5 see p. 181)

4 ...	P×P

Black could voluntarily give back his pawn with 4...P—K6 or 4...N—B3, but such moves do not test the accuracy of White's gambit.

5 N×P

5 Q×P is possible, but this would take away the square KB3 from White's KN, and KB3 is its most natural development square.

5 ...	P—KN3

This move strengthens Black's king's position. Also he prepares ...B—N2, followed quickly by ...O—O, tucking the king in the corner, well away from White's pressure on the open K and KB files.

(For 5...P—Q4 see p. 182)

6 B—KB4

A good developing move, which also prepares Q—Q2, followed by O—O—O.

6 ...	B—N2
7 Q—Q2	O—O

Both sides play according to plan.

8 O—O—O

Castling on opposite sides of the board always leads to a very fierce game. White will continue with moves like B—KR6 and P—KR4—R5, possibly sacrificing more pawns to get at Black's king. Meanwhile Black can keep his chances alive by playing ...P—Q4, ...P—QB4 and ...Q—R4, trying to open the QB file for his rooks, in combination with the pressure of his bishop from KN2 against the fortress of White's king.

A mistaken idea in this position is the immediate 8 B—KR6; e.g., 8...P—Q4; 9 B×B, K×B; 10 O—O—O, B—B4; 11 B—Q3, B×B; 12 Q×B, N—B3. This was played in a game between Bronstein and Alexander, Hastings 1953/54. White committed the error of exchanging too many pieces while he was material down. After 12...N—B3, Black had an extra pawn and a solid position and went on to win the game. 8 O—O—O is much stronger, since it avoids the premature exchange of pieces.

8 . . .   P—Q4

Black establishes a foothold in the centre. This is very necessary, but it does weaken his K4 square, which White promptly occupies with . . .

9 N—K5   QN—Q2

Challenging White's knight outpost at K5. In this position White has more space and active pieces. In addition he can attack with B—Q3 and P—KR4 – but Black has an extra central pawn in return, so the chances are roughly equal. This does not, however, mean that the game is likely to end in a draw, but that the position is so unbalanced that both sides have equal chances of winning.

This position, after move nine, is Russian analysis trying to improve on the Bronstein-Alexander game.

We must conclude that the Staunton Gambit can give White an overwhelming attack if Black goes wrong, but that it does not promise a great advantage if Black defends accurately. However, it does have an important psychological advantage over the positional treatments which we are about to analyse. Someone who plays the Dutch will want to get on with the job of attacking White's king. He will obviously feel very uncomfortable if he has to defend a difficult position in which it is his opponent who has attacking chances, as compensation for a sacrificed pawn.

So, you could try the Staunton Gambit to unsettle someone who wants to attack you.

---

4 B—KN5

4 B—KN5. This move is less consistent than 4 P—B3. Instead of sacrificing a pawn for the attack, White tries instead to regain his pawn. Play could continue:
    4...N—B3.
Developing a piece and threatening ...P—K4. (Incidentally, 4...P—Q4 fails to 5 B×N followed by Q—R5 ch and Q×QP.)
    5 P—Q5, N—K4; 6 Q—Q4, N—B2; 7 B×N.
7 B—R4, P—KN4!; 8 B—N3, B—N2, allows Black to develop his pieces quickly. The knight at KB2 easily protects the slight weakness of the Black KNP.
    7...KP×B; 8 N×P, B—K2; 9 O—O—O, O—O; 10 P—KB4, P—KB4; 11 N—N3, B—B3.
Black has an excellent position. His two

bishops on the open board are potentially very powerful. White is weak on the dark squares, and Black's KB could be very useful in an eventual attack against White's king.

5...P—Q4

5...P—Q4. Just how essential it is to protect the K side with ...P—KN3 can be seen from what occurs if Black plays 5...P—Q4, and then develops his pieces normally. Quick development is usually a principle to trust, but in this particular case it is more important for Black to concentrate on bolstering up the defences of his king.

6 N—K5!, B—B4; 7 P—KN4!.

Now Black's developed pieces must retreat in confusion.

7...B—K3; 8 P—N5, KN—Q2; 9 Q—R5 ch, P—N3; 10 N × NP, B—B2; 11 B—Q3.

Meeting 11...B × N with 12 B × B ch, P × B; 13 Q × P mate.

11...B—N2.

Covering the rook, but ...

12 R—B1!.

A brilliant move, threatening 13 R × B, K × R; 14 N × R dbl ch. After 12 R—B1, White has a winning attack; e.g., 12...P × N; 13 Q × P!, R—B1 (13...B × Q; 14 B × B mate); 14 Q × KB, and Black's position is shattered.

STONEWALL VARIATION

---

1 P—Q4	P—KB4
2 N—KB3	
2 ...	N—KB3
3 P—KN3	P—K3
4 B—N2	B—K2
5 O—O	O—O
6 P—B4	P—Q4
7 P—N3	P—B3
8 N—B3	Q—K1
9 N—K5	QN—Q2
10 N—Q3!	

| 1 P—Q4 | P—KB4 |
| 2 N—KB3 | |

This promises a lasting positional initiative and is therefore more trustworthy than 2 P—K4.

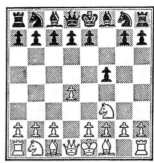

| 2 ... | N—KB3 |
| 3 P—KN3 | |

The best method of developing White's KB. P—KN3 not only strengthens the position of White's king, as a preemptive measure against Black's coming attack in that zone, but also places the KB on a fine square to support White's intended P—K4 at a later date.

3 ...   P—K3

We will examine the alternative development 3...P—KN3 in a subsequent section.

4 B—N2   B—K2
5 O—O

There is no point in delaying this. White is not well prepared for O—O—O.

5 ...   O—O
6 P—B4

Now that his king is safe, White claims some more territory in the centre.

6 ...   P—Q4

This is the move that gives the Stonewall its name. Black blockades the central zone with his triangle (stonewall) of pawns on Q4/K3/KB4 and gains a grip on White's K4 square. Black's reasoning is that with the centre fixed he can safely commence a wing action against White's king. However, Black's reasoning is fallacious, in view of the following:

(*a*) The centre is not entirely static, nor does Black exercise genuine control over White's K4 square. If White can arrange to play P—KB3 and P—K4 at the appropriate moment, Black will be forced to retreat and his backward pawn on K3 may become a serious weakness.

(*b*) If ever White can exchange his QB for Black's KB, Black will be woefully weak on the dark squares, and White's pieces will be able to use these dark squares to invade Black's position unchallenged. Even without this exchange Black is very weak on the dark squares — especially his own K4 and KB5 which could become havens for White pieces.

(*c*) It looks as if Black's pawns grant him control of the light squares, but also they severely impede the scope of his QB. This could be a major factor if an ending is reached.

(We will scrutinize 6...P—Q3 in the next section.)

7 P—N3

Another very good plan is 7 QN—Q2, followed by N—K5—Q3 and N(Q2)—KB3. That way White would dominate

Black's K4 square, which can no longer be protected by a pawn.
(For 7 N—B3 see p. 184)

7 ...   P—B3

Completing the light-squared Stonewall formation.

8 N—B3   Q—K1

Black prepares to feed over pieces for his attack on White's king – ...Q—K1—KR4 is a common link in this attacking chain.

9 N—K5   QN—Q2
10 N—Q3!

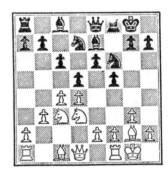

A very fine move indeed. Since Black's pieces are cramped in their development, White avoids any exchange of pieces (e.g., 10 N×N?, B×N), which might permit Black to free his restricted quarters. Furthermore, the knight – wonderfully centralized on Q3, observes all the important dark squares (QB5/K5/KB4). We can already state that White has a clear advantage, and this was exploited with superlative precision by White in a game between HÜBNER and MARIOTTI from Sombor 1970:
10...N—K5.
According to plan.
11 B—N2, B—Q3; 12 P—K3, P—KN4.
The "attack" continues. In fact this pseudo-aggressive move aggravates Black's palsy on the dark squares.
13 P—B3.
Proving Black's control over White's K4 to have been illusory.

13...N×N; 14 B×N, N—B3; 15 Q—K2, Q—R4.

This is as far as Black's attack ever gets.

16 B—N4!.

Achieving the vital exchange of dark-squared bishops. Positionally Black is now lost!

16...B×B; 17 N×B, P—R4; 18 N—Q3, P—N3; 19 N—K5.

Dark square invasion.

19...Q—K1; 20 Q—Q2, P—R3; 21 P—K4!.

This comes with all the more force for having been retarded. White easily regains his pawn.

21...BP×P; 22 P×KP, P×KP; 23 Q—K3, B—N2; 24 B×P, R—Q1; 25 B—N2, R—Q3; 26 R—B2, Q—Q1; 27 Q—Q3.

Black's position has been exposed as a shambles with weaknesses everywhere: if 27...R×P; 28 Q—N6 ch is lethal. If Black forestalls the incursion of White's queen with 27...Q—K1, then 28 R(1)—KB1, K—N2 (28...N—Q2; 29 R—B7!); 29 N—N4, N—Q2; 30 R×R, N×R; 31 Q—K3 (threatening a decisive check on K5); 31...N—N3; 32 N—B6, Q—K2; 33 N—R5 ch, K—R2; 34 B—K4, and Black is in a ghastly mess. In fact, Black was so depressed by these possibilities, that he conceded the game without a fight after White's 27th move.

The great American Master, Pillsbury, who was active at the end of the 19th century and the beginning of the 20th, once became involved in a conversation with a doctor, who was also a chess enthusiast. The doctor was amazed at the speed with which Pillsbury could comprehend the strengths and weaknesses of pawn structures.

Pillsbury then explained to the doctor that the pawn structure is the skeleton of every position and just as a doctor can recognize at a glance the defects in a diseased bone structure, so the chess Master can instantly grasp the defects of a diseased pawn structure.

If the reader studies the position after 27 Q—Q3 in the above game, he will gain some useful insights into the faculty of recognizing defects in chess board bone structures. A chess Master would at once dismiss Black's position as lost, in view of its many terrible weaknesses –

and these can be broken down as follows:

(a) The advance of Black's KNP creates a target for White's attack (e.g., by P—KR4). In addition, all the squares behind Black's KNP (KB3/KN3) lack pawn protection, and form a vacuum into which White pieces may be sucked. Already White's queen and knight are staring at Black's KN3.

(b) Observe the inviolability of White's knight, firmly entrenched before Black's backward and isolated KP.

White's only weakness is the QP on an open file, but Black is so tied down to defence of his own weaknesses that he has no time to exploit this. If Black's KNP were on KN2 and his KRP on KR2 then Black's only structural defect would be the KP, and he would have chances to draw the game.

---

7 N—B3

7 N—B3. Hübner's play in this game was such a convincing demolition of the positionally unsound Stonewall Variation that it hardly seems necessary to analyse alternatives. However, here is one example of Black's strategy succeeding against inept treatment by White. H. STEINER–BOTVINNIK, Groningen 1946:

7 N—B3.

There is nothing wrong with this. It is White's follow up that is at fault.

7...P—B3.

If 7...P×P, then 8 N—K5.

8 B—B4?.

From now on White begins to drift planlessly. 8 P—N3 is stronger. On KB4 White's QB is exposed to attack.

Furthermore, this square should be controlled by a knight, not occupied by a bishop!

8...Q—K1; 9 Q—B2, Q—R4; 10 QR—K1, QN—Q2; 11 N—Q2, P—KN4.

Catching White's dark-squared bishop whilst preserving his own intact. This is a positive step forward for Black, who now gains a measure of dark-square control.

12 B—B7, N—K1; 13 B—K5, N×B; 14 P×N, P—B5.

Botvinnik builds up a K-side attack in copybook style.

15 P×BP, NP×P; 16 N—B3, K—R1; 17 K—R1, N—N2; 18 Q—B1, B—Q2; 19 P—QR3, R—B2.

White has run out of ideas and can only watch while Black masses his pieces for the kill against White's king.

20 P—N4, R—KN1; 21 R—N1, N—B4; 22 N—Q1, R(2)—N2; 23 Q×P, R—N5; 24 Q—Q2, N—R5; 25 N—K3, N×N; 26 P×N.

26 B×N is positionally desirable but fails to 26...Q×P ch; 27 K×Q, R—R5 mate.

26...R—R5; 27 N—B1, B—N4; 28 Resigns.

The threat of ...B—B5 is unstoppable. Black triumphed on the dark squares.

FLUID CENTRE WITH 6. . .P—Q3

1 P—Q4	P—KB4
2 N—KB3	N—KB3
3 P—KN3	P—K3
4 B—N2	B—K2
5 O—O	O—O
6 P—B4	P—Q3
7 N—B3	Q—K1
8 R—K1	Q—N3
9 P—K4	P×P
10 N×P	N×N
11 R×N	

1 P—Q4	P—KB4
2 N—KB3	N—KB3
3 P—KN3	P—K3
4 B—N2	B—K2
5 O—O	O—O
6 P—B4	P—Q3

With this move Black still plans his K-side assault by means of ...Q—K1—KR4, etc., but 6...P—Q3 is considerably more flexible than 6...P—Q4, which we examined in the previous section. Black does not commit his pawns to a rigid formation after ...P—Q3 and in particular he does not weaken his own K4 square, as he does in the Stonewall. In some lines after...P—Q3, Black can even arrange to play ...P—K4.

However, White can still gain the advantage by aiming to force through P—K4 himself, which will open up lines to attack Black's backward KP.

7 N—B3

Clearly best, putting the knight into contact with the vital K4 square.

7 . . .   Q—K1

By now this theme should be familiar.

8 R—K1

Again preparing to play P—K4.

8 ...   Q—N3

Black modifies his plan in order to pick up pressure against White's projected P—K4. Black could also stop P—K4 by occupying the square with a piece, but after 8...N—K5; 9 N×N, P×N; 10 N—Q2, P—Q4; 11 P—B3, P—K6; 12 N—N1, Black's centre begins to collapse. White can safely undevelop his knight in this fashion since he will soon gain a powerful central pawn majority. If Black tries 11...P×KBP, then 12 N×P, and White has control of Black's K4 square in front of the backward KP; and 12...P×P; 13 N—K5, followed by Q—B2 and the recapture of the pawn, would leave Black's position riddled with weaknesses.

(For 8...Q—R4 see below)

9 P—K4

This looks crazy, but it isn't! A neat tactical point allows White to carry out this strategically important advance. But in fact it may be more effective to delay the move (see note).

(For 9 P—N3 see p. 187)

9 ...   P×P
10 N×P   N×N
11 R×N

Black's weak KP is exposed to White pressure on the open K file – and possibly from White's KB coming to KR3. However, Black's pieces are active and he can equalize the game by countering with ...P—K4 himself,

thus eliminating all his weaknesses.

Now 11...Q×R?; 12 N—R4!, and, amazingly, Black's queen is trapped in mid-board! So Black has to develop as quickly as possible with 11...N—B3, when there would follow: 12 Q—K2, piling up on the pawn; 12...B—B3; 13 B—Q2, P—K4!; 14 P×P, N×P; 15 N×N, B×N, with an equal position. Of course, it is a mistake to play 15...P×N?, since this would unnecessarily inflict an isolated pawn on Black's own position. But White can continue with 16 B—B3 (pressurizing the pawn); 16...B—B4; 17 N—R4, B×N; 18 R×B, QR—K1; 19 Q—K3, P—KR3; 20 P—QN4, Q—KB3; 21 P—N5, N—Q1; 22 P—B5! (22 Q×QRP is not worth it. White's queen is removed too far from the centre). White thus assures himself of the initiative both on the Q side and in the centre, and with his two raking bishops on the long diagonals he has a superb game.

8...Q—R4

8...Q—R4. Let us see what happens if Black carries on with his plan, ignoring White's threat to play P—K4. 8...Q—R4; 9 P—K4, P×P; 10 N×P, N×N; 11 R×N, N—B3; 12 B—B4 (preventing 12...P—K4); 12...B—B3; 13 Q—Q2, K—R1 (to avoid an embarrassing check on Q5 after ...P—K4); 14 QR—K1 and White dominates the centre. It is impossible for Black to free himself with ...P—K4, and if he develops his QB with 14...B—Q2, then 15 P—B5! is exceedingly painful.

9 P—N3

9 P—N3. 9 P—K4 is the most popular move in Master practice, but 9 P—N3 is the main alternative strategy for White. Having tied down Black's queen to observation of White's K4 square, White decides to develop all of his pieces on their most efficacious squares before effecting the advance P—K4.

9. . .QN—Q2.

Black plans to play . . .N—K5, firmly securing the key square, and the QN heads for KB3 to support this manoeuvre.

10 B—N2, P—B3; 11 Q—B2, N—K5; 12 P—K3.

12 N×N would be a blunder: 12. . .P× N; 13 N—Q2, P—K6!; 14 Q×Q, P× P ch, and Black wins. This is a common trap in the Dutch.

12. . .QN—B3; 13 P—B5!.

An important and typical move, striking at the dark squares. If Black accepts the pawn with 13. . .P×P, White will play 14 N—K5, Q—R4; 15 N×N, N×N; 16 B×N, P×B; 17 Q×KP, with a dominating position. The knight on K5 (cf. Hübner-Mariotti, p. 183) cannot be shifted, and Black cannot develop his Q side. After 13 P—B5!, White has a

definite plus. KEENE–CORDEN, Marlow 1971, concluded:

13. . .N—N5.

Black tries to beat a path to White's KB2 and KR2, but it is easy to fend this off, and White is left with all the traditional anti-Dutch positional advantages.

14 P×P, B×P; 15 R—KB1, N—N4; 16 N×N, Q×N; 17 QR—K1.

The final preparation for P—K4.

17. . .P—K4.

This does not help any more, since White now obtains a mobile central pawn-majority supported by his massed pieces.

18 P×P, Q—R3; 19 P—KR3.

White spots the mate.

19. . .N×P(K4); 20 P—B4, N—Q2; 21 P—K4!.

At last. White opens lines for the decisive assault.

21. . .N—B3; 22 P—K5, B—B4 ch; 23 K—R1, N—R4; 24 K—R2, P—KN4.

That pseudo-aggressive move again! Black hopes for an attack, but in fact he only violates the principle that one should not shatter the pawn defences around one's own king. White is quick to exploit this.

25 N—K2, B—N3; 26 N—Q4, P×P; 27 P×P.

Threatening Q—B4 ch and P—K6.

27. . .N×P.

A combination that goes sour.

28 Q—B1!, B—R4; 29 R×N, B×R; 30 R—N4 ch!.

The point Black has overlooked.

30. . .P×R; 31 Q×Q, P×P; 32 Q— N5 ch, K—R1; 33 N—B5!, Resigns.

After 33. . .B×N; 34 P—K6 ch, we see the full and fatal consequences of Black's 24th move, . . .P—KN4.

LENINGRAD VARIATION

1 P—Q4	P—KB4
2 N—KB3	N—KB3
3 P—KN3	P—KN3
4 B—N2	B—N2
5 O—O	O—O
6 P—B4	P—Q3
7 P—Q5!	P—B4
8 N—B3	N—R3
9 R—N1	N—B2
10 P—N3	P—QR3
11 B—N2	P—QN4
12 P—K3	R—N1
13 N—K2	B—Q2

1 P—Q4	P—KB4
2 N—KB3	N—KB3
3 P—KN3	P—KN3

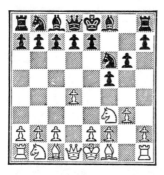

The characteristic move of the Leningrad Variation. It was elaborated in the 1950's by a group of Masters from Leningrad, who felt dissatisfied with the lack of strategic complexity for Black's side offered by the normal lines of the Dutch Defence.

Black's plan is to transpose into a version of the King's Indian Defence in which he has already achieved the advance ...P—KB4. However, the defects of the Leningrad are serious:

(a) As usual, the early ...P—KB4 by Black turns out to be a weakening of his own king position.

(b) White can play P—Q5 before Black is ready for ...P—K4. This means that Black will suffer from a hole on his K3 square. Alternatively if Black persists with ...P—K4, White can parry with P(Q5)×KP e.p., breaking up Black's pawn-mass, and inflicting more weak squares on Black's position.

(c) In view of Black's pawn structure, his QB often turns out to be a not very valuable piece, hemmed in by its own pawns.

4 B—N2	**B—N2**
5 O—O	**O—O**
6 P—B4	

Preparing to support P—Q5.

6 . . .	**P—Q3**

With the intention of 7...N—B3 and 8...P—K4, and Black would have a more than satisfying game, with very mobile pawns. So ...

7 P—Q5!

Achieving an important territorial conquest.

(For 7 N—B3 see p. 189)

7 . . .	**P—B4**

Black must change plans entirely. With the text he resolves to organize an advance on the Q side to gain some space for his pieces. If Black tries 7...P—K4, bypassing White's QP, which is cramping him badly, he ends up in a grisly situation: 8 P×P e.p.!, B×P; 9 N—Q4 (threatening B×P and N×B), 9...B—B1; 10 QN—B3, and White is well ahead in development. Black's QB has been forced to move twice, only to return to its original square, while White's KN has used this time to advance to a powerful central post.

8 N—B3	**N—R3**

Surprisingly, this is now the best square for the knight. It will come back to the centre at QB2, and help to force through ...P—QN4. But still, Black's position is far from satisfactory, in view of the positional defects in his camp outlined at move three.

9 R—N1

A very good move. White wants to develop his QB on the long dark diagonal (QR1—KR8), in the hope of exchanging this piece for Black's KB. The point of this manoeuvre would be to reduce the quantity of pieces defending Black's king. When White eventually opens the centre with P—K4, the retarded Black KP will then act as a barrier, hindering Black from moving defensive pieces over to aid his monarch.

But 9 P—N3? at once would fail to ...N—K5!. So White first moves his rook from the diagonal of Black's KB.

(For 9 N—K1 see p. 190)

9 ...	N—B2
10 P—N3	P—QR3
11 B—N2	P—QN4
12 P—K3	

Creating a square for the QN on K2, in order that it may eventually transfer to KB4 obscuring the hole at K6. White must never play QBP×QNP in such a situation since this would ruin his own pawn-chain by depriving his QP of vital support.

12 ...	R—N1
13 N—K2	B—Q2

(For 13...Q—K1 see p. 190)

White has a very good position. Black's sole counterplay resides in the QN file, which he can open with ...NP×P, but it is very simple for White to guard all the entry squares that might be used by a black rook or queen. Furthermore, if ever Black plays ...P—K4, the answer QP×P e.p. will leave him with a gaping wound at Q3 in the shape of a vulnerable backward pawn on an open file.

After 13 N—K2, B—Q2, the game KEENE-REE (played on top board of a match between England and Holland at Paignton 1970) witnessed the complete success of White's strategy: containment of Black's chances on the Q side, combined with a breakthrough in the centre and against Black's king.

14 B—B3, N—R1.
One of the worst squares on the board for a knight, but Black is running out of constructive things to do.

15 N—N5.
Glaring on the weakness at K6.

15...B—R3; 16 P—KR4, P×P; 17 P×P, R×R; 18 Q×R, Q—N3; 19 Q—B2.
White needs his queen for the attack on Black's king.

19...R—N1.
All dressed up but nowhere to go.

20 N—B4.
Now both knights are aimed at K6.

20...N—B2; 21 P—K4!.
With four of Black's pieces on the wrong side of his backward KP, this is the correct moment to strike.

21...B—N2; 22 P—K5, N—N5; 23 P×P, P×P; 24 B×B, K×B; 25 R—K1, N—K4; 26 N—Q3, R—K1; 27 Q—B3.
Those dark squares again. This is the justification for the manoeuvre begun by 9 R—N1!.

27...K—N1; 28 N×N, P×N; 29 R×P, R×R; 30 Q×R, P—R3; 31 P—Q6!, Resigns.

---

7 N—B3

7 N—B3. This natural developing move is not bad, but it does allow Black to play 7...N—B3 in reply, when he threatens ...P—K4. Now White must play 8 P—Q5, but after 8...N—K4; 9 N×N, P×N, Black does not have an

inferior position. Admittedly, his pawns are doubled, but they are very mobile, and Black can liquidate the liability at will by playing ...P—K3. Here is one example: **10 P—K4, P—K3; 11 P×KP, P—B3!; 12 P×P, P×P; 13 R—K1, Q×Q; 14 N×Q, P—K5,** and Black has no difficulties in regaining his pawn with an equal game.

---

9 N—K1

9 N—K1. This passive retreat of the knight to an inferior square was once played by the Russian Grandmaster, Korchnoy. On general principles this move cannot be good, since it puts a well-developed piece on an inferior square without gaining any advantage in compensation. KORCHNOY–TAL, World Championship Qualifying Match 1968, saw White's plan reduced to absurdity:

9...R—N1; 10 N—B2, N—B2; 11 P—QR4, P—N3; 12 R—N1, N—N5!; 13 P—R3, N—K4.

The point: White has problems with his QBP, since 14 P—N3, N×P! would lose a pawn.

14 N—R3.

Look at White's poor KN! It has taken up four moves just to reach this vile square, far away at the extremity of the world.

14...P—QR3; 15 B—Q2, B—Q2.

Black obviously has a good position at this stage. White has wasted too much time and achieved nothing. In order to drive away Black's superbly centralized KN on K4 (compare the position of White's KN!), White will have to weaken himself with P—KB4.

13...Q—K1

13...Q—K1. An interesting attempt to revert to a conventional Dutch K-side attack with ...Q—K1—KR4. But White is well armed to meet this:

14 B—B3.

Tempting ...P—N5, when White can prise open lines on the Q side.

14...P—N5; 15 B—N2, P—R3; 16 P—QR3!, P×P; 17 B×P, P—N4; 18 P—QN4.

A subsidiary point of 9 R—N1!.

18...P×P; 19 B×P, Q—R4; 20 N(2)—Q4, P—B5; 21 KP×P, P×P; 22 N—B6.

White has a decisive advantage – his knight on the 6th rank radiates power, and Black's KP is doomed (KEENE–HINDLE, English Counties Team Championship 1970).

14

MODERN DEFENCE

1 P—K4, P—KN3; 2 P—Q4, B—N2

This defensive sequence has only become popular at the highest level since the early 1960's, when the Russian Korchnoy used it as Black to beat Fischer, in a World Championship eliminating tournament. It is from this time that it has been employed frequently by specialists in active defensive systems, such as Botvinnik[1] and that is why we call it the Modern Defence. All over the world this defence is known under different names: in Yugoslavia it is called the Pirc; in Russia, the Ufimtsev; in Austria, the Robatsch – we believe that the term "Modern Defence" is simpler.

In former times this defence was frowned upon. In the 1930's the World Champion, the brilliant Franco-Russian Alexander Alekhine, wrote of 1...P—KN3: "This move is rightly considered inferior, as it concedes White the full control of the central squares."

Now all leading Masters recognize that this defence is fully playable, and it was even employed by Fischer in his World Championship Match with Spassky in 1972.

It is a highly sophisticated system which invites White to form a massive central pawn structure, but which aspires to the eventual demolition of that structure by means of undermining advances such as ...P—QB4. Black plans to pressurize White's Q4 in particular and soften White up along his dark-square diagonal (QR1—KR8) in general.

The particular subtlety and power of the Modern system will be revealed when we examine those lines in which White combats it with normal, naive development of his pieces (e.g., the Fork Trick line).

We must stress that this is a difficult defence to handle, but its counter-attacking results can be most satisfying if its secrets are mastered – the secret of destroying an established central pawn formation by pressure from the wings of the board. One outstanding problem connected with the Modern Defence is, that the proper method of play for Black often demands a violation of the very principles we have sought to inculcate in earlier sections of this volume. But the ability to appreciate the correct moment to abandon a general principle, forms one of the delights that go up to make the fascination and rich variety of chess.

[1] The Modern Defence is also a great favourite with one of the co-authors, Raymond Keene, who has used it to beat Grandmasters Gligoric and Donner.

Ostensibly the Modern Defence strategy may resemble that of the King's Indian Defence, but there is one important difference. The King's Indian Defence is a response to 1 P—Q4, while the Modern Defence is a response to 1 P—K4. Although White can continue (and often does) after 1 P—K4, P—KN3; 2 P—Q4, B—N2 with 3 P—QB4 (thus transposing into something resembling a King's Indian Defence), he will normally prefer to develop a piece with 3 N—QB3. Thus in the Modern Defence, Black not only has to cope with a great White pawn-centre (as in the King's Indian Defence), but also with the perils stemming from White's capacity for rapid development.

That we believe this task to be within Black's powers, is one indication of the infinite resources concealed in the sixty-four squares of the chessboard.

Note: Black can also introduce this defence with the move order 1 P—K4, P—Q3; 2 P—Q4, N—KB3, and only then . . .P—KN3; or he can kick off with 1. . .P—KN3, and follow with 2. . .P—Q3.

FORK TRICK VARIATION

1 P—K4	P—KN3
2 P—Q4	B—N2
3 N—KB3	
3 ...	P—Q3
4 N—B3	N—KB3
5 B—QB4	O—O
6 P—KR3	N×P
7 N×N	P—Q4
8 B—Q3	P×N
9 B×P	N—Q2
10 O—O	P—QB4!
11 P×P	Q—B2
12 P—B6	

1 P—K4	P—KN3
2 P—Q4	B—N2
3 N—KB3	

With this move White announces that he is content to develop his pieces normally on good squares, rather than to try for a pawn avalanche with 3 N—QB3 and 4 P—KB4.

3 ...	P—Q3
4 N—B3	

The other knight, too, enters play on its best square.

(For 4 B—QB4 see p. 194)

4 ...	N—KB3
5 B—QB4	

Another simple developing move that would be quite in place in most king's pawn openings that we have discussed (e.g., the Sicilian Defence or the King's Gambit). One might assume that White now stood very well, since all his pieces are going to reach good central squares within a few moves (e.g., O—O, followed by B—KB4, Q—Q2, QR—Q1, etc., with an ideal development). However, Black's subtle deployment of his forces allows him powerful counter-play.

(For 5 B—K2 see p. 195)

5 ...	O—O

Now Black threatens ...B—N5, followed by ...N—B3, with an annoying attack against White's QP. For example, should White play 6 O—O, there would follow 6...B—N5; 7 P—KR3, B×N; 8 Q×B, N—B3; 9 B—K3, N—Q2, and if 10 QR—Q1, then...P—K4; 11 P—Q5, N—Q5, with a good game for Black; or, 10 N—K2, N(2)—K4!; 11 P×N, N×P, and Black regains his piece with advantage. So ...

6 P—KR3

Preventing the pin, but now comes the fork trick, a common device in the Modern Defence for annihilating White's centre.

6 ...	N×P!

(For 6...N—B3 see p. 195)

7 N×N

The alternative 7 B×P ch, R×B; 8 N×N, would give Black the following advantages: (i) central pawn majority; (ii) bishop pair; (iii) the use of the half-open KB file for an attack against White's king.

7 ...	P—Q4

Thus Black regains his piece.

8 B—Q3

It is much worse to play 8 B×P, Q×B, since this would develop Black's queen to a powerful central square, cede Black the bishop pair, and also grant Black attacking chances against White's QP.

8 ...   P×N
9 B×P

If we sum up the result of White's very natural developing move 5 B—QB4, we see that his centre has been reduced, and his KB has been forced to move three times to end up on a square inferior to QB4.

9 ...   N—Q2

Black could also play 9...P—QB4; 10 P×P, Q—R4 ch, but White retains a development lead after 11 P—B3, Q×P(B4); 12 B—K3. After 10 P×P, Q—B2 is bad for Black. White can flout the rule concerning premature development of his queen by playing 11 Q—Q5, when it is very difficult for Black to regain his pawn; e.g., 11...N—R3; 12 P—B6!.

10 O—O   P—QB4!

This stroke at White's QP (note the co-operation of Black's KB pressing down the long dark-squared diagonal) is absolutely typical of Black's play in the Modern Defence. White's centre is finally liquidated and Black has at least an equal game.

11 P×P

11 P—Q5?, N—B3 would lose a pawn for White.

11 ...   Q—B2

Regaining the pawn. Also possible is 11...N×P of course.

12 P—B6

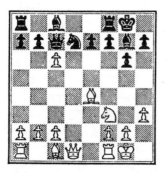

Since White cannot keep his extra pawn, he resolves to return it in order to inflict two isolated pawns on his opponent. However, this increases Black's control of the centre and in conjunction with Black's free play for his pieces and mobile K-side pawn majority gives Black an excellent game.

From this position the game GHIZDAVU–BOTTERILL, Graz 1972, continued:

12...P×P; 13 N—Q4, B—N2; 14 P—QB3, N—B4; 15 B—B2, P—K4; 16 N—N3.

White is driven back by Black's advancing pawns.

16...N—K3; 17 Q—K2, KR—K1; 18 KR—K1, P—KB4.

Black had the initiative. The advance of his K-side pawns will soon be supported by the Black QB, which will emerge after Black plays...P—QB4.

---

4 B—QB4

4 B—QB4. By playing 4 B—QB4, White can place his KB on a good developing square and avoid the fork trick after 4...N—KB3, by playing 5 Q—K2. However, Black can still equalize chances, preparing...P—Q4 with...P—QB3.

Here is one example of the great Russian Champion Mikhail Botvinnik obtaining a good position with Black in the game, GIPSLIS–BOTVINNIK, USSR Team Championship 1963:

4 B—QB4, N—KB3; 5 Q—K2, P—B3; 6 B—N3.

Getting the bishop out of the way of Black's coming...P—Q4.

6...O—O; 7 O—O, P—QR4.

Threatening to trap White's bishop.

8 P—QR4, B—N5.

Preparing to give bishop for knight – this is a good idea here, since Black plans to put all his pawns on light squares, and the position is a blocked one, so that the bishop pair is not very dangerous.

9 QN—Q2, P—Q4; 10 P—K5, KN—Q2; 11 P—R3, B×N; 12 N×B, P—K3.

Now Black has a French Defence position in which he can prepare to undermine White's pawn chain with ...P—QB4. But Black has one advantage here – he has already exchanged off his "bad" French QB. The Botvinnik game continued:

13 B—N5, Q—N3; 14 R—R3, P—QB4.

Black won in 32 moves.

---

5 B—K2

5 B—K2. This is less ambitious than 5 B—QB4, and Black has several methods of obtaining a satisfactory position. There is no chance in this relatively quiet position of castling on opposite wings so: 5...O—O; 6 O—O, and now Black has available 6...B—N5 or 6...N—B3, followed by ...P—K4, but Black's most solid and reliable course is as follows:

6...P—B3; 7 P—KR3.

So that White can develop his QB on K3 without being molested by ...N—N5.

7...Q—B2; 8 B—K3, QN—Q2; 9 Q—Q2, P—QN4.

Threatening...P—N5.

10 P—R3, P—K4.

Black has a very secure position. He can continue with ...B—N2, ...QR—Q1 and ...KR—K1, and White will experience great difficulty in making any impression at all on Black's fortress.

6...N—B3

6...N—B3. This move can lead to another example of the fork trick. After 7 O—O Black plays 7...N×KP; 8 B×P ch (now 8 N×N, P—Q4; 9 B—Q3 fails to 9...P×N; 10 B×P, and White's QP is en prise), 8...R×B; 9 N×N, P—Q4, with a position similar to that given in the note to White's seventh move in the main text.

Play continues: 10 N—B3 (if 10 N(4)—N5, R—B1, White's knight is in trouble), 10...P—KR3!, threatening ...P—KN4—N5 with a strong attack; e.g., 11 B—K3, P—KN4; 12 N—R2, P—K4!; 13 N—K2, P×P; 14 N×P, N—K4, when Black's bishops and mobile pawns promise him a great advantage.

WHITE STORMS BLACK'S KING

1 P—K4	P—KN3
2 P—Q4	B—N2
3 N—QB3	P—Q3
4 B—K3	

4 ...	N—KB3
5 P—B3	O—O
6 Q—Q2	P—B3
7 O—O—O	P—QN4
8 B—R6	P—N5
9 QN—K2	P—QR4
10 P—KR4!	Q—B2
11 P—R5!	P—K4
12 B×B	K×B
13 P×NP	BP×P
14 Q—R6 ch	K—N1
15 P×P	P×P
16 N—B4!!	P×N
17 B—B4 ch	R—B2
18 B×R ch	K×B
19 Q×RP ch!	

---

1 P—K4	P—KN3
2 P—Q4	B—N2
3 N—QB3	P—Q3
4 B—K3	

(For 4 P—KR4 see p. 197)

One of the most aggressive moves at White's disposal. Already White announces his intention of following up with Q—Q2, O—O—O, and P—KR4, "having a go" at Black's king.

4 ...	N—KB3

Preparing ...N—N5, to molest White's QB, which White prevents.
(For 4...P—QR3 see p. 198)

5 P—B3

Incidentally, this gives added protection to White's KP. On top of this White is also ready to reinforce the projected attack with P—KN4. This position could be compared with the Sämisch Variation of the King's Indian Defence. There too, White plots an annihilating assault against Black's castled king.

5 ...	O—O?

On this occasion we deliberately give an inferior move in the main text to rub in a most important principle: you must never castle into an attack if you have no counter-play in the centre, or against your opponent's king. Black has no such counter-play here and he is spectacularly punished for his crime. The correct play for Black will be found in the notes.
(For 5...P—B3 see p. 198)

6 Q—Q2

Preparing B—KR6 to exchange off Black's useful defensive bishop.

6 ...	P—B3

Black too organizes an advance against White's king, but it is painfully slow. It might be more helpful to develop a piece now; e.g., by 6...N—B3, followed by ...P—K4, gaining some influence in the centre.

7 O—O—O	P—QN4
8 B—R6	

Very much according to plan. In conjunction with P—KR4—R5, opening the KR file, this is a typical method of assaulting a castled king defended by a fianchettoed bishop.

8 ...	P—N5
9 QN—K2	P—QR4
10 P—KR4!	

By now Black's position is probably hopeless. There is no defence to White's automatic mating attack. Mastery of the technique of such attacks will prove a useful point-scorer for anyone engaging in club and tournament play.

| 10 . . . | Q—B2 |
| 11 P—R5! | |

It seems that this advance is not possible and that White had to prepare it with P—KN4. But this is not so. If now 11...N×RP, the sacrifice 12 R×N!, P×R; 13 Q—N5, leads to checkmate.

| 11 . . . | P—K4 |

Trying for counter-play in the centre, but it is very much too late.

12 B×B

Downing one defender.

| 12 . . . | K×B |
| 13 P×NP | BP×P |

Or 13...RP×P; 14 Q—R6 ch, K—N1; 15 Q—R8, finis.

14 Q—R6 ch   K—N1

Forced. 14...K—B2; 15 Q×RP ch, N×Q; 16 R×N ch, and 17 R×Q wins quickly for White. This theme recurs in the game.

15 P×P

Opening a file for the QR.

| 15 . . . | P×P |
| 16 N—B4!! | |

Brilliantly announcing the intervention of his KB. Black can only prevent B—B4 ch by means of 16...B—R3, but then comes 17 Q×R ch!, K×Q; 18 N—K6 ch, with absolute carnage.

| 16 . . . | P×N |
| 17 B—B4 ch | R—B2 |

17...N—Q4; 18 P×N; and 17...K—R1; 18 Q×R ch are hopeless too, of course.

18 B×R ch   K×B

Or 18...Q×B; 19 R—Q8 ch.

19 Q×RP ch!

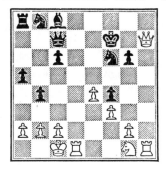

Now 19...N×Q; 20 R×N ch, K—K1; 21 R×Q, leaves White the exchange and a pawn up with a dominating position. So White must win.

This severe cautionary tale was from the game, MALACHI-BJÖRNSSON, Student's World Team Championship, Dresden 1969.

---

4 P—KR4

4 P—KR4. This represents an even more extreme and violent method of assaulting Black's king, but since Black has not yet committed his king to O—O, this immediate thrust is less effective than 4 B—K3. Black obtains a satisfactory game by means of the following pawn sacrifice:

4...N—KB3; 5 B—K2.
Still angling for P—R5.
5...P—KR4!.
Halting White's aggression.
6 P—B3.
To prepare B—K3.
6...N—B3; 7 B—K3.
7 P—Q5, N—K4, and if White continues to harry the knight with P—B4, the

piece can find a haven on KN5. This shows up a further defect of 4 P—KR4, which weakens the square KN4.

7...O—O.

Castling is good here now, but not earlier, since Black has adequate central counter-play.

8 Q—Q2, P—K4; 9 P—Q5, N—Q5!; 10 B×N, P×B; 11 Q×P, P—B3.

Black's two bishops, open lines, and control of the dark squares, give him more than enough for his pawn; e.g.,

12 P×P, P×P.

Threatening ...N—Q4, followed by ...N×N, shattering White's pawns.

13 Q—Q2, R—N1; 14 O—O—O, B—K3!; 15 Q×P, Q—R4.

Intending ...B×P, laying bare White's king.

16 P—R3, B—R3 ch; 17 P—B4.

17 K—N1, Q×N!.

17...KR—Q1.

And Black wins. We must conclude that 4 P—KR4 is premature and that it is Black who obtains attacking chances after this move.

4...P—QR3

4...P—QR3. This funny-looking move is a very modern idea with which there has not been much experience. It might seem that it violates the principles of development, but Black's plan is very deep. He calculates that he has just enough time to expand on the Q side before White can organize a really dangerous attack, and once Black has expanded on the Q side, White will not be able to play O—O—O, and so will be forced to alter his whole strategy.

Here is one example, from the game HARTSTON–KEENE, British Championship, Brighton 1972:

5 P—B3, N—Q2; 6 Q—Q2, P—QN4; 7 N—R3, B—N2; 8 B—K2, P—QB4; 9 P—Q5, KN—B3; 10 B—R6, O—O; 11 B×B, K×B.

Now it's too risky for White to play O—O—O, since his own king would be stormed by Black's advanced pawns; so he must castle on the same wing as Black, and that puts an end to his prospects of a mating attack by castling on opposite wings.

5...P—B3

5...P—B3. Much superior to 5...O—O. Black prepares an advance of his Q-side pawns and refuses to declare the future whereabouts of his king. This subtle strategy is good enough to guarantee Black a balanced game but we regard it as less ambitious.

Typical of further play from this position is: **6 Q—Q2, QN—Q2; 7 B—KR6, B×B; 8 Q×B, P—QN4,** gaining some useful space. After **9 O—O—O, P—N5; 10 N(B3)—K2, Q—N3,** Black has little to fear in the way of an attack against his king. His cautious play has robbed White of his normal target. In fact, White may have some problems when Black pushes forwards his own Q-side pawns. The relatively closed nature of the position means that Black's king is safe in the centre and he will only decide on ...O—O when White's queen has retreated to cope with Black's advance.

AUSTRIAN ATTACK

1 P—K4	P—KN3
2 P—Q4	B—N2
3 N—QB3	

3 ...	P—Q3
4 P—B4	N—KB3
5 N—B3	O—O
6 B—Q3	N—B3
7 P—K5	P×P
8 BP×P	N—KR4!
9 B—K3	B—N5
10 B—K4	P—B3
11 P×P	N×BP!
12 B×N	P×B
13 O—O	

---

1 P—K4	P—KN3
2 P—Q4	B—N2
3 N—QB3	

By far the commonest choice here. White develops a piece and retains the option of the aggressive P—KB4, building up a most imposing pawn centre.

3 ...	P—Q3
4 P—B4	N—KB3

In view of White's threatening central activity, Black develops his KN with the intention of castling as soon as possible.

5 N—B3

Typical development for White in the

Austrian Attack. White masses his pieces on their most aggressive central squares.

5 ...   O—O

(For 5...P—B4 see p. 200)

6 B—Q3

6 B—B4 looks more to the point, but it allows the fork trick with 6...N×P and...P—Q4.

(For 6 P—K5 see p. 201)

6 ...   N—B3

Black's strategy is to undermine White's vast pawn centre, so this obstruction of the QBP may appear anti-thematic. However, the immediate 6...P—B4 would fall flat after 7 P×P!, P×P; 8 P—K5, and White has a powerful wedge in the centre, while Black's QBP is looking rather silly with nothing left to do. 6...N—B3 is a more subtle method of pressurizing White's QP. Black plans ...B—N5 and ...P—K4, completing his development with gains of tempo.

(For 6...B—N5 see p. 201)

7 P—K5

White's centre rumbles forward to cut off the diagonal of Black's KB.

(For 7 O—O and 7 P—KR3 see pp. 201-2)

7 ...	P×P
8 BP×P	

The most ambitious. 8 QP×P, N—Q4; 9 N×N, Q×N gives White no more than an equal game. Superficially this position may resemble that given in the note examining 6...P—B4, but in this case Black has usefully developed a piece (N—QB3) instead of having a useless pawn on QB4, and this difference reacts in his favour.

8 ...   N—KR4!

Admittedly, this places a knight on the edge of the board, but here we have one of those situations when a rule must be broken in view of the other, overriding, compensating factors. All other knight moves are inferior. The point is that Black wants to undermine White's centre with ...P—KB3, and the square KN5 should be kept free for the QB, to intensify the pressure against White's central pawns. So 8...N—KN5 is inferior, as is ...N—K1, which merely obstructs the movement of Black's own pieces. Finally, 8...N—Q4 blocks off Black's own attack against White's QP, which is en prise after 8...N—KR4!

9 B—K3

White protects his pawn by developing a piece.

9 ...   B—N5

Once again threatening the White QP.

10 B—K4

Now the queen defends the pawn. Also, White can slip in B(K4)×QN eliminating an attacking piece, if the pressure becomes too great.

10 ...   P—B3

The thematic stroke at White's advanced centre. The pressure has reached such a peak that White must acquiesce in an exchange.

11 P×P

(For 11 Q—K2 see p. 202)

11 ...   N×BP!

Bringing back the knight to the centre and with gain of tempo on White's bishop, since Black threatens 12...N× B; 13 N×N, B×N, and ...N×QP.

12 B×N   P×B
13 O—O

White must castle before it's too late. In this position Black's pawns are broken (four pawn islands to two) but he has plenty of open lines for his pieces, good development, and the bishop pair.

We must assess chances as equal, especially in view of the possible continuation: 13...N—Q4; 14 N×N (what else?); 14...P×N; 15 P—KR3,

B×N; 16 R×B, R×R; 17 Q×R, Q—Q3, and Black follows up with ...P—K4, ironing out all of his weaknesses.

Neither side can claim any advantage after 17...Q—Q3.

5...P—B4

5...P—B4. This immediate assault on White's centre was Bobby Fischer's choice in his 1972 World Title Match. Black exploits the temporary under-protection of White's KP to meet 6 P×P, Q—R4; 7 P×P with 7...N×P!, and the pressure against White's QN leaves Black on top. Of course Black must not play 6 P×P, P×P?, since 7 Q×Q ch forces Black into a horrible tangle with his king stuck permanently in the middle of the board.

Probably the best way to handle this position for both sides was seen in the 17th game of the SPASSKY–FISCHER Match, Reykjavik 1972: 6 P×P, Q—R4; 7 B—Q3 (covering the KP), 7...Q× BP; 8 Q—K2 (in order to castle White must chase away Black's queen), 8...

O—O; 9 B—K3, Q—QR4; 10 O—O, B—N5; 11 QR—Q1, N—B3; 12 B—B4, and White has a slight advantage in development since Black has been forced to waste time with his queen in order to avoid an inferior pawn structure. However, White's advantage is not particularly significant in view of the solid nature of Black's position, and the game was eventually drawn.

6 P—K5

6 P—K5. This can lead to vast and crazy complications with 6...KN—Q2; 7 P—KR4 (having displaced Black's knight, White storms the fortress of Black's king), 7...P—QB4; 8 P—R5. A detailed analysis is quite beyond the scope of a book dealing with general principles. Suffice it to say that Black's resources are adequate to hold the balance, and if the reader desires to master all the secrets of this most hair-raising of variations, he should consult a specialist opening manual.

However, after 6 P—K5 Black can play more safely with 6...P×P; 7 QP×P, Q×Q ch; 8 K×Q, R—Q1 ch; 9 B—Q3, N—K1!. This is one position where the knight is well placed on the back rank, the more since Black's KR is not shut in on KB1. On K1 the knight supports an attack on White's KP, based on ...P—KB3 in conjunction with ...N—QB3 and ...B—KN5. If Black put his KN on KN5 or KR4 on move nine, it would be molested by White's K-side pawns. On 9...N—K1 Black stands well; e.g., 10 K—K2 (to break the pin on his KB), 10...N—QB3; 11 B—K3, N—N5; 12 B—K4, P—KB4!, with a

vigorous counter-attack. If White captures en passant then 13...N×KBP returns the knight to base in the centre, thus justifying Black's ninth move.

6...B—N5

6...B—N5. A weak move which results in premature surrender of the bishop pair. The intention is to reduce the defence of White's QP by eliminating White's KN and then pile on the pressure with...N—QB3. But it is more accurate to play...N—QB3 first.

6...B—N5 went right out of favour after FISCHER's brilliant win against BENKÖ in the 1963 USA Championship: 7 P—KR3!, B×N; 8 Q×B, N—B3; 9 B—K3, P—K4; 10 QP×P, P×P; 11 P—B5, P×P; 12 Q×P, N—Q5; 13 Q—B2, N—K1; 14 O—O, N—Q3; 15 Q—N3, K—R1; 16 Q—N4, P—QB3; 17 Q—R5, Q—K1; 18 B×N, P×B; 19 R—B6!!, K—N1 (19...B×R; 20 P—K5 gives mate); 20 P—K5, P—KR3; 21 N—K2, Resigns. If the Black knight moves, Q—B5 ends it all.

Note the role played in this by White's light-squared bishop.

7 O—O

7 O—O. A routine developing move which allows Black to carry out his plan: 7...B—N5; 8 B—K3, P—K4!, completing the assault on White's QP. Now 9 BP×P, P×P; 10 P—Q5, N—Q5 leaves White's KN tied up in an annoy-

ing pin, while 9 BP×P, P×P; 10 P×P, N×P; 11 B—K2 inflicts White with a weak, isolated blockaded KP.

After 7...B—N5, White's best is 8 P—K5, P×P; 9 QP×P, N—Q4; 10 N×N, Q×N; 11 P—KR3, with a roughly level game.

---

7 P—KR3

7 P—KR3. A very ambitious move which (a) prevents Black's putting pressure against the White QP based on ...B—KN5 and (b) prepares a massive pawn-storm with P—KN4. However, it wastes a crucial development tempo in a very sharp position, and Black can exploit this to commence an operation which instantly nibbles away at White's centre from the wings.

7...N—QN5!.
Moving the same piece twice, but this move is strong because it simultaneously unblocks Black's QBP and aims to obtain the Bishop pair.

8 B—K3.
Massing pieces in the centre is a stock response, but the retreat 8 B—K2 would have been more prudent.

8...P—N3; 9 P—R3, N×B; 10 P× N.

White relies on the doubled pawns to strengthen his centre, but in this case they are weak, since Black can launch a quick attack against the rear QP with ...B—QR3. 10 Q×N, P—B4 is also good for Black, who has the bishop pair in an open position. The manoeuvre N(KB3 or QB3)—N5, followed by N× B(Q3) or (K3), is one to be noted!

10...P—B4; 11 Q—Q2, B—QR3; 12 K—B2?.
Much stronger is 12 O—O!, with defensive chances. The text still plans P—KN4, but this "attacking" idea is premature in the sense that it should not be played at all, and Black easily puts an end to it. White should be thinking of defence now.

12...R—B1.
To meet 13 QR—KN1 with 13...P—B5; 14 P×P, R×P, and the threat of ...R×N and ...N×P ch halts White's aggression completely. From this point on we see Black increasing his advantage by virtue of his bishop pair in support of his mobile central pawns:

13 KR—QB1, N—Q2; 14 P—Q5, P—K3; 15 P×P, P×P; 16 R—K1, N—B3; 17 QR—Q1, P—Q4; 18 P×P, P×P; 19 P—Q4, N—K5 ch; 20 N×N, P×N; 21 N—K5, P— KN4!.
Black has a decisive advantage. White's centre is about to dissolve entirely (PENROSE–KEENE, British Championship, Blackpool 1971).

---

11 Q—K2

11 Q—K2. If White stubbornly refuses to relinquish his centre with 11 P×P, he can be overtaken by a horrible disaster.

For example in the game GLIGORIC-KEENE, Berlin 1971, Black replied to 11 Q—K2 with **11...P×P**, then **12 B×N, P×B; 13 Q—B4 ch, P—K3; 14 B—N5, Q—N1!**, and with this paradoxical move Black already achieved a winning position. There is a very real threat from Black's queen to White's QNP, and after **15 O—O—O, B×N; 16 P×B, P×P**, Black has more pawns and a good position, and went on to win the game without too many difficulties.

PSEUDO KING'S INDIAN VARIATION

1 P—K4	P—KN3
2 P—Q4	B—N2
3 P—QB4	

3 . . .	P—Q3
4 N—QB3	N—QB3
5 P—Q5	N—Q5
6 B—K3	P—QB4
7 KN—K2	Q—N3
8 Q—Q2	B—N5
9 N—R4	

1 P—K4	P—KN3
2 P—Q4	B—N2
3 P—QB4	

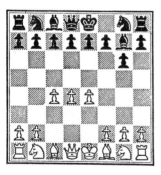

As we have seen, White normally takes the opportunity to develop a knight on his third move, but the text is also not uncommon, issuing an invitation to Black to transpose into the King's Indian Defence. However, Black can retain the contours of the Modern Defence by declining to develop his KN and concentrating instead on increasing pressure with his KB and QN against White's QP.

3 . . .	P—Q3
4 N—QB3	

It is best to develop the QN here. 4 N—KB3 would allow ...B—N5, augmenting the pressure against White's QP.

4 . . .	N—QB3

Developing the knight with a threat to White's QP. This is consistent with Black's plan of campaign outlined above. 4...N—KB3 would mean direct transposition to a King's Indian Defence.

(For 4...P—K4 see p. 204)

5 P—Q5

Attacking the knight is a natural reaction. 5 B—K3, defending the QP, is discussed in the notes.

(For 5 B—K3 see p. 204)

5 . . .	N—Q5

The dismal retreat 5...N—N1 hardly comes into consideration. Now Black has achieved his goal and occupied White's Q4 square with a piece ("playing into the opponent's half" is often good advice); but it will be a tough struggle to maintain the knight on its advanced post.

6 B—K3

Attacking the knight.

6 . . .	P—QB4

Supporting the knight without blocking the path of the KB by 6...P—K4.

7 KN—K2

White hopes to force the exchange of knights. Now 7...N×N; 8 B×N would mean that Black has wasted three moves (N—QB3—Q5×N) merely to develop a White piece (KB).

White could also play 7 P×P e.p., N×P, but Black could complete his development without further problems.

7 ...   Q—N3

This is a case where the early development of the queen is necessary. Otherwise Black would no longer be able to support his knight.

8 Q—Q2

White plans R—Q1, a further step to increase pressure against the knight.

(For 8 N×N see p. 205)

8 ...   B—N5

Attacking one of the pieces that threatens the knight. The attempt to support his knight by 8...P—K4 fails horribly: 9 P×P e.p., P×P; 10 R—Q1, P—K4; 11 N—Q5, Q—Q1; 12 N×N, BP×N; 13 B—N5, and White has an active position while Black has a "dead" point, instead of a piece, at his Q5.

9 N—R4

(For 9 O—O—O see p. 205)

By threatening Black's queen White finally breaks one of the links in the chain of pieces defending Black's knight. However, QR4 is not an attractive square for a knight, and Black can

exploit the displacement of this piece to reach an equal position: 9...Q—N5!; 10 Q×Q, N—B7 ch; 11 K—Q2, N×Q; 12 P—QR3, N—QR3; 13 R—QN1, B—Q2; 14 N(4)—B3, N—R3, followed by ...O—O and ...P—B4, and Black has good counter-play on the K side to make up for the chances White obtains with P—QN4.

4...P—K4

4...P—K4. This is another way of avoiding transposition to the King's Indian Defence, but White retains some advantage after **5 P×P, P×P; 6 Q× Q ch, K×Q; 7 P—B4,** followed by N—B3. Black's king is rather insecure in the middle of the board and, in view of White's possibilities of B—K3 and O—O—O, Black does not have a firm grip over White's Q4 as compensation.

This variation stresses that it is dangerous to forfeit early on, the right of castling one's king into safety.

---

5 B—K3

5 B—K3. Supporting the QP in this fashion leads to a sharp fight in which White advances on the Q side, and Black on the K side: **5...P—K4; 6 P—Q5, QN—K2; 7 P—B5, P—B4**, with chances for both sides. Note that after **6...N—Q5?; 7 KN—K2**, it is no longer possible to support the knight; e.g., **7...P—QB4; 8 P×P e.p., N×P**, and Black's backward QP is very weak.

White cannot copy the first variation above, here, with **6 P×P, P×P; 7 Q×Q ch**, since Black would recapture with his QN and then redeploy this piece on the excellent central square K3. Black would then have complete control over White's hole on Q4, which could not be protected by a pawn.

---

8 N×N

8 N×N. By playing this, White can force a draw if he so desires:

8...P×N.

8...B×N?; 9 B×B, P×B; 10 N—N5 wins a pawn for White.

9 N—R4, Q—R4 ch.

9...Q—N5 ch?; 10 B—Q2, and the Black queen goes! Anything else on move nine for Black loses the QP for no compensation.

10 P—N4, Q×P ch; 11 B—Q2, Q—R6; 12 B—B1, Q—N5 ch; 13 B—Q2. A draw by repetition.

---

9 O—O—O

---

9 O—O—O. A drastic method of

increasing the pressure against Black's knight, but it is risky to put the king at the wrong end of Black's fianchettoed KB.

9...N×N ch.

Black is quite happy to surrender his knight now in order to open the diagonal of his KB.

10 N×N.

An unfortunate retreat, but **10 B×N, B×B; 11 N×B, Q—R3** is very embarrassing for White, who would then have to weaken the pawn cover around his king with **12 P—QN3**, in order to cover all his pawns. Black could commence a vigorous attack with **12...Q—R6 ch; 13 K—N1, P—QR4**, which White could hardly hope to fend off.

10...Q—R3; 11 P—B3, B—Q2; 12 N—B3, Q—R4.

Black is now in a position to inaugurate a promising advance of his Q-side pawns against White's king.

The game DONNER–KEENE, from the international tournament at Palma de Mallorca 1971 concluded:

13 Q—B2, P—QR3; 14 B—Q2, N—B3; 15 R—K1, O—O; 16 K—N1, Q—B2; 17 P—B4, P—QN4!.

A powerful and typical pawn sacrifice to open files and diagonals against White's king.

18 P×P, P×P; 19 N×P, Q—N2; 20 N—B3, KR—N1; 21 B—B4, N—K1.

Bringing over the final piece for the attack.

22 R—K2, N—B2; 23 KR—K1, N—N4; 24 N×N, B×N; 25 P—QN3, R×P!.

Shattering White's defences – White resigned. If **26 K×R**, then **R—R1 ch** mates, while **26 Q×R, B×B** is truly horrible for White.

15

FLANK OPENINGS

1 N—KB3; 1 P QN3; 1 P—QB4

In previous sections we have witnessed White employing his birthright of the first move to commence the construction of a pawn centre with either 1 P—K4 or 1 P—Q4, and indeed, these natural, direct, and aggressive moves are the most popular choices at all levels of play.

But an alternative to this approach does exist in the highly subtle and indirect Flank openings. In these systems White does not go straight for the occupation of the centre with pawns – rather he observes the centre from the wings, normally by fianchettoing one or both bishops. Furthermore White restrains his central pawns in the hope that he may eventually conquer the central zone with even greater force by virtue of this retardation. In these systems Black is positively invited to occupy the centre with pawns, and White will then use his wing pawns (especially the QNP and QBP) as levers to deflect away Black's pawns from the middle of the board.

It will be seen that White does not neglect the centre when he uses a Flank opening, he merely disguises his attentions towards that zone. Ultimately he hopes to create a central pawn majority supported by his bishops bearing down on the centre from the flanks – cf. our comments in the chapter on The Importance of Pawns concerning the desirability of a mobile central pawn majority.

The reader will observe that the strategy for White in the Flank openings bears a certain resemblance to that employed by Black in the King's Indian Defence and the Modern Defence, and a close study of these three sections in conjunction, will certainly enrich the reader's understanding of this type of opening for Black and for White.

Here are the opening moves of a game played by one of the pioneers of Flank openings, Richard Réti, in which White's strategy of retarding his pawns succeeds to perfection (Réti-Rubinstein, Carlsbad 1923):

1 N—KB3, P—Q4; 2 P—KN3.
Hypermodern "indirectness" from White as opposed to Classical directness from Black.

2...N—KB3; 3 B—N2, P—KN3; 4 P—B4, P—Q5; 5 P—Q3, B—N2; 6 P—QN4.
Golombek in his book on Réti writes: "The Black QP is to be deprived of its natural support by a pawn on QB4 and will eventually have to be exchanged, when White will conquer the centre with a force all the greater for having been retarded."

6...O—O; 7 QN—Q2, P—B4; 8 N—N3, P×P; 9 B—N2.

No hurry! Black's QP must eventually fall into White's hands.

9...N—B3; 10 QN×P, N×N; 11 B×N, P—N3; 12 P—QR3, B—N2; 13 B—N2, P×P; 14 R×P, Q—B2; 15 Q—R1, N—K1; 16 B×B.

Exchanging off one of the defenders near Black's king.

16...N×B; 17 O—O, N—K3; 18 R—N1, B—B3; 19 P—Q4.

White has now achieved a central pawn majority which Black cannot touch. He won the game on move 50 after he had crushed Black by advancing his centre like an avalanche.

The Flank openings are too numerous to analyse exhaustively; here we will confine our investigation to the following four:

1 P—QN3: the Nimzowitsch/Larsen Attack.

1 N—KB3, followed by P—QB4: the Catalan/Réti System.

1 N—KB3, followed by P—KN3 and P—Q3: the King's Indian Attack.

1 P—QB4: the English Opening.

An important advantage of 1 N—KB3 and 1 P—QB4 is the possibilities they offer of transposition into other openings. Thus, if you want to play a Queen's Gambit against a Nimzo-Indian expert without allowing his favourite defence, you could try 1 P—QB4, N—KB3; 2 N—QB3, P—K3; 3 N—B3!, and if 3...B—N5 you don't need to play 4 P—Q4, while if he plays 3...P—Q4 then you can play 4 P—Q4 with equanimity.

NIMZOWITSCH-LARSEN ATTACK

1 P—QN3

1 . . .	P—K4
2 B—N2	N—QB3
3 P—QB4	N—B3
4 N—KB3	P—K5!
5 N—Q4	B—B4
6 N×N	QP×N!!
7 P—K3	B—B4
8 Q—B2	Q—K2
9 B—K2	O—O—O

1 P—QN3

Employed spasmodically by the great writer and master Aron Nimzowitsch, the popularity of this opening increased dramatically when it was adopted by Bent Larsen, one of the most successful tournament players of modern times.

1 . . .   P—K4

The testing reply, after which White will have great difficulty in preventing his opponent from forming a broad pawn-centre with ...P—Q4. After 1...P—Q4, 2 B—N2 prevents 2...P—K4.
(For 1...P—Q4 see p. 209)

2 B—N2

Developing the QB with gain of tempo against Black's KP. In fact, the assault on Black's bold KP forms one of the main themes of White's future strategy.

2 . . .   N—QB3

Best, defending the pawn by developing a piece. Moving the pawn out of range of White's QB with 2...P—K5 would be silly. The obstruction to the scope of White's QB would vanish and the pawn on K5 would be exposed to attack (e.g., P—Q3; N—QB3).

3 P—QB4

This is one way of discouraging Black from playing...P—Q4.
(For 3 P—K3 see p. 210)

3 . . .   N—B3

Once again Black threatens...P—Q4, since he can now recapture with a knight on Q4.

4 N—KB3

Still holding up ...P—Q4 and consistent with the attack against Black's KP, but very risky, since White falls behind in development after Black's next move.
(For 4 P—K3 see p. 210)

4 . . .   P—K5!

Now, this is a very good move since it happens with tempo-gain on White's knight.

5 N—Q4

5 N—KR4 would leave the knight looking very lonely at the edge of the board.

5 . . .   B—B4

Developing, but White can double Black's pawns.

6 N×N   QP×N!!

Black knows just when to break all the rules. First he invited doubled pawns and now he recaptures away from the centre. Ordinarily this would be idiotic, but here Black has ample compensation in the shape of (i) open lines for his pieces; (ii) a vast lead in development; (iii) pressure against White's backward QP. 6...NP×N looks more normal, intending to build up the centre with ...P—Q4, but Black sees that the most important thing is to bring his QB out with the utmost speed.

7 P—K3	B—B4
8 Q—B2	Q—K2
9 B—K2	O—O—O

Now White can never free himself by advancing his QP, and Black has much the better of it. This position arose on board one in the second round of the World *v* USSR Match in 1970. LARSEN played White and SPASSKY Black. The game continued:

10 P—B4?.
Weakening the pawn structure around his king. You should be very careful about moving your KBP, KNP or KRP two squares forward if you have not castled or have already castled K side. Development by 10 N—B3! was imperative.

10...N—N5.
Black immediately exploits the weakness to open the diagonal for his queen to go to KR5.

11 P—N3.
Preventing the check.

11...P—KR4.
The usual way of storming against a pawn on KN3. Now it is especially effective, since there is no White bishop on KN2 to aid the defence.

12 P—KR3, P—R5!.
Commencing a brilliant attack in the course of which Black sacrifices two pieces; but its success is only credible, with White's king stuck in the centre and no Q-side pieces developed.

13 P×N, P×P; 14 R—N1.
14 R×R, R×R; 15 K—B1, Q—R5 is clearly hopeless for White.

14...R—R8!!.
A move of genius. No amount of general principles can teach you how to find a move like this. You have to see it! But general principles can teach you how to build up strong positions – the combinative vision to finish off your winning games with sparkling sacrifices, comes with talent and experience. The finale is superb:

15 R×R, P—N7; 16 R—B1, Q—R5 ch; 17 K—Q1, P×R(Q) ch; 18 Resigns.
Had White played 16 R—N1, Black would have won as follows: 16...Q—R5 ch; 17 K—Q1, Q—R8; 18 Q—B3, Q×R ch; 19 K—B2, Q—B7; 20 P×B, P—N8(=Q).

1...P—Q4

1...P—Q4. Black has many reasonable replies to 1 P—QN3. 1...N—KB3 is possible, as is 1...P—QB4 and even 1...P—QN3. But 1...P—Q4 is reliable; e.g., 1...P—Q4; 2 B—N2, N—KB3; 3 P—K3, P—KN3, and Black's KB comes out on KN2 to challenge the long dark diagonal. Black would follow up with ...O—O and ...P—QB4, or, the super-solid ...P—QB3.

One thing Black should not do is play 1...P—Q4; 2 B—N2, P—QB4; 3 P—K3, N—QB3, since 4 B—N5, followed by N—KB3, would give White a Nimzo-Indian Defence with colours reversed and therefore an extra move.

---

3 P—K3

3 P—K3. Continuing the fight against Black's KP by means of B—QN5. White makes no attempt to prevent the formation of a massive Black pawn centre after 3...P—Q4, but rather regards the centre as a target.

Play might continue: **3...P—Q4** (...P—Q3 is more circumspect); **4 B—N5, B—Q3** (developing a piece to protect the KP). Now White has two flanking blows available to undermine Black's centre – P—KB4 and P—QB4.

(a) **5 P—KB4, Q—R5 ch!; 6 P—N3, Q—K2; 7 N—KB3, QB—N5** (LJUBOJEVIC–PORTISCH, Teesside 1972). Black has a very solid position. White is very weak on the light squares near his king. That was the point of 5...Q—R5 ch.

(b) **5 P—QB4!, P×P; 6 N—KB3,** **P×P; 7 Q×P,** with good compensation for a pawn. This sacrifice is a suggestion of Larsen. Alternatively White could play safe with 6 B×BP or 6 P×P. Neither move looks bad.

We must conclude that 3 P—K3 is superior to Larsen's 3 P—QB4, which he played against Spassky. Spassky's win against Larsen was given in the main text to emphasize the evils of under-development, and also to highlight Spassky's subtle appreciation of the correct moment to break the rules.

---

4 P—K3

4 P—K3. This can transpose into a Sicilian with reversed colours. It is certainly safer than Larsen's 4 N—KB3.

Here is a possible line: **4...P—Q4; 5 P×P, N×P; 6 B—N5,** and White will try to inflict doubled pawns on Black in the QB file at the cost of giving up his light-squared bishop.

CATALAN

The Catalan opening is a kind of Queen's Gambit where White fianchettoes his KB.

1 N—KB3	P—Q4
2 P—B4	P—K3
3 P—KN3	N—KB3
4 B—N2	B—K2
5 O—O	O—O
6 P—Q4	QN—Q2
7 Q—B2	P—QN3
8 P×P	N×P!
9 N—B3	B—N2
10 N×N	B×N
11 P—K4	B—N2
12 B—B4	

1 N—KB3	P—Q4

(For 1...N—KB3 see p. 213)

It is a natural reaction to occupy the centre with pawns after White's first move, and as 1...P—K4 is impossible in view of 2 N×P, 1...P—Q4 is the next best.

2 P—B4

Attacking Black's QP and hoping to lure it away from its central post. After 2...P×P; 3 P—K3, White could transpose (by following with B×P and P—Q4) into a favourable version of the Queen's Gambit Accepted.

2 ...	P—K3

Stolidly refusing to give any ground in the centre.

(For 2...P—Q5 see p. 213)

3 P—KN3

White intends to continue with P—Q4 after a few more moves, going into a kind of Queen's Gambit Declined, Orthodox Defence, but with his KB developed on KN2. White hopes that his bishop on KN2 will help to increase the pressure against Black's QP.

3...	N—KB3

If 3...P×P, then 4 Q—R4 ch and Q×P(B4), when White's queen is quite well placed on the open QB file. Black prefers to concentrate on the defence of his QP, the focal point of his position. All his pieces are now developed to have some contact with this point. The opening turns into a grim fight for control of this square.

4 B—N2	B—K2

A typical mistake here would be ...B—B4. This looks like a good square for the bishop, but in fact its a serious error, for two reasons:

(a) the bishop blocks Black's QBP which should advance to free his game;

(b) White will soon play P—Q4, attacking the bishop and gaining development tempi.

5 O—O	O—O
6 P—Q4	

Going into the Queen's Gambit position. If Black antithematically surrenders his central grip with 6...P×P, White retrieves his pawn with 7 N—K5 or 7 Q—B2. After the latter move 7...P—QN4 is impossible: 8 P—QR4, P—QB3; 9 P×P, P×P; 10 N—N5!, winning a rook. This is a trap the reader should note.

6 ...	QN—Q2

6...N—B3 can be played, but has the defect of obstructing Black's QBP.

7 Q—B2   P—QN3

The normal paths of development for Black's QB are not available, so Black brings it out via QN2. Incidentally, the QB on N2 is also pointing at Black's Q4 square.

(For 7. . .P—B3 see p. 214)

8 P×P

Opening up the QB file for White's queen.

8 . . .   N×P!

There are several drawbacks to 8. . .P×P:

(*a*) It permanently blocks the QR1—KR8 diagonal for Black's QB.

(*b*) Both 9 B—B4 and 9 N—K5 would give White some initiative.

(*c*) Worst of all, after 8. . .P×P White can exploit the hole on QB6 with 9 Q—B6!, tying Black up in knots; e.g., 9. . .R—N1; 10 B—B4!. After 8. . .N×P; 9 Q—B6, R—N1, the move 10 B—B4 is no longer any good, so Black has time to expel White's queen with . . .N—QN5 or . . .B—N2.

After the text White has a central pawn majority but Black is well developed and has chances to equalize.

9 N—B3   B—N2

Of course not 9. . .N×N; 10 P×N, strengthening White's centre.

10 N×N

To gain a tempo for central advance by attacking Black's QB, since 10. . .P×N would, once again, block the diagonal of this piece.

10 . . .   B×N
11 P—K4   B—N2
12 B—B4

Developing a piece with gain of time by attacking the QBP. The opening phase is completed and White has a slight pull.

We are following the game KEENE-ROBATSCH, from top board of a match between England and Austria in the West European Team Tournament at Madrid 1971:

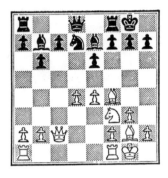

12. . .P—QB4.

Necessary, to challenge White's centre before White places his rooks on the central files Q1 and K1.

13 P—Q5, P×P; 14 P×P, B—KB3.

14. . .B×P is impossible – 15 QR—Q1, N—B3; 16 N—N5, threatening R×B, and if 16. . .P—N3, then 17 B—K5 wins material. 15. . .B—QB3; 16 N—N5, B×N; 17 B×QB is also very good for White. In view of all this, White succeeds in maintaining a powerful passed pawn in the centre.

15 P—KR4.

Supporting an attack on Black's king by N—N5. 15. . .B×QP; 16 QR—Q1 is still good for White.

15. . .R—K1; 16 N—N5, N—B1; 17 QR—Q1, B—Q5.

To cut the support of the passed pawn.

18 B—K3!, P—KR3.

18. . .B×B; 19 P×B uncovers an attack from White's rook against Black's KB2.

19 N—K4.

A fine central square for a knight.

19. . .B×B; 20 P×B, N—N3.

Black's knight, too, strives for its own K4 square, from which it can never be shifted. This would provide Black with good compensation for White's strong, passed QP, but its not to be. 20. . .Q—K2 first was essential. Now White has the opportunity for a stroke which destroys the shelter of Black's king, which he already weakened with 18. . .P—KR3.

21 R×P!!, K×R; 22 R—KB1 ch, K—K2.

Or 22. . .K—N1; 23 N—B6 ch!, P×N; 24 Q×N ch, K—R1; 25 Q×RP ch, K—N1; 26 R×P, and White wins.

23 P—Q6 ch.

The passed pawn begins to make its presence felt.

23...K—Q2; 24 R—B7 ch, N—K2.
Or 24...K—B1; 25 R—B7 ch, K—N1; 26 R×B ch, K×R; 27 N×P dis. ch, and wins.

25 Q—R4 ch, K—B1.
25...B—B3; 26 B—R3 mate.

26 P—Q7 ch!.
The passed pawn deals the final blow.

26...Q×P; 27 B—R3!, Resigns.
27...Q×B; 28 Q×R ch, with imminent mate.

1...N—KB3

1...N—KB3. Black is under no obligation to occupy the centre at once. He can also play possum with this move or even 1...P—KN3. Here is a typical continuation:

1 N—KB3, N—KB3; 2 P—B4, P—KN3; 3 P—KN3, B—N2; 4 B—N2, O—O; 5 O—O, P—B3.
5...P—Q3 transposes to a King's Indian Defence.

6 P—Q4, P—Q4.
Really threatening 7...P×P, since the pawn on QB3 already supports ...P—QN4.

7 QN—Q2, B—B4; 8 P—N3.
The bishop must be developed in this fashion.

8...QN—Q2; 9 B—N2, N—K5.
Black has a solid position and approximate equality. White can gain a slight initiative by playing 7 P×P, P×P; 8 N—B3, N—K5; 9 N—K5, N×N; 10 P×N, N—B3; 11 N×N, P×N, since he has the move in a symmetrical position, but this hardly promises a tangible advantage, let alone winning chances for White.

2...P—Q5

2...P—Q5. Dogmatically claiming space in the centre; but the move is very risky since Black's advanced QP is open to undermining attacks:

3 P—KN3, P—QB4.
Necessary to support his QP. If 3...N—QB3, Black would have a considerably weaker hold on White's QN4 square, and White would achieve this advance by means of the manoeuvre: N—QR3—B2/P—QR3/R—N1/P—QN4. White would follow up with P—QN5, chasing away Black's QN, and then play P—K3, nibbling at the QP. 3...P—QB4 obviously slows down White's process of achieving P—QN4.

4 B—N2, N—QB3; 5 O—O, P—K4; 6 P—Q3, B—K2; 7 N—R3, N—B3; 8 N—B2, O—O; 9 P—QR3.
Preparing a slower P—QN4 backed up by P—K3, attacking Black's pawn-chain. Chances are about equal.

However, White has a most promising pawn sacrifice available on move seven, which severely weakens Black's centre; this sacrifice involves a typical exchange of two wing pawns for a more valuable centre pawn:

7 P—QN4!, P×P; 8 P—QR3, P×P; 9 Q—R4, B—Q2; 10 B×P, N—B3; 11 Q—N5!.
White has a powerful attack; e.g., 11...B×B; 12 N×B, Q—K2; 13 Q×NP. This motif is also known from the Four Pawns Attack in the King's Indian Defence.

Such blows from the wing against a

pawn centre are entirely characteristic of the Flank openings.

7...P—B3

7...P—B3. A solid continuation popular in tournament play. Black devotes his energy towards supporting his QP. White can gain a spatial advantage by force now, but Black has very good chances to equalize the game.

8 P—N3.

8 B—B4 is playable too. With the text White covers his own QP in preparation for P—K4.

8...P—QN3.

Black's set-up looks passive, but it is very difficult to penetrate his defences before he completes the development of his men, and plays the necessary freeing advance...P—QB4.

9 B—N2, B—N2; 10 N—B3, R—B1.

Putting a rook opposite the opponent's queen is often a good idea.

11 QR—Q1, Q—B2.

All in the interests of...P—QB4, which Black is now ready to play. To forestall this, White must strike in the centre.

12 P—K4, P×KP; 13 N×P, N×N; 14 Q×N.

This position has come about on countless occasions in tournament games, and Black normally holds the draw. Best is 14...P—QB4; e.g., 15 Q—K2, P×P; 16 N×P, B×B; 17 K×B, Q—N2 ch, and although White has the nominal advantage of a three-two Q-side pawn majority it is hard to exploit this.

White can also try 15 P—Q5, but Black can still minimize White's advantage with 15...B—KB3 (challenging White's powerful QB); 16 Q—B2, P×P; 17 P×P, Q—Q3!, blockading White's passed QP.

This is an idea of the Yugoslav Grandmaster Matanovic, who once lost a game by playing 17...B×B (intending...Q—Q3 next move), overlooking the "Zwischenzug" (in-between move) 18 P—Q6!, and after 18...Q—Q1; 19 Q×B, White's far advanced QP was like a fishbone stuck in Black's throat.

KING'S INDIAN ATTACK

1 N—KB3	P—Q4
2 P—KN3	N—KB3
3 B—N2	P—QB4
4 O—O	N—QB3
5 P—Q3	
5 . . .	P—K3
6 QN—Q2	B—K2
7 P—K4	O—O
8 R—K1	P—QN4
9 P—K5	N—K1
10 N—B1	P—QR4

11 P—KR4	P—R5
12 B—B4	P—R6
13 P—N3	B—N2

---

1 N—KB3

(For other moves see p. 216)

The same initial move as the Catalan, but in the King's Indian Attack White plans to continue with P—Q3 and P—K4 rather than P—QB4.

1 ...	P—Q4

(For 1...N—KB3 see p. 216)

2 P—KN3	N—KB3
3 B—N2	P—QB4

Occupying the centre with pawns in the traditional fashion.

4 O—O	N—QB3
5 P—Q3	

Announcing a King's Indian Attack formation. White's opening moves are very flexible and it was also possible to play here 5 P—B4 or even 5 P—Q4, with immediate pressure against Black's pawn centre.

5 ...	P—K3

Securing the QP as in Black's anti-Catalan play.

(For 5...P—K4 see p. 216)

6 QN—Q2	

To support P—K4. 6 N—B3 would also achieve this, but would allow the exchange of queens if Black played ...QP×P at the necessary moment, and White needs queens on the board for his attack.

6 ...	B—K2

The best square. 6...B—Q3 would expose the bishop to a potential fork after White had played P—K4.

7 P—K4	O—O
8 R—K1	P—QN4

The stage is set: White attacks on the K side by means of P—K5, driving away Black's KN, followed by P—KR4—R5—R6. Black counters this strategy by marching his pawns towards White's Q wing.

9 P—K5	N—K1

9...N—Q2 is, of course, well playable.

(For 9...N—Q2 see p. 217)

10 N—B1	

This looks a bit odd but the move is well founded. White has two ideas in mind, either N—B1—K3—KN4, or, N—B1—KR2—KN4. On KN4 White's QN supports the thrust of KRP and generally aids in the assault on Black's king.

10 ...	P—QR4
11 P—KR4	P—R5
12 B—B4	

Note the quantity of White's pieces in contact with the key cramping pawn at K5. This gives evidence of a co-operation amongst White's pieces that will become of great significance if the K side is ever opened up.

12 ...	P—R6

Creating dark-square holes in White's Q-side pawn structure. White obviously cannot play P×P, since his isolated QRP would become very exposed.

13 P—N3	B—N2

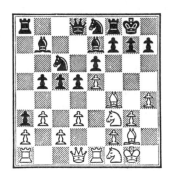

Both sides have implemented their attacks in the most efficient manner possible. As so often in these obscure

Flank openings, the position reached is, objectively speaking, not favourable to either party. It is purely a matter of taste whether one prefers Black's position or White's at this stage. For example, the prominent East German Grandmaster, Uhlmann, is a great upholder of Black's chances in such typical situations, while the Rumanian Grandmaster, Gheorghiu, takes precisely the opposite view.

Perhaps we should regard the White attack as the more dangerous for the following reasons: after White has pushed his KRP as far as it will go, he can arrange to play B—KN5, forcing off Black's KB. Then White can play over his knights to occupy the key dark squares KN5 and KB6, where they molest Black's king. Black's assault on the opposite wing does not jeopardize anything so important as the White king.

OTHER MOVES

White can play the move order of the King's Indian Attack in a variety of ways; e.g., 1 P—KN3, 1 P—Q4, or even 1 P—K4. For example, 1 P—K4, P—K4; 2 N—KB3, N—QB3; 3 P—Q3, followed by QN—Q2 and P—KN3; or 1 P—K4, P—QB4; 2 N—KB3, P—Q3 (or P—K3 or N—QB3); 3 P—Q3; or even 1 P—K4, P—QB3; 2 P—Q3, P—Q4; 3 N—Q2, etc. Finally, 1 P—K4, P—K3; 2 P—Q3, P—Q4; 3 N—Q2, and this is, in fact, just about the most popular method of introducing the King's Indian Attack – i.e., as an anti-French weapon. However, by continuing 3...N—KB3; 4 KN—B3, N—B3; 5 P—KN3, P×P; 6 P×P, P—K4!; 7 B—N2, B—QB4, Black levels out the pawn formation and obtains an easy development. The move lost with the KP is a small price to pay for this.

1...N—KB3

1...N—KB3. Once again this is well

playable, and if White continues with a King's Indian Attack it is safe, if unambitious, to copy his moves: 2 P—KN3, P—KN3; 3 B—N2, B—N2; 4 O—O, O—O; 5 P—Q3, P—Q3; 6 P—K4, P—K4; 7 QN—Q2, QN—Q2; 8 P—QR4, P—QR4; 9 N—B4, N—B4, and White has drawn little profit from his extra move (FILIP-PETROSIAN, World Championship Qualifying tournament 1956). Black even went on to win this game by playing ...N—KR4 and ...P—KB4, setting in motion a K-side pawn avalanche, well before White thought of the idea.

5...P—K4

5...P—K4. This invasion of the centre is extremely hazardous. Now we have a pure King's Indian Defence with colours reversed, and of course, White has an extra tempo. A very good plan for White now would be 6 B—N5, followed by N—B3 and KN—Q2, putting severe pressure on Black's QP. More constrained, but also not bad, is 6 QN—Q2, followed by P—K4. Compare the chapter dealing with the King's Indian Defence.

9...N—Q2

9...N—Q2. As we pointed out in the main text, this move is well playable, but as an illustration of the dynamic power concealed in White's King's Indian Attack formation, here are the moves of two games with 9...N—Q2 in which Black suffered disastrous reversals. We would emphasize that this was not the fault of 9...N—Q2.

(*a*) **10 N—B1.**

According to plan.

10...P—QR4; 11 P—KR4, P—N5; 12 B—B4, B—R3.

Black could defend more securely with 12...R—K1; 13 N—N5, N—B1, covering K3 and KR2.

13 N—N5, Q—K1.

Also dubious.

14 Q—N4, P—R5??.

Carried away by his Q-side advance, Black overlooks White's threat.

15 N×KP!.

After ...P×N; 16 Q×KP ch, Black loses many pawns. (BRONSTEIN–UHLMANN, Alekhine Memorial Tournament, Moscow 1971.)

(*b*) The game LEE–RADULOV, Sinaia 1965, followed the above game until:

11...P—R5; 12 P—R5, P—N5; 13 P—R6.

Achieving one objective.

13...P—N3; 14 B—B4, P—R6; 15 P—N3, B—R3; 16 Q—Q2.

Preparing B—KN5.

16...R—B1; 17 N(B1)—R2, N—R2; 18 B—N5!.

Gaining complete control of the K-side dark squares.

18...N—N4; 19 Q—B4, R—B2; 20 N—N4.

The storm gathers around Black's king.

20...N—Q5; 21 B×B, N×N ch; 22 B×N, Q×B; 23 B×P!.

As so often in the King's Indian Attack, White breaks through with a sacrifice on Q5.

23...P×B; 24 P—K6, N—N3.

White has discovered an attack from his queen on Black's rook.

25 Q×R!!, Q×Q; 26 N—B6 ch.

Triumph of the dark squares.

26...K—R1; 27 P—K7, Q—N1; 28 P×R(Q) ch, Q×Q; 29 R—K8.

An easy winning position for White.

ENGLISH

1 P—QB4	P—QB4
2 N—QB3	N—QB3
3 P—KN3	P—KN3
4 B—N2	B—N2
5 N—B3	N—B3
6 O—O	O—O
7 P—Q4!	P×P
8 N×P	N×N
9 Q×N	P—Q3
10 B—N5	

---

1 P—QB4	P—QB4

(For 1...P—K4 see p. 219)

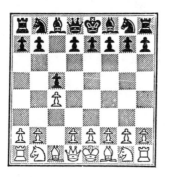

The English opening, 1 P—QB4, strikes from the flank at the square Q5, which White later hopes to control and dominate with his pieces. In the previous sections dealing with Flank openings, we looked at lines where Black resolutely opposes White's oblique lateral pressure by establishing a chain of pawns in the centre. In this section we analyse a different type of response for Black, to wit: imitation of White's moves.

2 N—QB3

Increasing the pressure against Q5 ...

2 ...	N—QB3

... while Black treats White's Q4 square in the same fashion.

3 P—KN3

The White KB is also to be developed into contact with the Q5 square. This play around the key point Q5 gives White's opening manoeuvres a primary objective and theme. Once this objective has been achieved a middle game plan will arise naturally, as if of its own accord, from the pointed strategic disposition of White's pieces.

3 ...	P—KN3
4 B—N2	B—N2
5 N—B3	

This natural development of the KN on KB3 is superior to the more passive alternative 5...P—K3 intending KN—K2. Then Black can obtain full equality simply by copying White's moves; e.g., 5 P—K3, P—K3; 6 KN—K2, KN—K2; 7 O—O, O—O; 8 P—Q4, P×P; 9 N×P, N×N; 10 P×N, P—Q4; 11 P×P, N×P; 12 N×N, P×N, with a drawn position.

5 ...	N—B3
6 O—O	O—O
7 P—Q4!	

This central advance promises White some advantage since the White queen is also brought into contact with Q5. Furthermore, 7 P—Q4 opens up lines for White to complete his development. The slower 7 P—N3, intending to develop all the bishops on long diagonals, is an error here: 7...N—K5!; 8 B—N2, N×N; 9 B×N, B×B; 10 P×B, and White has allowed his pawns to be doubled for no visible compensation.

(For 7 P—Q3 see p. 220)

7 ...	P×P

It is dangerous to prolong the imitation: 7...P—Q4; 8 QP×P, P×P; 9 Q—R4, and Black's QBP is in trouble; e.g., 9...B—K3; 10 N—KN5!, a well-known method of molesting a bishop on K3. If Black allows N×B he will lose the bishop pair and have his pawns shattered, while if the QB vacates K3 the QBP will fall.

(For 7...P—Q3 see p. 220)

8 N×P

Now Black has problems in the completion of development for 8...P—Q3; 9 N×N, P×N; 10 B×P would hand White a free pawn. So Black must play ...

8 ...   N×N
9 Q×N   P—Q3

... in order to develop his QB.

10 B—N5

These moves were played in the eighth game of the 1972 Fischer-Spassky World Championship Match. White (Fischer) has a small plus in view of his free development and firm grip on the square Q5.

Here is one possible continuation, which shows how this abstract advantage of a grip on a key square can be utilized to gain something more tangible and concrete:

10...B—K3.
Spassky's move in the game, but it would have been more logical to play ...P—KR3 at once to chase away White's QB.

11 Q—B4.
Black threatened 11...N—Q4, disclosing an attack from the Black KB on White's queen, followed by ...N×N, saddling White with very weak doubled pawns.

11...Q—R4; 12 QR—B1, QR—N1; 13 P—N3, KR—B1; 14 Q—Q2, P—QR3; 15 B—K3, R—B2.
Spassky played 15...P—QN4 whereupon 16 B—R7! won the exchange.

16 N—Q5!.

Threat: Q×Q.
16...Q×Q; 17 B×Q, N×N; 18 P×N, R×R.
He cannot move his QB first because his rook is en prise.
19 R×R, B—Q2; 20 R—B7.
White establishes a rook on the 7th rank. Such an invasion of Black's position should be sufficient for White to win. Black would have done better with the humble 17...R—Q2, allowing White's powerful knight to remain on Q5, but the strength radiated by this piece would also have guaranteed a White advantage.

1...P—K4

1...P—K4. The most forthright reply to the English, giving a type of Sicilian Defence with colours reversed. Here is one possible example which has occurred in tournament play:
1 P—QB4, P—K4; 2 N—QB3, N—KB3; 3 P—KN3, P—Q4; 4 P×P, N×P; 5 B—N2, N—N3; 6 N—B3, N—B3; 7 O—O, B—K2. Now 8 P—Q3 would give a pure reversed Dragon Sicilian, while with 8 P—QR3, intending P—QN4/B—N2/R—B1/and N—K4—QB5, White could strike out on an independent path, exploiting his control of the squares (especially QB5) in the QB file.

A commoner method for Black after 1 P—QB4, P—K4, is to keep the centre closed and to prepare a K-side pawn avalanche with ...P—KB4. Meanwhile White will push forwards to the attack on the other wing with P—QN4, P—QR4, P—QN5, P—QB5, etc., hoping to open lines for his pieces to invade Black's position. Here is a typical sequence:

1 P—QB4, P—K4; 2 N—QB3, N—QB3; 3 P—KN3, P—KN3.
Apart from allowing ...B—N2, the pawn on KN3 is good preparation for ...P—KB4.

4 B—N2, B—N2; 5 P—Q3, P—Q3; 6 N—B3, P—B4; 7 O—O, N—B3; 8 R—N1, O—O; 9 P—QN4, P—KR3.
To get in ...P—KN4, allowing ...Q—K1—KR4.

10 P—N5, N—K2; 11 P—QR4.
The chances for both sides are about equal. It is a matter of personal taste as to which side you prefer.

7 P—Q3

7 P—Q3. A much slower and less effective method than 7 P—Q4. Again White aims for P—QN4, but with his pawn on QB4 Black can easily block this threat: **7 P—Q3, P—Q3; 8 R—N1,** and Black can safely copy: after **8...R—N1; 9 P—QR3, P—QR3; 10 P—QN4, P×P; 11 P×P, P—QN4; 12 P×P,** P×P, White can claim no advantage from this symmetrical position.

7...P—Q3

7...P—Q3. This move is quite playable if Black does not want to surrender his hold on the centre with 7...P×P.

Following 7...P—Q3 with 8 P×P, P×P gives White nothing, so his best move is **8 P—Q5,** driving Black's QN to QR4. **8...N—K4; 9 N×N, P×N,** would leave Black with an inferior pawn structure. **8...N—QR4; 9 N—Q2.**

In this position Black's knight on the edge is not a liability, since it supports an assault on White's QBP by means of ...P—QR3/ ...R—QN1/ ...P—QN4. Furthermore, Black can undermine the spearhead of White's pawn-chain by means of...P—K3, or he can block the centre with...P—K4. These possibilities give Black good compensation for the offside position of his QN and White's superior control of space in the centre.

16

SOME OTHER OPENINGS

Alekhine's Defence

1 P—K4, N—KB3, Black's knight encourages the advance of White's central pawns in the hope that the advanced pawn centre will be vulnerable to an early counterattack: **2 P—K5, N—Q4; 3 P—QB4, N—N3; 4 P—Q4, P—Q3; 5 P—KB4, P×P; 6 BP×P, N—B3; 7 B—K3.** Current opinion favours White's central domination over Black's counterattacking chances.

Benkö Gambit

1 P—Q4, N—KB3; 2 P—QB4, P—B4; 3 P—Q5, P—QN4. In this offshoot of the Benoni Defence, Black sacrifices a pawn in return for active piece play and attacking chances on the Q side. Play normally continues **4 P×P, P—QR3; 5 P×P, B×P** and now, irrespective of how White completes his development, Black plays . . .P—Q3, . . .P—KN3, . . .B—KN2, . . .O—O, followed by development of his queen and QN and then . . .KR—QN1, with strong pressure on the Q side. The **Blumenfeld Counter Gambit** is a similar but inferior system in which Black plays an early . . .P—K3 in conjunction with the pawn sacrifice.

Bird's Opening

1 P—KB4. This is a Dutch Defence with a move in hand. White's strategy is to play N—KB3, P—K3, O—O followed by P—QN3 and B—N2 (to increase his control of the K5 square) and then attack on the K side with Q—K1—R4.

Bishop's Opening

1 P—K4, P—K4; 2 B—B4. Belongs to the same family as the Giuoco Piano to which it can transpose (by 2. . .N—QB3; 3 N—KB3). Can also transpose to the King's Gambit or Vienna Game.

Blackmar/Diemer Gambit

1 P—Q4, P—Q4; 2 P—K4?!, P×P; 3 N—QB3, N—KB3; 4 P—B3, P×P and now either **5 N×P** or **5 Q×P**, according to whether White wishes to sacrifice one or two pawns for a rather tenuous lead in development. We must condemn this gambit as unsound, since it gives up material and weakens White's K side for no tangible gains. It has found virtually no favour with chess masters.

Budapest Gambit

1 P—Q4, N—KB3; 2 P—QB4, P—K4?!; 3 P×P, N—N5. This continuation was popular in the 1920's but has now disappeared from Master praxis. It is only dangerous for White if he tries to hang on to his extra pawn at all costs; but with **4 P—K4, N×KP; 5 P—KB4** White gains a spatial advantage and Black will have to lose time with his wandering knight. Even the quiet **4 N—KB3, N—QB3; 5 N—B3** leaves White on top, since Black will have expended three moves with his king's knight merely to see it exchanged.

Centre Counter (Scandinavian) Game

1 P—K4, P—Q4; 2 P×P. If Black recaptures immediately he suffers from the usual defect of bringing the queen out too soon: 2...Q×P; 3 N—QB3, and White has a lead in development. The usual method of recapturing the pawn is 2...N—KB3, and if 3 P—QB4, P—B3; 4 P×P, N×P, and Black's lead in development is more important than White's extra pawn. But by 3 P—Q4, N×P; 4 P—QB4, White takes control of the centre and emerges from the opening with an advantage in space.

Centre Game

1 P—K4, P—K4; 2 P—Q4, P×P. White usually continues with 3 Q×P, N—QB3; 4 Q—K3, hoping that the open lines will give him sufficiently active play to compensate for moving his queen twice in the opening. An unsound continuation is the Danish Gambit, 3 P—QB3, P×P; 4 B—QB4, P×P; 5 B×NP, when White's lead in development is not sufficient to compensate for the two pawn deficit.

Four Knights Game

1 P—K4, P—K4; 2 N—KB3, N—QB3; 3 N—B3, N—B3 (if Black plays a different third move the opening is called the Three Knights Game). Once a favourite with ex-World Champion Botvinnik, this is a rare example of a symmetrical opening which does not offer any tangible advantage to White. Simple, classical development is the rule.

Greco-Counter (Latvian) Gambit

1 P—K4, P—K4; 2 N—KB3, P—KB4?. A reversed King's Gambit with one tempo less. Must be doomed against correct play, but its numerous complications have sometimes proved the better of Master players. 3 B—B4, P×P; 4 N×P, Q—N4; 5 P—Q4, Q×P; 6 Q—R5 ch, is the most effective refutation.

Morra Gambit

1 P—K4, P—QB4; 2 P—Q4, P×P; 3 P—QB3. White offers a pawn in return for which he gets only one tempo and the use of his Q1—QR4 diagonal. 3...P×P; 4 N×P, N—QB3; 5 N—B3, P—Q3; 6 B—QB4, P—QR3, (not 6...B—N5?; 7 B×P ch, K×B; 8 N—N5 ch, and 9 Q×B regaining a piece); 7 O—O, N—B3; 8 B—KN5, P—K3; 9 Q—K2, P—R3; 10 B—R4 (or 10 B—K3, N—KN5!; 11 B—Q2, KN—K4, with a very solid position and an extra pawn); 10...P—KN4!; 11 B—KN3, N—KR4; 12 KR—Q1, N×B; 13 RP×N, P—N5. Black has an excellent game as well as an extra pawn.

Nimzowitsch Defence

1 P—K4, N—QB3. Conforming with its inventor's principle of controlling the centre with pieces rather than occupying it with pawns, this defence is contrary to the principles taught in this book: 2 P—Q4, P—Q4; 3 N—QB3, and now with 3...P—K3 Black reaches an inferior variation of the French Defence (he has blocked his QBP and will not, therefore, be able to play the thematic counter...P—QB4). Another possibility is 3...P×P; 4 P—Q5, N—N1; 5 B—KB4, N—KB3; 6 B—B4, when White's lead in development and his active position more than outweigh the (temporarily) sacrificed pawn.

Old Indian Defence
1 P—Q4, N—KB3; 2 P—QB4, P—Q3; 3 N—QB3, P—K4; 4 P×P. 4 N—B3
is the most common alternative. 4...P×P; 5 Q×Q ch, K×Q; 6 N—B3,
KN—Q2; 7 P—KN3, P—KB3; 8 B—N2, P—B3 (making an escape square
for the king and depriving White of the use of his Q5 and QN5 squares);
9 O—O, N—N3. The chances are about even.

Petroff Defence
1 P—K4, P—K4; 2 N—KB3, N—KB3. A passive, symmetrical defence which
announces Black's intention to bore his opponent into defeat. A typical
continuation is 3 P—Q4, N×P; 4 B—Q3, P—Q4; 5 N×P, when White's
initiative is intact and his opening advantage remains.

Philidor's Defence
1 P—K4, P—K4; 2 N—KB3, P—Q3. An inflexible move which restricts the
development of Black's KB. Black relies on a solid, passive, defensive
position to withstand White's spatial advantage: 3 P—Q4, N—KB3 (3...
P×P; 4 Q×P, N—QB3; 5 B—QN5, B—Q2; 6 B×N, is also better for
White - his queen is no longer vulnerable to harassment); 4 N—B3, QN—Q2;
5 B—QB4, B—K2; 6 O—O, O—O; 7 Q—K2, P—B3; 8 P—QR4. White has
the better prospects.

Pirc Defence
1 P—K4, P—Q3; 2 P—Q4, N—KB3. This is almost identical in strategy to
the Modern Defence which was discussed in detail in chapter 14. The two
defences frequently transpose. The difference in move order has the effect,
in the Pirc, of compelling White to defend his KP on move three thereby
giving him less flexibility. White normally plays 3 N—QB3, and after 3...
P—KN3, the game leads into the same channels as the Modern Defence.

Ponziani Opening
1 P—K4, P—K4; 2 N—KB3, N—QB3; 3 P—B3. White hopes to use his
third move as the foundation for a strong pawn centre, but by active play
(3...N—B3!) Black can equalize with ease.

Réti Gambit
1 N—KB3, P—Q4; 2 P—B4. If Black advances his QP with 2...P—Q5,
White has a Benoni formation with an extra tempo. If Black captures with
2...P×P, White can regain the pawn by 3 N—R3, followed by 4 N×P, or
by 3 Q—R4 ch and 4 Q×BP.

Scotch Game
1 P—K4, P—K4; 2 N—KB3, N—QB3; 3 P—Q4, P×P. White opens up
the game at once in order to give his pieces easy development. The disadvantage of releasing the tension so soon is that White's aims become clear
cut, and Black has no real problem in finding a satisfactory plan of development.

Vienna Game
1 P—K4, P—K4; 2 N—QB3. This usually becomes a gambit opening (after
2...N—KB3; 3 P—B4) and is similar to the King's Gambit in character.
The play can become very complicated and exciting.

INDEX OF OPENINGS

List of Openings

(Covering all Important Variations in each Opening)

Sicilian	Pirc	Dutch
King's Indian	Alekhine	Larsen's
Grünfeld	Ruy Lopez	Queen's Gambit
Nimzo-Indian	Benoni	King's Gambit
English	French	Queen's Indian
Reti	Caro-Kann	Benko Gambit
	(additions will be made)	

All "Chess Opening" theory is in a perpetual stage of change, some lines being successfully challenged and discarded, other lines improved, new and promising lines being continually discovered as thousands of games are played in current grandmaster tournaments.

Not only can your own game in your favorite Openings be greatly improved by study of the 100 current games in the Openings section selected by you, but you will gain new and valuable insights into the middle game play and end game play flowing naturally from each line through the individual game annotation and analysis-in-depth by the many world-famed grandmasters who will be serving on our Board of Contributing Editors.

The average cost of each full-size section containing all we have just described should be modest, but **send no money**— only your name and address on a postcard—so that you will be entered as a subscriber to receive announcements and full descriptions of each Openings section as they become ready for shipment. There is no charge for entering this subscription, and it puts you under no obligation. You later order only what you wish to order.

But you can help us (and yourself) by listing on the postcard the **5 top choices of Openings** you would like to see covered. This informal "straw poll" will guide us in the order of publication of individual Openings sections.

We are now preparing publication of sections covering some of the most popular Openings and commencing work on all the rest, and to receive announcements of each section as it becomes available, merely send your full name and address on a postcard to:

Dept. 10

R.H.M. SURVEY OF CURRENT CHESS OPENINGS

Albertson, New York 11507

In Europe write to R•H•M PRESS LTD. • P.O. Box 55 London N13, England 5BE

8 of the 10

Top-Rated Chess Grandmasters in the world are on the Board of Contributing Editors of the Chess division of R·H·M Press

including the
new world champion,
Anatoly Karpov
and four previous
world chess champions,
Boris Spassky, Tigran Petrosian,
Mikhail Botvinnik and Mikhail Tal.

R.H.M. Chess Books

The French Defence
A classic monograph, indispensable to anyone who plays the French or 1 P-K4.

The Battle of Chess Ideas
The second edition of Saidy's lively description of the modern chess giants, updated to include a chapter on Karpov.

The Najdorf Variation—Sicilian Defence
The most popular variation in chess theory brilliantly explained by four of the world's top Grandmasters.

The Life and Games of Mikhail Tal
Possibly the greatest chess book ever written. 100 brilliantly annotated games and a scintillating auto-biography—all from the pen of the attacking genius from Riga.

Psychology in Chess
Why do you make mistakes? How does your personality affect your play? How can you improve? How to avoid time trouble. How to train.

Practical Chess Endings
Keres explains the ideas behind all the basic endings in great detail.

Portoroz/Ljubljana Grandmaster Chess Tournament 1975
Anatoly Karpov's first tournament after being crowned World Champion.

The Life and Games of Viktor Korchnoy
100 annotated games and an absorbing autobiography by the world's number two Grandmaster.

The Chess Opening For You
Larry Evans is possibly America's best chess writer and this is a unique contribution to the chess opening.